AVON COUNTY LIBRARY

BRISTOL
REFERENCE LIBRARY

BRISTOL CITY COUNCIL
LIBRARY SERVICES

THIS BOOK IS FOR USE
IN THE LIBRARY ONLY

BR75

4008 P&S

C.L.74

3596 P&S

The War Decade

An Anthology of the 1940s

compiled by

ANDREW SINCLAIR

Hamish Hamilton · London

HAMISH HAMILTON LTD

Published by the Penguin Group
27 Wrights Lane, London w8 5TZ, England
Viking Penguin Inc., 40 West 23rd Street, New York,
New York 10010, USA
Penguin Books Australia Ltd, Ringwood, Victoria, Australia
Penguin Books Canada Ltd, 2801 John Street, Markham,
Ontario, Canada L3R 1B4
Penguin Books (NZ) Ltd, 182–190 Wairau Road, Auckland 10,
New Zealand

Penguin Books Ltd, Registered Offices: Harmondsworth,
Middlesex, England

First published in Great Britain by Hamish Hamilton Ltd 1989

Selection copyright © Andrew Sinclair, 1989

Designed by Craig Dodd
Filmset in Erhardt

Printed in Great Britain by Richard Clay Ltd, Bungay, Suffolk

A CIP catalogue record for this book is available from the British
Library

ISBN 0-241-12567 7

Contents

CONTENTS

CONTENTS

v

CONTENTS

CONTENTS

CONTENTS

CONTENTS

9 After the War Was Over

10 The End of the War Decade

CONTENTS

xi

Acknowledgements

The author and publishers would like to thank all the writers, publishers and literary representatives, who have given permission to include the poetry and prose in this anthology. While every effort has been made to find copyright holders, this has not always been possible, and the publishers will be glad to make good any omissions in future editions. Writers whose work is printed here are listed in alphabetical order below.

Jack Aistrop: 'The Naked Boy and the Brigadier' from *Bugle Blast, an Anthology from the Services* eds. Aistrop & Moore, Allen & Unwin, 1943. Drummond Allison: 'For Karl Marx' from *For Your Tomorrow*, Oxford University Press, 1950. Kenneth Allott: 'Black Out' and 'Departure' from *Collected Poems* by Kenneth Allott reprinted by permission of Martin Secker & Warburg Ltd. Brian Allwood: 'Ack Ack Said the Instructor' and 'Pilot' from *More Poems from the Forces* ed. K. Rhys, Routledge, 1943. Barry Conrad Amiel: 'Poem' from *Poems From India*, Oxford University Press, 1946. Patrick Anderson: 'Armaments Worker' from *The Best Poems of 1943* ed. Thomas Moult, Jonathan Cape, 1944. John Arlott: 'Music-Hall' from *Of Period and Place*, Jonathan Cape, 1944. Honor Arundel: 'Morning Shift' from *New Lyrical Ballads*, Nicholson and Watson, 1945; reprinted by permission of Alex Mc-Crindle. John Atkins: 'War Aims: Planning' from *New Lyrical Ballads*, Nicholson and Watson, 1945; reprinted by permission of the author. W. H. Auden: 'The Novelist' reprinted by permission of Faber & Faber Ltd from *Collected Poems* by W. H. Auden. Bruce Bain: 'NAAFI At The Drome'. Donald Bain: 'War Poet'. A. D. Bass: 'Here in a Hillside Camp' from *For Your Tomorrow*, Oxford University Press, 1950. John Bayliss: extract from 'Epilogue, Testament and Prophecy', from *Poetry of the Present* ed. A. Grigson, Phoenix House, 1949. Audrey Beecham: 'Song', from *Poetry London*, 1, November 1940. Jack Beeching: 'Spring Offensive 1940' and 'The Millionaire' from *Tribune*, Spring, 1940. Elizabeth Berridge: extract from 'Conversation' from *Little Review Anthology, 1946*, Eyre & Spottiswoode. John Betjeman: 'In Praise of Dirt', *Lilliput*, reprinted by permission of the estate of Sir John Betjeman and John Murray Ltd. C. P. Billot: 'Temporary Uniform' from *Poems of the Forces*, Fortune Press, 1946. Donald Bishop: 'Colour Bar' from *Little Review Anthology*, 1945, Eyre & Spottiswoode. D. Van Den Bogaerde: extract from 'Steel Cathedrals', Chatto and Windus. David Bourne: 'Parachute Descent' from

Airforce Poetry, The Bodley Head. Elizabeth Bowen: 'Calico Windows' from *Soho Centenary*, Hutchinson, 1945, reprinted by permission of Curtis Brown, London; extract from *The Heat of the Day* reprinted by permission of the estate of Elizabeth Bowen and Jonathan Cape Ltd. Jocelyn Brooke: extract from 'Soldier's Song' from *December Spring*, John Lane/The Bodley Head, 1946, reprinted by permission of the estate of Jocelyn Brooke. Harry Brown: extract from *A Walk in the Sun* and 'This is Merely Part of the Studio Tour' from *Poems*, Martin Secker & Warburg Ltd. Frances Buckland: Diary 'The Life of a Land Girl' from *Lilliput* April, 1941. Michael Burn: 'To a Forced Voice' from *Poems to Mary*, Rupert Hart-Davis, 1953, reprinted by permission of Grafton Books, a division of William Collins & Sons. Ritchie Calder: extract from *The Lesson of London*, Secker & Warburg, 1942. Mel Calman: extract from 'Memoirs of an Evacuee' from *The Evacuees*, ed. B. S. Johnson, Gollancz, 1968, by permission of Mel Calman. Norman Cameron: 'Punishment Enough' and 'The Verdict' from *Collected Poems*, reprinted by permission of the Executor of the Norman Cameron Estate and The Hogarth Press. Lord Campbell of Alloway, QC (Alan Campbell): extract from 'Prison Life' from *Colditz Cameo*. Roy Campbell: 'One Transport Lost' from *Collected Works*, reprinted by permission of Francisco Campbell Custodio and Ad. Donker (Pty) Ltd. Elias Canetti: extract from 'August 1945' from *The War Province*, Andre Deutsch, 1985. Maurice Carpenter: 'Machine Shop: Nightshift'. Charles Causley: 'Song of the Dying Gunner' and 'Armistice Day' from *Collected Poems 1951–75*, Macmillan Ltd. Robert A. Chaloner: 'Home Front – 1942' from *More Poems from the Forces* ed. K. Rhys, Routledge, 1943. Robert Conquest: 'Poem in 1944' and '1944 and After' from *New and Collected Poems* © 1988 Robert Conquest, Century Hutchinson, 1988; reprinted by permission of Curtis Brown, London. Herbert Corby: 'Daylight Operations', 'No Answer' and 'Reprisal'. Timothy Corsellis: 'What I Never Saw' from *Poems of This War by Younger Poets*, eds. P. Ledward and C. Strang, Cambridge University Press, 1942; 'News Reel of Embarkation' from *Poems from the Forces* and 'In Memoriam – A.N.C.W.' from *More Poems from the Forces* (1943), both volumes ed. K. Rhys, Routledge. Cyril Connolly: extract from 'The Condemned Playground', from *Essays: 1927–44*, Routledge, 1945. E. Denyer Cox: 'Aviator' from *Poems from the Forces* ed. K. Rhys, Routledge, Chapman & Hall Ltd. R. N. Currey: 'Boy With a Rifle' and 'Unseen Fire' from *This Other Planet*, Routledge, 1945; 'Troops' Cinema' and 'Unconsidered Bodies' from *Poems From India* (1946), reprinted by permission of Oxford University Press. Donald Davie: extract from 'Rejoinder to a Critic' from *A Winter Talent and Other Poems*, © Donald Davie 1957,

Routledge, & Kegan Paul, 1957. Cecil Day Lewis: extract from 'On Writing "In the Shelter"' from *Cecil Day Lewis: An English Literary Life* by Sean Day Lewis, Weidenfeld & Nicolson, 1980; 'Stand-To', 'Will It Be So Again?', and 'Watching Post' from *Collected Poems*, 1954, reprinted by permission of the executors of the estate of C. Day Lewis and The Hogarth Press and Jonathan Cape. Paul Dehn: 'New Age' from *The Fern on the Rock: Collected Poems 1935–65*, Hamish Hamilton, 1965, copyright © 1965 by Paul Dehn, reprinted by permission of London Management. Patric Dickinson: 'To a Fireman-Poet' and 'Bombers: Evening' from *Theseus and the Minotaur*, Jonathan Cape Ltd, 1946; reprinted by permission of the author. Keith Douglas: extract from *Alamein to Zem Zem* and 'How to Kill', copyright © Marie J. Douglas, 1978; reprinted from *The Complete Poems of Keith Douglas* edited by Desmond Graham (1978) by permission of Oxford University Press; 'The Prisoner', 'The Aristocrats', 'Landscape with Figures', 'Vergissmeinnicht' and 'Simplify Me When I'm Dead' from *Collected Poems*, Faber & Faber Ltd, 1966. Clifford Dyment: 'From Many a Mangled Truth a War is Won' from *Collected Poems*, Dent, 1970. D. J. Enright: 'The "Black" Country' from *The Laughing Hyena and Other Poems*, Routledge & Kegan Paul, 1953; reprinted by permission of Watson, Little Ltd. Ken Etheridge: 'To a Young Soldier' from *More Poems from the Forces* ed. K. Rhys, Routledge, 1943. Bernard Evslin: 'My Right Leg Was Germany' from *Penguin New Writing*, April, 1946. Gavin Ewart: 'When a Beau Goes In', 'The Bofors A.A. Gun' and 'Officers' Mess' from *The Collected Ewart, 1933–1980*, Century Hutchinson Ltd. Stephen Fenlaugh: 'Troop Ship' from *Poems from India*, Oxford University Press, 1946. Constantine Fitzgibbon: extract from *The Blitz*, Macdonald & Co Ltd, 1970. Olivia Fitzroy: 'Fleet Fighter' reprinted by permission of Viscount Daventry. Keith Footit: 'Two Pairs of Shoes' from *For Your Tomorrow*, Oxford University Press, 1950. G. S. Fraser: extract from *A Stranger And Afraid*, Carcanet Press Ltd, 1983. Roy Fuller: 'Obituary of R. Fuller', 'ABC of a Naval Trainee', 'The Legions', 'The Middle of a War', 'A Wry Smile', 'War Letters', 'During a Bombardment by V-Weapons', 'The Divided Life Re-Lived' and '1984', from *The Last Season*, Martin Secker and Warburg Ltd; extract from Introduction to *Kenneth Allott Collected Poems*, Martin Secker & Warburg Ltd, 1975. David Gascoyne: 'The Post-War Night' reprinted from David Gascoyne's *Collected Poems 1988* by permission of Oxford University Press. John Gawsworth: 'Bayonet Instruction'; reprinted by permission of the Estate of T. I. F. Armstrong ('John Gawsworth'). Francis Gelder: 'A Ballad of 1941' from *Poems of the War by Younger Poets* eds. P. Ledward & C. Strang, Cambridge University Press. Wilfred Gibson:

'When the Plane Dived', 'Shells' and 'The Soldier Poet' from *The Alert*. Robert Gittings: 'September 3rd, 1939' from *Wentworth Place*, William Heinemann Ltd, 1950. Virginia Graham: 'My Bonny', 'Switch It Off', 'VJ Day' and 'A Thought For Denman Street' from *Consider the Years, 1938–1946*, Jonathan Cape. David Graves: 'In Conclusion'. Graham Greene: extract from *The Third Man: The Screenplay* reprinted by permission of Faber & Faber Ltd; extract from 'At Home' from *The Lost Childhood and Other Essays*, reprinted by permission of Laurence Pollinger Ltd. Bernard Gutteridge: 'In September 1939' and 'My Platoon' from *Traveller's Eye*, Routledge & Kegan Paul. Stephen Haggard: 'The Mantle' from *I'll Go to Bed at Noon*, Faber & Faber, 1944. J. C. Hall: 'Journey to London' and 'The Reunion' from *The Summer Dance and Other Poems*, John Lehmann Ltd, by permission of J. C. Hall. Charles Hamblett: 'Bombs on My Town' from *Poems from the Forces*, Fortune Press, 1946. Norman Hampson: 'Corvette' from *More Poems from the Forces* ed. K. Rhys, Routledge, 1943. Christopher Hassall: extract from 'Sonnet XXVII' from *Crisis*, William Heinemann Ltd; 'Hats, Demob Depot, York', 'Banned Area' and 'Medical' from *The Slow Night and Other Poems*, Arthur Barker Ltd, 1949. Desmond Hawkins: 'Night Raid' from *Poetry in Wartime*, Faber & Faber. John Heath-Stubbs: 'The Pearl' and 'Funeral Music for Charles Wrey Gardiner' from *Collected Poems*, Carcanet. Hamish Henderson: extracts from 'End of a Campaign', 'Interlude: Opening of an Offensive' and its footnote from *First Elegy*, reprinted by permission of the author. J. F. Hendry: 'Midnight Air-Raid' from *The Bombed Happiness*, Routledge, 1942. Raynor Heppenstall: 'Instead of a Carol', from *Poems 1933–1945*, Martin Secker & Warburg, 1946. Richard Hillary: extract from *The Last Enemy*, reprinted by permission of Macmillan, London and Basingstoke. Brian Howard: 'Gone to Report' from *Horizon 5 March 1940*. Edward Hyams: extract from *William Medium*, The Bodley Head Ltd, 1947. John Jarmain: 'El Alamein' and 'Thinking of War' and 'Prisoners of War' from *Poems*, William Collins Sons & Co., Ltd, 1945. Randall Jarrell: 'The Death of the Ball Turret Gunner' and 'A Camp in the Prussian Forest' reprinted by permission Faber & Faber Ltd from *The Complete Poems* by Randall Jarrell. Séan Jennett: 'Raid' and 'I Was A Labourer in the Smoky Valley' from *The Cloth of Flesh*, Faber & Faber; reprinted by permission of the author. Elizabeth Jennings: 'The Second World War' from *Collected Poems*, Macmillan Ltd. C. E. M. Joad: extract from 'The Face of England, Etc.' from *Horizon*, 29. Robert Joly: extracts from 'To Lazarus' and 'Hospital: October 1941' from *For Your Tomorrow*, Oxford University Press, 1950. P. J. Kavanagh: 'Beyond the Headlines' from *Collected Poems* reprinted by kind permission of Katherine B. Kavanagh c/o Peter

Fallon, Loughcrew, Oldcastle, County Meath, Ireland. Sidney Keyes: 'War Poet' and 'To Keep Off Fear' from *Collected Poems*, Routledge, 1945. Lincoln Kirstein: extract from 'Foresight' from *Rhymes and More Rhymes of a PFC*, New Directions Publishing Corp, New York, 1964, reprinted by permission of the author. Uys Krige: 'Midwinter' from *More Poems from the Forces* ed. K. Rhys, Routledge, 1943. James Laughlin: extract from 'When Does the Play Begin' copyright © 1953 by James Laughlin. Laurie Lee: 'The Armoured Valley' and 'Poem: The Evening, The Heather' from *The Sun My Monument*, The Hogarth Press. John Lehmann: extract from *I Am My Brother*, Longmans. Ben Levy: 'Pin-Up' from *Poems From India*, Oxford University Press, 1946. Alun Lewis: 'The Journey' and 'Goodbye' from *Ha Ha Among the Trumpets*, 'Lady in Black' from *Selected Poetry and Prose*, 'Raiders' Dawn' and 'All Day It Has Rained' from *Raiders' Dawn*, 'Goodbye' from *Selected Poetry and Prose*, George Allen & Unwin Ltd, 1966; extracts from 'Night Journey' and 'The Earth Is a Syllable' from *In the Green Tree*; all reprinted by permission of Unwin Hyman Ltd; from 'Lance Jack' from *Leaves in the Storm*, Lindsay Drummond, 1947. Jack Lindsay: 'Two Pulls' and 'Squadding' from *New Lyrical Ballads*, Nicholson and Watson, 1945. Lawrence Little: extract from 'Signals Section' from *More Poems from The Forces*. ed. K. Rhys, Routledge, 1943. Colin McIntyre: 'Motor Transport Officer' and 'Infantryman' © Colin McIntyre, from *From Oasis Into Italy*, Salamander Oasis Trust, Shepheard-Walwyn Ltd. Julian Maclaren-Ross: 'A Sentimental Story' from *The Stuff to Give the Troops*, and 'He Died for his Country' published in *Lilliput*, reprinted by permission of Alan Ross. M. Macnaughton-Smith: 'Raiders Over Troy'. Louis MacNeice: extract from preface to epigram from *Holes in the Sky* reprinted by permission of Faber & Faber Ltd; 'Bar-Room Matins', 'The News-Reel', 'Bottleneck', 'Convoy', 'Swing-Song' and 'Hiatus' reprinted by permission of Faber & Faber Ltd from *The Collected Poems of Louis MacNeice*. H. B. Mallalieu: 'At the Range' and 'State of Readiness' from *More Poems From the Forces* ed. K. Rhys, Routledge, 1943. John Manifold: 'Camouflage' from *Poems from the Forces* and 'The Deserter' and 'Nightpiece' from *More Poems from the Forces* (1943), both volumes ed. K. Rhys, Routledge; 'Defensive Position' from *Modern British Poetry* ed. L. Untermeyer, Harcourt Brace Jovanovich, New York. Fred Marnau: '1939, October'. J. G. Meddemmen: extract from 'L.R.D.G.' © J. G. Meddemmen, from *Return to Oasis*, The Salamander Oasis Trust, Shepheard-Walwyn Ltd. J. G. Millard: 'Arakan Box' from Penguin *New Writing*, 25, 1943. James Monahan: 'The Feckless Years', 'Ghosts' and 'Prisoners' Return' from *Far From the Land*, Macmillan Ltd. Malcolm Muggeridge: extract from 'The Beginning of the Forties' from *The Windmill*, reprinted by permission of the author. Edwin Muir: 'Reading in Wartime' reprinted by permission of Faber & Faber Ltd from *The Collected Poems of Edwin Muir*. Paul Nash: extract from 'Aerial Flowers' from *Little Review Anthology*, Counterpoint-Publications, Oxford 1947. Kenneth Neal: extract from 'Hale, YMCA' from *Poems of This War by Younger Poets*, eds P. Ledward & C. Strang, Cambridge University Press, 1942. Howard Nemerov: 'August 1945' and 'Peace in Our Time' from *The Collected Poems of Howard Nemerov*, University of Chicago Press, 1977, reprinted by permission of the author. Norman Nicholson: 'Cleator Moor' from *Five Rivers* reprinted by permission of Faber and Faber Ltd. Daphne Nixon: 'In These Five Years', Fortune Press 1946. Julian Orde: extract from 'The Changing Mind', *Aquarius* 17/18. Mervyn Peake: 'The Consumptive, Belsen, 1945' from *Poems*, Faber & Faber Ltd; 'Palais de Danse' and 'London 1941' from *Shapes and Sounds* by Mervyn Peake, The Bodley Head; by permission of the estate of Mervyn Peake. Geoff Pearse: 'At Sea' © The Salamander Oasis Trust, from *Return to Oasis*, Shepheard-Walwyn Ltd. Alfred Perles: 'Soldiers and Civilians'. J. B. Pick: 'The Train' from *Modern Reading*, 9, 1944. William Plomer: 'The Bungalows' and 'The Flying Bum' from *Collected Poems* reprinted by permission of Jonathan Cape Ltd on behalf of the estate of William Plomer. Paul Potts: 'My Work' from *New Lyrical Ballads*, Nicholson & Watson, 1945. J. B. Priestley: extract from 'The War – And After', *Horizon*, 1, 1940, reprinted by permission of the Peters Fraser & Dunlop Group Ltd. F. T. Prince: 'Soldiers Bathing' from *The Doors of Stone: Poems 1938–1962*, Rupert Hart-Davis, 1963; reprinted by permission of Grafton Books, a division of William Collins & Sons. V. S. Pritchett: extract from *Midnight Oil* reprinted by permission of Chatto & Windus Ltd. John Pudney: 'For Johnny', 'Combat Report' and 'Missing' from *Ten Summers*, John Lane/The Bodley Head, 1942. David Raikes: 'Let It Be Hushed' from *For Your Tomorrow*, Oxford University Press, 1950. Kathleen Raine: 'Heroes' from *Collected Poems*, Hamish Hamilton, 1956. Arnold Rattenbury: 'Calendar Song' from *New Lyrical Ballads*, Nicholson & Watson, 1945. Henry Reed: 'Lives' and 'The Lessons of War' from *A Map of Verona*, Jonathan Cape, 1946; reprinted by permission of John Tydeman, literary executor to H. Reed Estate. Keidrych Rhys: 'Alarm, Alarm' from *More Poems from the Forces* ed. K. Rhys, Routledge, 1943. John Rimington: extract from 'Fear' © The Salamander Oasis Trust, from *Return to Oasis*, Shepheard-Walwyn Ltd. Charles Ritchie: extract from *The Siren Years: Undiplomatic Diaries 1937–1945*. W. R. Rodgers: 'Escape', 'War-Time' and 'The Raider' from *AWAKE! and Other Poems* © W. R. Rodgers 1941, Martin Secker & Warburg Ltd, reprinted by permission of Lucy Rodgers Cohen. Alan Rook: 'Song of a Technical Soldier', 'Radar', 'Night Patrol', 'Messdeck', 'Bombed City' and 'Memory' from *These Are My Comrades*, Routledge, 1943. Alan Ross: extract from *The Forties*, Weidenfeld & Nicolson, 1950, 'Demobilization', 'Stateless Persons' and 'J.W.51B' reprinted by permission of the author. Joyce Rowe: 'Dieppe', from *New Lyrical Ballads*, Nicholson & Watson, 1945. Sagittarius (Olga Katyin): 'The Passionate Profiteer to His Love' from *Quiver's Choice*, Jonathan Cape, 1945. C. R. Sanderson: 'Poem', 'To Peter' and 'Grantchester – Again' from *Poems of the Forces*, Fortune Press, 1946. Clive Sansom: 'September Holiday' from *The Witnesses*, Methuen, 1956. William Sansom: extracts from *Westminster at War* (Faber & Faber, 1947) and 'Fire and Water' from *N.F.S. Anthology* (Lindsay Drummond, 1942). Vernon Scannell: extract from *The Tiger and the Rose*, Hamish Hamilton 1971. Francis Scarfe: 'Ballad of the Safe Area', 'Grenade' and '25-Pounder' from *More Poems from the Forces*, ed. K. Rhys, Routledge, 1943. Paul Scott: 'Tell Us the Tricks' from *Poets Now*, Favil Press, reprinted by permission of the estate of Paul Scott. Tom Scott: 'Canteen' reprinted by permission of the author. George Scurfield: 'Song and Dance' from *Poetry London*, 4, Jan–Feb 1941; 'The Bitter Mangoes' from *Return to Oasis*, The Salamander Oasis Trust, Shepheard-Walwyn Ltd. Ian Serraillier: 'The New Learning'. Louis Simpson: 'Memories of a Lost War' from *Good News of Death and Other Poems*, Charles Scribners, New York. John Singer: 'Cities Are People' from *Little Review Anthology*, Eyre & Spottiswoode, 1946. C. H. Sisson: 'The Writer' and 'On the Way Home' from *Collected Poems*, Carcanet Press Ltd. Edith Sitwell: 'Dirge for the New Sunrise' from *Collected Poems*, Macmillan Ltd. William Soutar: extracts from 'The Permanence of the Young Men' and 'Revelation' from *Poems of the War Years* ed. M. Wollman, Macmillan Ltd, 1948. Bernard Spencer: 'Behaviour of Money' © Mrs. Anne Humphreys 1981; reprinted from Bernard Spencer's *Collected Poems* ed. Roger Bowen (1981) by permission of Oxford University Press. Stephen Spender: extracts from 'The Prisoners', *Citizens in War – and After, World Within World* (Hamish Hamilton) and 'September Journal' reprinted by permission of the author. G. W. Stonier: extract from *Round London with a Unicorn*, Turnstile Press, 1951. Randall Swingler: extract from 'Sixty Cubic Feet' from *New Lyrical Ballads*, Nicholson and Watson, 1945, reprinted by permission of Chatto & Windus. Julian Symons: 'Homage To Our Leaders', 'Conscript', 'Pub' and extract from *Notes from Another Country* © Julian Symons 1943, 1972. A. S. J. Tessimond: 'Smart-Boy', 'Song in a Saloon Bar', 'London' and 'The British' from *Collected Poems of A. S. J. Tessimond*,

Whiteknight Press, by permission of H. Nicholson (editor and literary executor). Dylan Thomas: 'A Refusal to Mourn the Death, By Fire, of a Child in London' and 'Lament' from *Collected Poems 1934–1953*, Dent, 1988. R. S. Thomas: 'Homo Sapiens 1941' from *Song at the Year's Turning*, Rupert Hart-Davis, 1955; reprinted by permission of Grafton Books, a division of William Collins & Sons; also 'Propaganda'. J. Alan Thompson: 'Military Honours' from *Poems of the Forces*, Fortune Press, 1942. Frank Thomson: 'Allotrias Diai Gynaikos' and 'Tent-Pitchers' from *For Your Tomorrow*, Oxford University Press, 1950. Ruthven Todd: 'Letter About War', from *Until Now*, The Fortune Press. Henry Treece: extracts from 'To Certain Ladies, on Going to the Wars' from *The Black Seasons*, Faber, 1945, and from 'The End of the War in Europe' from *Leaves in the Storm: a Book of Diaries*, Lindsay Drummond, 1947. Vic Turner: 'Country-Town in War-Time' from *Little Review Anthology*, 1943, Eyre & Spottiswoode. Keith Vaughan: extracts from *Exiles in Khaki;* and 'V-E Day' from Penguin *New Writing*, No. 25, 1945. E. A. Walmsley: '1914' © The Salamander Oasis Trust, from *Return to Oasis*, Shepheard-Walwyn Ltd. J. B. Warr: 'Stepney 1941' from *Poems from the Forces* ed. K. Rhys, Routledge; 'War Widow' from *Air Force Poetry* eds J. Pudney & H. Treece, John Lane/The Bodley Head, 1944. John Wedge: 'Night Patrol' from *Poems from the Forces* and 'Action Stations' from *More Poems from the Forces* (1943), both volumes ed. K. Rhys, Routledge; also from 'War Widow' from *Air Force Poetry* ed. J. Pudney and H. Treece, John Lane/The Bodley Head, 1944. Victor West: 'La Belle Indifférence' © Victor West, from *Return to Oasis*, The Salamander Oasis Trust, Shepheard-Walwyn Ltd. Tom Wintringham: 'Embarkation Leave' from Penguin *New Writing*, 28, 1946. Michael Wishart: extract from *High Diver*, Blond & Briggs; reprinted by permission of Century Hutchinson Ltd. George Woodcock: 'The Agitator' from *The Kestrel and Other Poems of Past and Present*, Ceolfrith Press, 1978. Rollo Wooley: 'The Search' from Penguin *New Writing*, No. 30, 1947. David Wright: 'V.J. Day' and 'The Fall of France' from *New Poems*, *P.E.N. Anthology* ed. Nott, Lewis and Blackburn, 1957; 'A Stroll in Soho', 'A Ballad for Hard Times' and 'On a Friend Dying' from *To the Gods the Shades*, Carcanet, 1976. Peter Yates: 'November News: 1941' from *Poems*, Chatto & Windus Ltd. Andrew Young: 'Field Glasses' from *The Collected Poems of Andrew Young*, Rupert Hart-Davis, 1960.

Illustrations

The author and publishers would also like to thank the following for permission to use their illustrations: Mrs. Eric Fraser for *War Calls the Tune* (page 3), *Go To It – Shipbuilding* (page 153) and *Music While You Work* (page 179) – all these originally appeared in *Radio Times*; David Langdon for 'Now 'ere you 'ave a more or less perfect example of what 'appens to a feller what's never troubled to master the art of unarmed combat' (page 95); Brooke Bond Oxo Ltd for Oxo advertisement *Strengthen the Home Front* (page 215); *Punch* magazine for *The Sign* (page 255); Osbert Lancaster and John Murray (Publishers) Ltd for 'Don't be so stuffy, Henry! I'm sure that if you asked him nicely the young man would be only too pleased to give you the name of a really GOOD tailor who doesn't worry about coupons!' (page 287); The Royal College of Art for drawing by John Minton (page 317).

Introductory Note

This anthology illustrates the experience of the war decade as seen by the writers and poets and artists of the nineteen-forties. The stimulus of war provoked a sea change in the arts in Britain. Many new voices were heard in the explosion of democratic culture that centred round the pubs and drinking clubs of the West End of London. Because of the short attention possible for those serving in the armed forces, the age was that of the small magazine, of light verse and the serious poem, of the sketch and the cartoon, of the newsreel and the short story. This anthology uses these disparate sources to create pictures of the period from its beginning until the dispersal of this brief culture at the end of the decade.

The selection of pieces is the personal choice of the editor, derived from his wide reading for his book about the arts in the 1940s, *War Like a Wasp*. There are many pieces by unknown authors, while some famous poems have been excluded, usually for reasons of length. For instance, the finest of the war poems, the later of T. S. Eliot's *Four Quartets*, have not been included, as they should be read as a whole. The editor has preferred pieces that describe the war and post-war experience rather than rural or religious poetry, which may be timeless in its commentary. He has also preferred the evidence of those who knew London, where the culture of the period was centred. Above all, he has tried to select pieces that capture the feel and the shock of the years of the war decade. He regrets only the omissions he has had to make among the tens of thousands of just and true and spare descriptions of that extraordinary time.

Andrew Sinclair

I
The Coming of
the War

When Nazi Germany supported by Russia invaded Poland on the First of September 1939, and when Britain and France declared war on Germany two days later, the coming of the war had long been expected. In some ways, it was a relief. The twenty-one years which had passed since the end of the Great War had seemed only an interval. They had been wasted. Or so James Monahan felt:

THE FECKLESS YEARS

The wounded took the stone-eyed girls,
danced on a maudlin floor
to music that broken nerves had chosen.
And the time was after war.

They danced for twenty years. They danced
to the hammering, same refrain,
louder and louder as though they sought
to drown the sound of pain –

until it became the lullaby
of a world that had buried sorrow
beneath the muddied pool of pleasure;
so would have killed the morrow.

The feckless years! For testament
They left their sons a scourge.
A war has been their epitaph.
A crooner sang their dirge.

Even the aesthete Brian Howard saw the waste of the 'twenties and the 'thirties.

GONE TO REPORT

For twenty-one years he remained, faithful and lounging
There, under the last tree, at the end of the charming evening street.
His flask was always full for the unhappy, rich, or bold;
He could always tell you where you wanted to go, what you wanted
    to be told,
And during all the dear twenty-one years he remained exactly
    twenty-one years old.
His eyes were the most honest of all, his smile the most naturally
    sweet.

5

Many, many trusted him who trusted no one. Many extremely clever
Persons will kill themselves unless they find him. They search
Sparkling with fear, though the whole quarter. They even enter the Church.
Crowds, across all Europe, are beginning to feel they've been left in the lurch.
But it's worse than that. It's something they couldn't tell anyone, ever.

He's abandoned his post because he was the greatest of all informers,
And now he's gone to report. He never had a moment's leisure.
He was paid so many powers that one shakes with shame
To think of them. Time, the Army and Navy, Pain and Blame,
The Police, the Family, and Death. No one will escape. He got every name.
And he wasn't at all what he said he was. Mr. Pleasure.

Some blamed their fathers' generation, as E. A. Walmsley was to do from the desert front:

1914

They said, 'It shall not happen twice. We'll fight
To make the world a better place.' They died
And I was born. Foolish, I thought them right.
They lied.

Christopher Hassall and others put the blame on themselves. They had not stopped the coming of the wary.

from CRISIS

Look at the searchlights! There's a fire in heaven
And we have turned our hoses on the sky.
Look at that flock of birds, daring to fly
Across the luminous torrent, never driven
To earth, but coming thickly on in tens,

Twenties and hundreds, silvering overhead.
– Your dare-all birds are aeroplanes, I said,
Whose passengers are heavy fountain-pens.
– What will they write?
　　　　　　　Death-warrants.
　　　　　　　　　　Who must die?
Since you demand an answer: You and I.
My friend grew pale. Is this our Judgement-Day?
How have we sinned? How have these Things intruded
On our sweet sleep? Who made them, anyway?
Startled, we both replied together – YOU DID.

*And some such as Edward Hyams's hero William Medium greeted the war
as a job and as security.*

from *WILLIAM MEDIUM*

With what a sense of relief and release did I greet the outbreak of
war on the following day! Here, at last, after years of the sultry
oppression which precedes the storm, came the lightning, the thunder,
the rain; and, like millions of others, while outwardly grave, I welcomed
the storm.

For what had the peace meant to so many? It had meant semi-
starvation on a grudged dole. Or hard work, at uncongenial labour, for
a bare living wage, without any security. These facts are notorious.
But there are others: no young man or woman, of whatever class,
could say that, when he or she left school, there would be interesting
and remunerative work to do. But what would happen now that the
war had come? There would be a sense of purpose and community of
interest. The youth, leaving school, would face not misery, not boredom, but dangerous adventure, which is congenial to a young man, if
he be sufficiently fed. He would not have to run errands for some
grinding shopkeeper, serve a dull apprenticeship to some discouraged
tradesman, wear out a seat in a bank or municipal office. On the
contrary, he could look forward to comradeship, to quick promotion,
to authority; could see himself as pilot of a great aircraft, as holding
rank, as being well-paid, as being able to marry, as having a servant.
He might even come to the command to one of H.M. ships, sail the
seven seas, fight heroic battles. The man who, hitherto, had found
himself a public nuisance, would now be a public pet. The woman
who had been bound to the terrible and unremitting grind of housekeep-
ing and breeding children, on an inadequate income, would go into the

7

factory, enjoy amusing and friendly company, high pay and regular hours, for the first time in her life.

The most terrible indictment of our moral condition in 1939 which it is possible to make, is that Hitler and his kind were perfectly right to exalt the notion of war to their young men; it was, unquestionably, and all cant put away, preferable to the arid peace which we had made.

Once the war was declared, the question was how to react to it. As a girl, Elizabeth Jennings was afraid.

THE SECOND WORLD WAR

The voice said 'We are at War'
And I was afraid, for I did not know what this meant.
My sister and I ran to our friends next door
As if they could help. History was lessons learnt
    With ancient dates, but here

Was something utterly new,
The radio, called the wireless then, had said
That the country would have to be brave. There was much to do.
And I remember that night as I lay in bed
    I thought of soldiers who

Had stood on our nursery floor
Holding guns, on guard and stiff. But war meant blood
Shed over battle-fields, Cavalry galloping. War
On that September Sunday made us feel frightened
    Of what our world waited for.

Bernard Gutteridge was also afraid, as most people were who lived in the cities. They expected to be destroyed immediately by air raids and bombs.

IN SEPTEMBER 1939

The last war was my favourite picture story.
Illustrated London News bound in the study;
The German bayonet we believed still bloody

But was just rusty. Privacy of death.
My uncle's uniform meant more than glory;
Surprise that grief should be so transitory . . .

All the predictions of adolescence had
Disposed of glory in their realist path:
There'd be no need to duck and hold your breath.

Now, looking as useless and as beautiful
As dragonflies, the plump silver balloons
Hang over London also like zany moons.

Yet from the blacked-out window death still seems
Private, not an affair that's shared by all
The distant people, the flats, the Town Hall.

But some remember Spain and the black spots
They shouted 'Bombers' at. That memory screams
That we know as a film or in bad dreams.

Fear will alight on each like a dunce's cap
Or an unguessed disease unless death drops
Quicker than the sirens or the traffic stops.

*Robert Gittings and W. R. Rodgers saw the war as a matter for the
generations to resolve.*

SEPTEMBER 3rd, 1939

Eating an apple from an English tree
With Autumn at our feet, we are at war.
It might be madness on a martian star
For all the evidence that eyes can see –
Wasps at their prey of plums, intent as we,
But wiser in their limits – calendar
Of ripeness everywhere but us, who are
Seasonless, reasonless, mortal and unfree.

No words can put this right. Our proper place
Is now our proper selves. The only hope
For man is still man though mankind be cursed.

9

Horror may slash the earth's and every face
With hate. Yet if we fill our harmless scope
We, the last Adam, need not be the worst.

Robert Gittings

WAR-TIME

Now all our hurries that hung up on hooks,
And all our heels that idly kicked in halls,
And all our angers that at anchor swung,
And all our youth long tethered to dole-lines,
And all our roots that rotted deep in dump,
Are recollected. In country places
Old men gather the children round them now,
As an old tree, when lopped of every bough,
Gathers the young leaves into itself, a frilled stump.

W. R. Rodgers

Louis MacNeice was in the United States of America in 1939 before he returned to work at the British Broadcasting Corporation. He took a jaundiced view of war reports and propaganda.

BAR-ROOM MATINS

Popcorn peanuts clams and gum:
We whose Kingdom has not come
Have mouths like men but still are dumb

Who only deal with Here and Now
As circumstances may allow:
The sponsored programme tells us how.

And yet the preachers tell the pews
What man misuses God can use:
Give us this day our daily news

That we may hear behind the brain
And through the sullen heat's migraine
The atavistic voice of Cain:

'Who entitled you to spy
From your easy heaven? Am I
My brother's keeper? Let him die.'

And God in words we soon forget
Answers through the radio set:
'The curse is on his forehead yet.'

Mass destruction, mass disease:
We thank thee, Lord, upon our knees
That we were born in times like these

When with doom tumbling from the sky
Each of us has an alibi
For doing nothing – Let him die.

Let him die, his death will be
A drop of water in the sea,
A journalist's commodity.

Pretzels crackers chips and beer:
Death is something that we fear
But it titillates the ear.

Anchovy almond ice and gin:
All shall die though none can win;
Let the Untergang begin –

Die the soldiers, die the Jews,
And all the breadless homeless queues.
Give us this day our daily news.

Such disillusion was shared by those leading literary figures, John Lehmann and Stephen Spender, who had been Marxists and supporters of Russia in the 'thirties. Now they found themselves uneasy patriots with Communist Russia on the side of Nazi Germany. Lehmann wrote in I AM MY BROTHER:

On September 1, 1939, when the news came through that Hitler had opened his attack on Poland, I had the feeling that I was slipping down into a pit, clutching at grass on the ledges but failing to stay the accelerating descent into darkness. This feeling must have been shared by many others. It was more than the knowledge that we should obviously be at war ourselves within a few days: listening to the broadcasts of Hitler's speeches, it seemed to me that the frightening irrational note in his voice, the lunatic evil that I had become more and more acutely conscious of since the invasion of Austria, had drowned everything else. It had led me deeply to distrust both the school of thought that held that he could be handled on traditional foreign-policy lines, and the other, that everything the Nazis did could be explained on orthodox Marxist lines as part of a shrewdly ruthless plan for capitalist expansion. Now it afflicted me like nausea; and I am certain that I knew from that moment, in spite of the hopes of last-minute withdrawal we all talked about during the tense forty-eight hours between the two decisions, that war to the ruinous end, until either Hitler was destroyed or we ourselves were finished for ever, had become inevitable.

And yet the upper part of our minds clung to straws: I remember during that morning Stephen Spender came in to see me, and like prisoners tapping every corner of a cellar into which they have been flung in the hope of finding a loose stone, we went through every tiniest possibility of escape we could imagine in the situation. He was oppressed with the same weight of foreboding as I was, and though we made our usual jokes to one another, melancholy kept falling on us like a fog . . .

When the actual declaration of war came on the 3rd, the immediate uppermost sensation was, curiously enough, relief. The whole point, after all, of the movement I and my friends had belonged to and believed in was that Hitler must be thwarted and stopped by every means possible. War we dreaded, but war was better than giving in to Hitler if it came to that. It had not been prevented; but at least England was going to show that her – perhaps too tardy – threats were no bluff, and the whole nation was in it at last. We were not alone; and yet, ironically enough, the country we had so lightly thought to be the great champion and leader of our cause was not one of our allies. Even in those early days, before the partition of Poland, the attempt of the comrades to prove that what had broken out was just one more imperialist war was an eye-opener for those who were not too ir-remediably blinded to read the signs.

All the same, the blow was grim enough. Everyone, except possibly those who scented in the war the chance to infuse meaning into lives that had hitherto been meaningless, had his own hardships and disappo-intments to bear. For those who were younger than I was, there was the prospect of an early call-up, the unassessable danger of the front line and a sponge wiped right over the immediate hopes of their careers. During those September days I saw many of them, and was struck by the quiet, undemonstrative way they were taking it, haunted by the slightly dazed look that would come over their faces. For me, there seemed to be an end to many things: a new life had come, and almost everything that mattered in the old life had to be tied up like letters in bundles, and locked away in a drawer for the duration – or for ever.

Because he felt unable to write, Stephen Spender forced himself to keep a diary during the first month of the war.

from SEPTEMBER JOURNAL

SEPTEMBER 3rd.

I am going to keep a journal because I cannot accept the fact that I feel so shattered that I cannot write at all. Today I read in the paper a story by Seymour Hicks of a request he gave to Wilde after his imprisonment, to write a play. Wilde said: 'I will write a wonderful play with wonderful lines and wonderful dialogue.' As he said this, Hicks realised that he would never write again.

I feel as if I could not write again. Words seem to break in my mind like sticks when I put them down on paper. I cannot see how to spell some of them. Sentences are covered with leaves, and I really cannot see the line of the branch that carries the green meanings . . .

The most dangerous deception the emotions can practise on you is to pretend to be timeless and absolute. On top of despair, they impose a boredom, which tells you that nothing is or ever will be worth doing, that all the words have broken into the separate letters of the alphabet and cannot be put together again. The whole of your life, they say, will be like this. Your unhappiness is no longer just a sensation, it is a fern growing through your whole body, and separating the brain. Not only is it going to be impossible for you now to do anything but just stare, without crystallizing your disparate sensations, but today too is expanding into an infinity of boredom. It is now ten o'clock, and one o'clock will not come: or not until a whole sea of empty agony has flooded your mind.

That is how Wilde must have felt sitting with his two boys at his marble-topped table in a café. That is how hundreds of people waiting for the News Bulletins on the wireless feel today. But there is another waiting which is not just the emptiness of waiting. That is the patient faith of waiting. Realising that everything is only an episode in the whole story, and that although one has no control over the episodes, one can gradually form the whole pattern, however terrible the setbacks of moments and even of years.

I must put out my hands and grasp the handfuls of facts. How extraordinary they are! The aluminium balloons seem nailed into the sky like those bolts which hold together the irradiating struts of a biplane between the wings. The streets become more and more deserted and the West End is full of shops to let. Sandbags are laid above the glass pavements over basements along the sidewalk. Last night during the blackout there was a tremendous thunderstorm. We stood at the bottom of Regent Street in the pouring rain, the pitch darkness broken intermittently by flashes of sheet lightning which lit up Piccadilly Circus like broad daylight.

SEPTEMBER 4th.

Personally, I prefer Chamberlain's line to all this sanctimoniousness, which is that he has done his best to give Hitler everything but now feels that he can give nothing more. I dislike all the talk about God defending the right. God has always defended the right, and after such a long experience, he of all people should realise the utter futility of it. Personally, if I were a close adviser of God, I'd press him to decide the issue one way or the other once and for all and not go on playing this cat and mouse game between right and wrong.

The whole point of being a man is that there is no omnipotence on one's side. One doesn't have to choose between good and evil, right and wrong, but between various kinds of evil. It is not a conflict between God and the Devil, Christ and Judas, but between the systems represented by Hitler and Chamberlain.

With all humility, I am on the side of the Chamberlain system against Fascism. The fundamental reason is that I hate the idea of being regimented and losing my personal freedom of action. I carry this feeling too far, in fact, I must admit I carry it to the point of hysteria – i.e. the point where I would really fight. I dread the idea of being ordered about and being made to do what I don't want to do in a cause I hate. This fear has even forced me into a certain isolation, in which I find that the personalities of my fellow beings often impose a restraint and unwelcome sense of obligation on me.

There you are, you analyse your hatred of Fascism and it comes to a desire to be left alone. At school you allowed the other boys to take your possessions from you, but finally there was something which you fought for blindly – the possibility of being alone. When you felt that they were compelling you to be like them, and never to get away from their system and their standards, you bit and scratched. The same is true of all your relations with people. When you feel that another personality is obstructing the development of your own, you feel an embarrassment which is really the repression of rage . . .

Of course, there is a great deal to be got out of refusing to touch evil, in the way of saving one's own soul and being an example to future generations. But actually, personal salvation and getting myself into a morally correct position superior to my contemporaries, don't appeal to me, perhaps because I don't believe in a system of rewards and punishments in an after life. If I ran away it would be because I wanted to save my skin or get on with my work, not because I felt that even the world at war was unendurably wicked.

SEPTEMBER 29th.

The world suffers from the worst and least necessary of mental illnesses – homesickness. The papers are filled with photographs, and have been now for years, of those who have been driven out of their homes – the endless rustle of shuffling peasant feet through the dust all night along the road outside Malaga, the family with their possessions piled up in a cart outside a burning Polish farmhouse, the widow searching amongst the ruins of her house for a souvenir. They are driven from the little hole which surrounded and comforted them, into the elemental world of alien stones and light.

Most homeless of all, little shreds of matter from distant countries that have nothing to do with them, are driven through their flesh. The whole universe of Outside enters their bodies – a fragment of a bomb, a bullet.

After that, in the world today there is the desolation of ideas. In times of war and revolution, the great comfort has always been that in place of home there is the home of the idea. Patriotism suddenly becomes the home. One goes out into the street and finds that everyone is friendly, everyone is a brother or sister of everyone else, because the family of the homeland is threatened. The home of the idea, patriotism, revolutionary fervour, can knit people together into a spasmodic unity which is even stronger than the happiest family life. But today, for hundreds of people, even that consolation is denied to them. The greatest desolation in the world is produced by the confusion of ideas.

Many can no longer fight for their country with any conviction, which is to fight for the home of the Past. And the Home of the Future, Revolution, is so compromised that only the most ideological thinkers are able to want to fight for that, either. The world appears a desert. There is no woman, there are no children, there is no faith, there is no cause.

The moon shines above the London streets during the blackouts like an island in the sky. The streets become rivers of light. The houses become feathery, soft, undefined, aspiring, so that any part of this town might be the most beautiful city in the world, sleeping amongst silk and water. And the moon takes a farewell look at our civilization everywhere. I have seen it as an omen in Valencia, Barcelona, and Madrid, also. Only the houses were not plumed, feathery, soft, there: the moon was brighter, and they seemed made of white bone.

Neither Spender nor Lehmann was to serve in the armed forces during the war, although Spender did join the Auxiliary and the National Fire Services. To Michael Burn and Drummond Allison, it was not enough to speak out and refuse to fight.

TO A FORCED VOICE

It is not enough to mouth elegies to tractors,
If you return each evening and hang your hat
In the neat white cloakroom of your neat white flat.

It is not enough to blast the people to battle,
If you have never had part in a battle yourself.
It is not enough to take from the dustered shelf

The anger of others and bottle it up as your own,
And chatter like parrot and monkey of golden morns.
You are following feet that have walked on the world's thorns,

And if your heart has never worn ragged clothes,
And if it has never been wounded, whatever the pain,
All you can shout of the struggles of others is vain.

Michael Burn

FOR KARL MARX

O Marx, who showed ideas made out of matter,
Who saw the soldier and the missionary
As servants not of flags but the exporter,
Who stood God with the phantom and the fairy,

Who could reveal the gold behind the talkers;
I am not deaf to all truth I encounter
Though every minute thought like some eggtimer's
Sand seep away, though never I recover

My eagerness to learn. But from my Father's
Laborious ways to wealth there still remain
Some scorns for spoil the foredoomed victory gathers

Urging allegiance where your books ordain
Annihilation, and my troth is plighted
With guilty classes sure to be defeated.

Drummond Allison

Ruthven Todd was called up against his will to serve in uniform. His mood was widespread.

LETTER ABOUT WAR

I walked to-day in that grey city
Where the soft balloons spangle the blue sky
Down to the pale horizon, broken
By the spires of churches, where some pray
That their god, if he has not forsaken
Them, should rise in anger, without pity.

Yesterday I walked between hedges
Of hawthorn twisted like a net, where the fields'
Chocolate earth was crisp as glass
From a Christmas tree, where the frozen stream folds
Like linen, and there was ice
In the morning round the window's edges.

In this place I am one of many,
To die for four shillings and an oath gabbled
On a station-platform, for a dream,
For vague words a gouty old man babbled;
To be nothing but a name,
One of a multitude crushed by weight of money.

I am not expected to think;
But to be content with a future ending to-morrow
Or the day after – if I am lucky
Enough to know god intimately, to borrow
That time to strut, cocky
As a child, in a new uniform. My pen and ink

Are treason. My dear,
I write these few lines to state to you
I will not play the hero in a dream
Or die to prove a falsehood more untrue
Nor to increase the fame
Of old men who have no future, whose end is near,

Whose page in history
Is booked already, but the verdict hidden;
I do not wish to solve the mystery
Of death for such as have forbidden
Life for the living.

The point was, the war had to be fought. The question was, what was the fight for? J. B. Priestley, the most influential of all the wartime broadcasters, tried to give some answers.

from THE WAR – AND AFTER

People still write to me to say that we are at war because we like war. This is not true. Apart from some young Nazi hotheads and officers hoping for quick promotion, nobody now likes and wants war. The Nazis based their whole technique on this fact. In a really belligerent world they could never have brought off their remarkable series of *coups*. The trick was to threaten war in a world ready to pay almost any price for peace. The Nazis did not want war but the spoils of it. Collecting those spoils was rapidly becoming the national industry of the Third Reich.

Other people, who applauded Leftish writers like myself when we said that Britain should make a stand against the Nazis, now revile us as warmongers because we believe in the stand that Britain is now making. Why? Can you disintegrate the Gestapo by passing a few resolutions in Hampstead? We passed thousands of resolutions, spoke eloquently of peace and goodwill, but the dark stain spread over the map of Central Europe, the Gestapo moved in, and the refugees came thick and fast. Bernard Shaw says it is all right now, because his friend

Stalin has everything under control. Well, Stalin may have made special arrangements to see that Shaw comes to no harm, but the rest of us in Western Europe do not feel quite so sure of our fate, especially those of us who do not share Shaw's curious admiration for dictators . . .

What do human beings want most? The answer appears to be, Security and Freedom. Security comes first, for if you do not know when your children will have their next meal, you are not interested in the refinements of political theory. (This fact is apt to be overlooked by the democracies.) On the other hand, the point at which the demand for security changes into the desire for freedom is soon reached. (This fact is overlooked by the totalitarian states.) Security-at-the-expense-of-freedom only seems to apply with most people to elementary needs and does not apply to radio sets, cars, tiled bathrooms, antique furniture, collections of etchings, and the like. Freedom, by which I do not mean anything transcendental but the absence of the censor, the informer, propaganda-at-all-costs, forced labour, and the whole dreadful para-phernalia of the police state, comes long before these things are reached, at least among the healthy-minded. It seems nothing while you have it. But it seems everything when you have lost it. Ask the nearest refugee.

It may be, however, that there is something in the modern world, no matter whether it accepts capitalist democracy, communism, Nazism, Fascism, that is bent on rapidly reducing the number of the healthy-minded, is addling the wits of man, is making it harder and harder to be easy, merry, affectionate and wise. It may be that all this fuss about machinery does some damage to the imagination, that life in our huge idiotic cities poisons the psyche, that too many people secretly regard their own activities with contempt, that we are creating an atmosphere, in peace as well as in war, in which the spirit cannot flower freely, that our inability to answer the major questions of life and our frequent pretence that therefore they do not still exist are producing profound and terrible conflicts. Perhaps where we need it most, we have no Maginot Line.

However bad the prospect of war might be, there was certainty that the country would outlast it. As John Bayliss declared:

from EPILOGUE: TESTAMENT AND PROPHECY

And I say to you who have seen
war like a wasp under a warm apple
rise and sting the unwary,
that its breed shall multiply

and fill the air with wings, and dapple
disaster on the bright sky,
and worse things shall be than have been.

But there shall yet be better.
Out of the almond-tree and the acacia
shall come back beauty, out of the cornfield
a few shall comfort them
when all things else have failed;
and though the cities be quiet
and the streets wet
with the river's rising and the sea's invasion
and their buildings flat as the bomber's vision,
there shall be farms in the far country
shall end fear: and ruin yield
a better sight than the grey sentry.

2

Waiting and Training

" Of course you realise that it's all very informal."

Malcolm Muggeridge found it difficult to take the first year of the war too seriously.

from THE BEGINNING OF THE 'FORTIES

It was the period which has come to be known as the phoney war. Every circumstance of war was present except warfare. Armies existed, apparently in battle-array; uniforms were worn, both at home and abroad; fortifications were dug, passwords were exchanged, trumpets were sounded, canteens were organised, songs were sung – washing to be hung on the Siegfried Line, rabbit to be made to run, run, run, or of the tenderer sort 'Somewhere in France with you'. The champions were in the ring, proclaiming what they would do to one another, asserting their prowess, but carefully refraining from coming to grips, until the onlookers across the Atlantic grew impatient, and began to complain that their attention had been gained on false pretences, and that the whole effort was a hoax, a sort of 'Royal Nonesuch' advertising itself as for adults only and constituting nothing.

So strange a situation has rarely existed. Clouds were dark and menacing; the wind had dropped, and there was the stillness which precedes a mighty storm, and still the first heavy drops of rain did not fall, still it seemed that, after all, no storm might come. Was it, perhaps, on the part of all concerned a sense of the awful consequences which would follow the explosion when at last it came? In the same way, suicides find pretexts to put off the fatal act upon which they have decided – to-day will not do because the laundry has not come, or because someone is coming to tea; another time, when all has been prepared, no shilling is available to put into the gas-meter. Thus Europe, preparing for its act of suicide, delayed, in the faint, and for the most part unconscious, hope that, after all, the suicide might be unnecessary. Something would surely happen to prevent it. Somehow, somewhere, something would happen to make the dreaded event unnecessary. Meanwhile, seal up the windows, write the last will and testament, prepare to turn on the little tap and efface a life which had become futile and burdensome.

In England, Neville Chamberlain was still Prime Minister. His flock remained faithful, though the tumultuous enthusiasm aroused by his return from Munich with Hitler's signed undertaking not to resort to war had diminished considerably under the stress of actually going to war with Hitler. He had become a somewhat melancholy figure. His rage at the manner in which he had been deceived was too personal to be impressive – like the rage of an elderly vicar who, after a romantic marriage with a youthful church-worker, finds that she has deceived him with the choirmaster. His denunciations of the Nazis were now unbridled, but late, and in politics timing is all . . .

Certain changes had been made in the composition of the Cabinet when war broke out, the most notable of which was the inclusion of Mr. Churchill as First Lord of the Admiralty. After a decade of exclusion from office, he found himself again exercising authority, and the experience was invigorating. Like a music-hall star banned from the stage, and then once more stepping into the limelight, seeing an audience again spread out before him and waiting expectantly to be delighted, he began a performance more remarkable than any even he had ever given; a performance which, before it had finished, would earn him undying glory, and if not the gratitude, at least the applause of his fellow-countrymen. His broadcasts on the activities of the Royal Navy accustomed them to a voice which they were to get to know very well indeed, beneath whose heavy cadences they were to shelter from fearful dangers, and which was to arouse, encourage, stimulate and reassure them when all other circumstances were calculated to have an opposite effect. Amidst much unreality, what Mr. Churchill said seemed real. Compared with other microphone emanations, his words had a solid quality – like a glass of beer after a soda-fountain concoction. Whatever anyone else might be doing, Mr. Churchill and the Royal Navy had found the elusive war and were fighting it. His only possible rival as a broadcaster was Haw-Haw across the water, whose venomous accents were reaching the peak of their popularity; turned on nightly in large numbers of homes, and listened to with a kind of guilty fascination – that venom, that insistence, like Lear's, that *all* should change or cease, also finding an echo in many hearts.

Malignancy and resistance to malignancy provided, indeed, at this stage the only reality the war had – two voices, one lean and venomous, the other deep-throated, rich. All else seemed dream-like, shadowy – silky B.B.C. announcer . . . uniforms multiplying, savings appealed for, the foot of Nelson's column bearing the legend 'Save for the Brave', torches required even by itinerant prostitutes who would otherwise have passed unnoticed through the blacked-out streets, required by everyone in that bitterly cold winter.

In Germany, enthusiasm was still high, and prospects appeared excellent. The Führer announced that he would continue to wear his old corporal's tunic until the final victory was gained, and announced in a New Year message that Germany was 'fighting for the creation of a new Europe, for, unlike Mr. Chamberlain, we are convinced that this new Europe cannot be created by the senile powers of a decaying world'. Poor, bellowing, little Führer – what he did not understand was that he, too, belonged to the decaying world, and would achieve no new Europe, but rather the old one's final destruction. His rage was as vacuous as what it was directed against. The trumpets blew, and the walls of Jericho obediently fell down, becoming a heap of rubble. It was rubble, not a new Europe, he was to leave behind him – towns transformed into rubble, heaps of liberated dust.

At the beginning of the 'forties, however, his fury was still young and in the spring. Nothing had gone wrong. Every one of his ventures had succeeded, and it seemed that the mystique of his luck had provided Germany with a religion, and Germans with the will to go on from victory to victory. His associates, notably Mussolini, were dazzled, and against their own judgment surrendered themselves to his purposes; his opponents were dazed, and from their defensive positions awaited his next move. Like the Ancient Mariner, he held them all with his glittering eye – strange, incandescent phenomenon of a departing world, twilight monstrosity, wild sudden glare in the sky before darkness finally descends.

From his Bavarian eyrie, up in the mountains, he surveyed the world, waiting for guidance as to what he should do next. Generals were in attendance, patiently listening to long, turgid discourses; prime ministers, and even monarchs, were content to wait their turn to be received by him, and the whole world still anxiously hung on his words, thinking to find in them the key to what he intended. He had to decide. The very success with which the Nazi theory of leadership had been preached put him in this position – that he alone could decide. Like many another, he was the victim of his own deception, imprisoned in his own vanity and deceit. Führer he had demanded to be, and Führer he now was; the one and only. A Keitel or Jodl would execute his orders, might even respectfully proffer advice, or respectfully criticise his projects; but he must take the decision, he alone, or the spell would be broken.

Even in the light of all that has subsequently been disclosed in captured documents at Nuremberg, in the revelations of personal associates, it is still impossible to know exactly what went on inside that strange, confused mind. Like Joan of Arc, he heard voices; like Macbeth he attached great importance to supernatural signs and omens, and kept his own staff of astrologers and seers. In his intentions, he faltered and changed; yet in the end, somnambulistic, he led us all to our doom with the sleep-walker's sureness of foot and of purpose. A general will to destruction found expression in his will. He focused the despair of a civilisation which had lost its way, and the destructive rage of all those for whom life has no significance beyond its phenomenon, no satisfaction other than in its appetites.

If, from his mountain eyrie, he looked eastwards, he saw the multitudinous Slavs who were destined, he thought, to become the instruments of German dominance; the vast kingdoms of his new ally, Stalin. If he looked westwards, he saw the ranged forces, such as they were, of his enemies, temptingly vulnerable and loot-worthy, a prize which would satisfy, at once, his pride and his cupidity. They deserved destruction because, in their weakness and folly, they had refused to accept the inevitability of his triumph. They had despised and rejected him, and must now receive their punishment. Eastwards, the rage of superiority, and westwards of inferiority – where should he strike first? He hesitated, certain only that at all costs he must avoid engaging both at the same time. In the end, it was just that he must do, thereby achieving at last his own ruin.

In the West, the forces of democracy prepared themselves for battle, and noisily announced their determination to go on until final victory was achieved. Trenches were dug and defences constructed, and Mr. Chamberlain congratulated the B.E.F. on the 'good humour with which they were facing the conditions of active service in the winter weather'. Officers with many decorations and wearing riding-breeches supervised the positions which had been prepared, and discussed plans of campaign; maps were pinned on boards, and orders of battle marked on them, and occasionally patrols actually made contact with the enemy. War correspondents, having exhaustively described the excellent arrangements made for moving troops abroad, the good humour of the men, the adequacy of the rations, the amount of wine provided to French soldiers, moodily wondered when something would happen for them to write about, and grumbled at having to describe a war which would not come to pass. General Ironside, whose name and physique were reassuring, announced that all was prepared to deal with an enemy offensive, and that the Allied armies desired nothing better; and General Gamelin issued laconic communiques which daily reported no change in the situation.

The war which General Ironside and General Gamelin expected was a dream war – like the vast armies and splendidly caparisoned knights which Don Quixote described to Sancho Panza as they looked down on a flock of sheep. For this dream war, as General Ironside said, all was indeed prepared. As, however, it never happened, the preparations for it were in vain. Don Quixote valiantly charged his imaginary armies, performing incredible deeds of valour, until the shepherds, annoyed by his antics, began to aim stones at him, and brought him bruised and bewildered to the ground.

This was soon to happen. Meanwhile, Sancho Panza continued to be convinced. At the Mansion House, the Prime Minister, he, too, a knight of the Woeful Countenance, dwelt on the battles which were to be fought and the victories which were to be won in the war that could never happen. 'Nowhere but in the City of London,' *The Times* commented, 'could such an audience be assembled. The heads of the National Church and the Roman Communion in England, Cabinet Ministers, principal officers of all the fighting services and of the various auxiliaries that war, or the preparation for war, has called into being – these were interspersed with the leaders of finance, commerce and industry, and the dignitaries of the City itself, headed by the Lord Mayor and Lady Mayoress.'

It seemed formidable enough.

Some troops left to join the British Expeditionary Force in France.

1939, OCTOBER

The land is freezing, soldiers line the station
who have forgotten where their country is.
The girls are dreaming of heroic actions
and they know more of Death and Victories.

You stand at the station, waving your tears.
The train leaves, now smoke is all you can see.
No angels now, to go down on their knee
and love: they also know fear.

Horror is knocking at every door
and through our window throws its grudge.
The blind man must be led over the bridge,
but we are tired and cannot see any more.
The grass grows yellow and the seas are weary,
tonight the night is filled with jazzy blare.
On the dark waters swims the moon, the ferry
taking with it the fear and the war.

Fred Marnau

Less than four in a hundred people who were conscripted refused to fight.
Louis MacNeice tried to explain some of their reasons.

BOTTLENECK

Never to fight unless from a pure motive
And for a clear end was his unwritten rule
Who had been in books and visions to a progressive school

27

And dreamt of barricades, yet being observant
Knew that that was not the way things are:
This man would never make a soldier or a servant.

When I saw him last, carving the longshore mist
With an ascetic profile, he was standing
Watching the troopship leave, he did not speak
But from his eyes there peered a furtive footsore envy
Of these who sailed away to make an opposed landing –
So calm because so young, so lethal because so meek.

Where he is now I could not say; he will,
The odds are, always be non-combatant
Being too violent in soul to kill
Anyone but himself, yet in his mind
A crowd of odd components mutter and press
For compromise with fact, longing to be combined
Into a working whole but cannot jostle through
The permanent bottleneck of his highmindedness.

Louis MacNeice

*Some who did not wish to volunteer, such as Cecil Day Lewis, joined the
local Home Guard to watch against the coming of the enemy.*

WATCHING POST

A hill flank overlooking the Axe valley.
Among the stubble a farmer and I keep watch
For whatever may come to injure our countryside –
Light-signals, parachutes, bombs, or sea-invaders.
The moon looks over the hill's shoulder, and hope
Mans the old ramparts of an English night.

In a house down there was Marlborough born. One night
Monmouth marched to his ruin out of that valley.
Beneath our castled hill, where Britons kept watch,
Is a church where the Drakes, old lords of this countryside,
Sleep under their painted effigies. No invaders
Can dispute their legacy of toughness and hope.

Two counties away, over Bristol, the searchlights hope
To find what danger is in the air tonight.

Presently gunfire from Portland reaches our valley
Tapping like an ill-hung door in a draught. My watch
Says nearly twelve. All over the countryside
Moon-dazzled men are peering out for invaders.

The farmer and I talk for a while of invaders:
But soon we turn to crops – the annual hope,
Making of cider, prizes for ewes. Tonight
How many hearts along this war-mazed valley
Dream of a day when at peace they may work and watch
The small sufficient wonders of the countryside.

Image or fact, we both in the countryside
Have found our natural law, and until invaders
Come will answer its need: for both of us, hope
Means a harvest from small beginnings, who this night
While the moon sorts out into shadow and shape our valley
A farmer and a poet, are keeping watch.

The anti-aircraft gunners watched the sky, waiting for the enemy to come.

STATE OF READINESS

The moon rises late:
After sudden warning we wait,
The guns manned, searching among the stars.
At last, perhaps, our hour has come. Cars
Shoot past with urgent messages. We stand
Eager and glad, rifles steady and cool in hand.
For months nothing has happened. Now the sky
Turns hostile. Around us searchlights pry
Into thin clouds. Tonight the enemy, unseen,
Is real. We know these tedious past days have been
Prelude to battle: and if the time is near,
No dearer thoughts shall resurrect our fear.
For this we have waited. If the air should fill
With mushroom parachutes we will
Forsake all memory, all promises to break
On future days, for battle's compelling sake.
We have been ready. Though the warning prove
As false as any, we have abjured our love,
All dreams or hopes, to keep alert and sure.

The drone of planes continues and clouds endure
The searchlight's naked steel. Flares fall,
Hang in the sky. Flashes of guns appal
The quite air. But as the minutes pass
Talk dies out, rats scurry through the grass.
We grow tired, long for cigarettes. Our minds return
To windows where familiar lights still burn.
Our thoughts resume their island voyages:
Raiders give place to homelier images.
                    The moon is full and shines
On tree and hill. In the farm a dog whines;
The routine of life continues while we wait;
Less eager and less certain. Our moons rise late.

H. B. Mallalieu

Lone raiders appeared over Britain to test the country's defences.

RAIDERS' DAWN

Softly the civilized
Centuries fall,
Paper on paper,
Peter on Paul.

And lovers waking
From the night –
Eternity's masters,
Slaves of Time –
Recognize only
The drifting white
Fall of small faces
In pits of lime.

Blue necklace left
On a charred chair
Tells that Beauty
Was startled there.

Alun Lewis

THE RAIDER

There, wrapped in his own roars, the lone airman
Swims like a mote through the thousands of eyes
That look up at him ironing-out the skies,
Frocked and fanged with fire, by nagging fingers
Of guns jagged and jogged, with shell-bursts tasselled.

Does ever the airman's eye, speeding on
To grim conclusion, alight and loiter
Curiously on the country below?
Or does his gaze easily dissolve
Upon the moving surfaces, and flow
Evenly away like rain on rivers?

Or, roaring back over our armoured rims,
Does his view take in only the bloom and boom
Of bomb beneath him, noting how neatly
It mopped up a map-point town or snouted out
This tip or else that tap-root of resistance?

Yet, pity him too, that navigator
Who now in archipelago of steel
Nears that place where hooked upon barbed air he'll
Halt, hang hump-backed, and look into his crater.

W. R. Rodgers

While working on two collections of Poems from the Forces, *Keidrych Rhys served in an anti-aircraft battery.*

ALARM, ALARM

I remember vapour-trails over Gillingham – wavy
And the monument to the builder of the Japanese navy,
And oil burning in black columns down Thameshaven way;
Queer happenings on Gravesend range; Croydon's day.

Detling divebombed – and Hawkinge – we got two;
I saw convoys screaming up the Channel's blue.
Connect dodged shells a lamp's smashed splendour with
A boy's M.M. earned defending Martlesham Heath.

A plotting board with one-five-o hostile;
The Italian raid; patrolling the beaches, Deal,
Oxney, Shakespeare Cliff and the invasion warning.
From pier-extension to Dovercourt, Felixstowe in Spring!

Joking and blood in a Nissen hut in South Ronaldsay:
The Flow; trips in a drifter to bird-splashed Hoy:
The *Prince of Wales* through an OSDEF telescope;
The leave-boat; a crofter snuffling his stony-crop hope.

Norwich. All this I remember and more oh much more.
Digging planes King's Bench Walk The 'Temple' burning
But nothing nothing that I can compare
To love like a bell through Yarmouth flying!

The men were putting on uniform and leaving the women, and Audrey Beecham knew the hurt of it.

SONG

There's no more talk and ease
No more time to do as you please
Pressure of men on roads, of boots and heels,
Lorries and guns, and birds again
This winter will freeze.

War comes flooding like a tide
O where shall we run, shall hide?

Setting out or turning back,
The old wound split in new strife,
A new wound is a new eye
A festering wound a womb of different life.

Where shall we hide but in the wound?

In England, the countryside was untouched except by the spoiling army camps and Nissen huts disfiguring the landscape. Jack Beeching thought of the soldiers in France.

SPRING OFFENSIVE 1940

Soon come young lambs, and the yellow
Daffodils. Then the tractor-plough
Will shave the frozen squares of fallow.

Soon we shall see hopscotch of bull and cow,
Then leggy calves, and the trees all pure bud green.

As my blood beats I think of French fields. How
Their rivers will thaw, their cuckoos sing, and then
Come screaming shells, and bright bayonets and dead men.

In France, Alan Rook had to be an expert gunner before the retreat to Dunkirk.

SONG OF A TECHNICAL SOLDIER

Do we die
in this far country?

Light of heart and quick of fancy
nimble as a young man's wit,
lightly took the boat and sailed
to do or die for Liberty.

Gaily passed a waiting winter
calling 'See you back next year!'
wheeling guns into position
calculating arcs of fire.

What is this heroic madness
being serious to plan?
Who can hope to stay the cyclone
fighting war without an aim?

So the road is neverending:
so the guns are spiked and lost:
so is sullen death eclipsing
heart before we reach Dunkirk.

33

Do we die
in this far country?

The Fall of France shook the British from their complacency. Everyone remembered, as David Wright did, the bad news announced.

THE FALL OF FRANCE

In Stoke Newington, 1940,
Evening fades again in dust.
Balloons at anchor in the sky
Catch the last light of a lost

Day in London, 18 June.
There by stone museum lions I'd
Seen a man close a newspaper:
'Those bloody frogs have let us down!'

So cut back to the red brick house
Where I met a face from Europe,
A refugee Jew's, a carpenter,
Shoring a hopeless timber prop

Against a boarded kitchen-window
To keep a blast, or Hitler, out;
I looking from an island at
Eyes of no hope, blank with it.

At home, the men volunteered or were conscripted into wearing uniform, usually in camps in the country. Rayner Heppenstall saw them as beasts of the field.

INSTEAD OF A CAROL

The winter hardens. Every night I hear
The patient khaki beast grieve in his stall,
His eyes behind the hard fingers soft as wool.
His cheerful morning face puts me in mind
Of certain things were rumoured far and near
To hearts wherein there fretted and repined
A world that came to its last dated year.

George Scurfield chose to see military training as a song and dance

SONG AND DANCE

I

In the sweet morning over the Kentish hills
comes the sergeant's voice
crying, like a cow in the wilderness –
Bring back, oh bring back,
my baby to me.

Over the hills and into the Kentish river
the sergeant's voice carries
making the blackberries
drop from their branches
and the leaves fade,
fade, fade, my little green jade.

Who sadly spoilt the flow
of the sergeant's beautiful voice
made soldiers fall to vice
and some women to folly.

Into the ruins of a darkened tower
the silence of evening is creeping,
while soldiers in the countryside
are weeping, quietly, softly weeping
– Bring back, oh bring back
my baby to me.

II

Look at the sloping shaping hill
Of huts, trenchscars, and mud
camouflage acts and the scent of blood,
says the soldier
– staring out of the window.
Look at the grey gangrene of the grass
the trapeze of the trees
the becastled river and the maze
of sandbags and wire
– staring out of the window.

35

The steam rises out of the stupid ground
covering over the history of shouts
the whistle of the wind over the huts –
Sleep soon –
– staring out of the window.

*To C. P. Billot, wearing battledress was only a camouflage, not a license
to kill.*

TEMPORARY UNIFORM

These men are soldiers only
Khaki-deep; nothing remains of murder
Under the mud-coloured, sand-coloured
Temporary uniform.
Only the strong clean flesh, the self,
The stamping heart in the chest,
Get into bed with their wives.

This battledress is not
Case-hardening, but enamel peeling
At animal heat, the grim cataract
Draws over the heart, the eyes,
The necessary camouflage for devotion.
The children buried in bombed cities   .
Share flesh with burning heroes by the tanks.

Though a rifle is steel
And wood, trees and the earth
Are never symbols of death;
Under the drab shapes of essential slaughter
The heart pants for its lover,
The eyes for a garden's colours
And the quiet hills at evening.

*As for serving in the forces, the first week was generally the worst. An
anonymous diarist wrote for the popular magazine* Lilliput:

THE FIRST WEEK

Out of the Diary of a Recruit

MONDAY. Letters come at 4 p.m. We cluster round the Orderly Corporal, hoping against reason, like sparrows about a dead horse. There can't possibly be anything for us. We only got here this morning. We put on Battle Dress at 1.30, and have got our first military flavour. It's only a flavour as yet. We are no more like soldiers than a fishy fork is like fish. Bits of our first Army haircut cling to our ears. A Corporal looks in at us and says, 'Why should England tremble? My God.' We are in our Hut: thirty beds made of three boards and two trestles; some brooms and a shovel. We have been told to make ourselves at home. One man has already filled half of a fourpenny pad with his new sorrows, and, concluding with, 'But don't worry, Dear Mum, I am quite all right,' asks for a stamp. Nobody talks. It is raining. There is nothing round here but mud and grass. The grass is dead. No doubt it is better off. Somebody keeps asking: 'But *do* they put Something in the Tea?' A Sergeant says: 'Anybody here like potatoes?' Four of us pluck up courage to say 'Yes.' 'Then come and peel some,' says the Sergeant. He adds: 'All joking aside, I'm looking for somebody who can sing or play the piano.' Three more leap up eagerly. One says he can play an accordeon. 'You'll do,' says the Sergeant. 'Come and help with the dustbins.' The day ends. Lights go out. A man from Worksop screams in his sleep. Another, from Kent, stops breathing with a sharp *Khuk*, and then struggles desperately, finally getting his breath back with a *Wahooooo!*

TUESDAY. An Officer informs us of Army Law. Everything is illegal, particularly Mutiny, Drunkenness, Insubordination, Gambling, Filthy Talk, Unclean Habits and Boots, Desertion, Neglect of Duty, Answering Back, Dumb Insolence, Stealing, Looting, Failure To Respect Womanhood, Murder, Cowardice, Swapping Kit, Bribery, Idleness, Possessing Playing Cards, Bringing Alcohol Into Barracks, Masquerading As An Officer Or N.C.O., Fighting Whilst On Active Service, and Urinating Outside The Hut But Not In The Proper Place. The only indoor game officially permitted is Lotto, or Housie-Housie. If we want to go and drink, we must do so in the proper place: in Barracks, the Naffy. If we want to go and desert, we must be prepared to face the consequences. These consequences make Parkhurst seem like the wide open spaces. The Sergeant asks if we are getting used to it. We enthusiastically cry, 'Oh yes.' To-morrow we shall be given our first taste of the Square. In the meantime, to occupy our minds, there is some swabbing to do. We swab. We receive a Stab In The Arm to inoculate us against diseases. We have one Anti-Vaccinist who swears he will die a thousand deaths rather than submit. But when he opens his mouth to protest, words will not come. He is stabbed. We go to the Naffy. Compared with the pies, the tea seems good. *Night:* The man from Worksop dreams he is saving my life in deep water.

WEDNESDAY. The Square. The Sergeant says: 'What a shower of tripe you are! What horrible men! Gimme loaves to turn into fishes. Gimme water to turn into wine. But turn you into Soldiers, . .! Groo! Why do some mothers have sons?' We leave the Square, sore of foot and heart, for Weapon Training. Then, P.T. The Staff Sergeant looks at us and we sweat in anticipation. Rumour has it that he once put his fist through a galvanised iron wash-bowl. He makes us run round and round, and jump up and down, and fall flat, and skip-jump, and carry each other in our arms, and crouch, and stretch, and breathe in and out, and hop, and hang on bars, and roll over on mats, and vault over horses. Wednesday is a short day, a half-holiday. The man with the fourpenny pad fills a foolscap envelope with a catalogue of atrocious sufferings, but, concluding, asks how you spell 'Enjoyable'. We are led out in due course for a Medical. We have to appear, nakedly, before the M.O. I do not know what he is looking for: he doesn't seem to find it. He looks bored. Somebody asks what these examinations are for. A theorist suggests that once upon a time a lady called Sweet Polly Oliver joined the Army, and since then they cannot be too careful. It seems that there is a little town in reach of an infrequent bus, and that in this little town there are Goings On. Our informant makes it sound like Hollywood in the 1920's. Research lays bare the fact that in the little town nothing whatever goes on. There is a tea-shop which is usually shut, and a cinema to which *Broadway Melody* has just come. The girls, it appears, are all engaged to N.C.O.'s. Such as are not know soldiers only too well. *Night:* The man from Worksop dreams of a Charlie Chaplin film he once saw.

THURSDAY. P.T. Square. Weapon Training. Square. Shepherd's Pie for Dinner. Lecture on Hygiene: contagious diseases are catching, and also illegal. More Square. Gas Masks fitted in gas-chamber. Tear-gas makes our eyes water. We pretend to weep, saying 'Boo-Hoo'. Tea. Hut. Bed. Man from Worksop talks in sleep of Uncle's Tumour in Throat, 'Big as a Babby's Head'. Stiff all over.

FRIDAY. As we rise, we cry 'Eek.' Our muscles are knotted. Man from Kent claims that, such is the rush in the wash-house, he cleaned man from Worksop's teeth. P.T., 'to loosen us up'; then Square, to tighten us up; then more of the same. *Afternoon:* some fatigues, concerned with dead leaves. We are acquiring a technique of keeping a lookout while relaxing. *Evening:* The Man with the Fourpenny Pad has come down to seven lines. We had biscuits for tea: he enclosed one in envelope, saying, 'This is the kind of thing we get. But don't worry. I am quite at home.'

SATURDAY. Half-day. Most of us sleep. Others, fearing fatigues, hide about Camp. I don't know what's happened: I have been asleep. P.T., and Drill have got me in the legs. I do not believe I have much longer to live. Worksop has been talking for three hours about how they had to give him salt-water after his wedding-breakfast. The rain is heavier. The mud is deeper. It is amazing how soft the beds are now. Perhaps this is because deal is a nice soft wood. Or it may be the air. One sleeps.

SUNDAY. Sunday like any other Sunday, except that there is Church. Day of rest, apart from scrubbing out hut, beds, utensils, windows, stove, coal-tub, buckets, and anything else that is washable. An examination of the Library reveals *Little Arthur's England*, *Angela's First Term*, the *Complete Works of Mrs. Humphrey Ward*, *Trixie's Fairy*, *The Pilgrim's Progress*, 198 pages of a *Life of Nelson*, and a bound volume of *Household Words*. We talk of wine, Relativity, women, Hitler, song, Ann Sheridan, children, bicycles, mothers, beetroots, gangsters, tumours, sergeants, ghosts, Godfrey Winn, the potentialities of nurses, dum-dum bullets, the weather, toffee-apples, and the War. Soon we shall go to bed. Then Lights Out will sound. Then the man from Worksop will start to talk of his friend's grandmother who married again at eighty-nine. Then we shall sleep, accepting, with incredulous astonishment, the certainty that tomorrow will be Monday and we've been here a whole week.

Another private wrote to the intellectual magazine Horizon *of his experiences in the army.*

from OURS IS NOT TO REASON WHY

CIVVY STREET

In the Condemned Row the greatest breach of taste is to protest innocence. Moral questions are meaningless after the verdict. In the ante-chamber of death there is only one hope for innocent and guilty alike – Reprieve.

The change from civilian to Army life is almost as great. For the civilian there exists a complex of moral and political motives. Am I a coward? Am I right to seek exemption? How best can I serve my country, class, family or self? The civilian is an agent.

Strip off that mufti; put on the battle dress; make the agent a mere executant; and all these problems vanish, like cobwebs in candleflame. Conscript or volunteer, it makes no difference. The fish is hooked and struggles to get away.

It is not just mufti that we put off and pack in our bags to take home on our first leave: it is a hundred things, which civilians do not treasure because they take them for granted. Career, for example. I do not mean only the young architect or sculptor, taken from the work to which he has devoted years of thought, at the moment when he is beginning to find himself. I mean also the careers of the lorry-drivers and clerks and commercial travellers and bricklayers, personally as important as an artist's life work. Few civilians realize how much the casual contacts of their daily life mean to them: the friendship with the paper boy outside the suburban station, the waitress in the café, the regulars in the local pub. They make a social landscape in which the humblest civilian can freely move, an individual, sketched by his clothes, possessions and habits.

The same man, conscripted, is a number, two identification discs on a string round the neck, a uniform, and a military haircut. His dress, his feet, his hair, his face and his penis are inspected by authority. His standard of living is reduced, and what is even more important psychologically, his spending power is curtailed. Liberty of action is replaced by the authoritarianism of the detail board. He cannot go where he wishes in his free time without a pass. He has to obey all orders he receives, even if they are foolish or unjust. (He may complain afterwards.) Initiative and will power, exercise of which gave him his greatest pleasure in life, now reside in higher authority. He is parted from his family, and stripped of his responsibilities. Civilians sometimes envy soldiers because they are assured of food, a small wage, rent and clothing. But there are few soldiers who would not surrender that meagre security in return for the demands which civilian life places on their resourcefulness.

In peace time the Army recruited men from those who had failed in civilian life, the bankrupts, love-lorn and misfits. The intelligence quotient of these recruits was not high, and rigid discipline was necessary to extort from them the unquestioning obedience on which the morale of a mercenary army is based.

We conscripts, however, had most of us succeeded in adjusting ourselves to civilian life. We held our jobs because we were good at them. We made our way in the world because we could think for ourselves. Our employers appreciated the fact that we could form our own judgements, instead of having to run to them for advice. We were paid for intelligence, not blind obedience.

We realize that fighting is a new job for us and, to start with, most of us are quite eager to learn. But we expect to be taught fighting as we were taught other trades, not as we were taught the Creed. As we are fighting for Democracy, we expect to be treated, not necessarily as equals but as thinking human beings. The military way of saying something is, 'You will do this'. We prefer the civilian way, 'You will do this, because . . .'

We were everything under the sun in Civvy Street, dustmen, actors, scammel drivers, chartered accountants, shopkeepers. But it is amazing the unity which we develop, subjected to the same treatment. The Army tries to turn us into professional soldiers; but the formulae based on training failures as mercenaries fail with us. Potentially we can be finer soldiers than the regulars; but only if methods are devised to use our full powers, our initiative, invention, resourcefulness. To the regular there may be comfort in the attitude, Theirs not to reason why, theirs but to do and die. But the reason why is very important to us, if we have to do and die.

The attempt to train responsible citizens as obedient mercenaries produces a state of mind which is either incomprehensible or appalling to many civilians. On the one hand, the return to Civvy Street becomes the common dream: to get back into mufti at almost at any cost. You should see our envy for the man with hammer toes, or flat feet, our admiration and good wishes to the chap trying to work his discharge by aggravating his duodenal ulcers. You should see the rapture with which a conscript goes back to work with the A.F.S. or the demolition squads. Of course, it is back to the wife and the children, better wages, freedom of movement. But it is, also, back to a life of individual responsibility, a man whose name is more important than his registration number and whose thoughts can find expression in his work.

On the other hand, we accept the military position. If it is not ours to reason why, we shall refuse to reason why. We shall leave the head and heart aches of the war to our superiors. We shall be utterly irresponsible, doing exactly what we are told, no more, and, if possible, less. We shall augment our wages whatever ways we can, like true mercenaries, fighting because we are paid and are jailed if we desert. It is not *our* war; but *their* war, 'they' being vaguely our officers with cars and cultured accents, the politicians and the big business men, the people who write the tripe about us that we read in daily newspapers.

41

One day 'they' will decide not to have a war any longer; some think it will be next month, others in 1950. But all wars must end sometime. Then we shall go back to Civvy Street, that spacious boulevard which our thoughts fill with benign sunlight. With what nostalgia we talk of Civvy Street, the lore of our trade, the names of roads in London suburbs, pubs we frequented, pigeons we bred for racing! So Adam and Eve must have talked of Eden, after the expulsion. Our faces lighten and our voices grow vivid in the recollection of the past. But when we talk of the future, after the war is over, our joy is suddenly shot with anxiety, the sort of terror the first couple would have felt, if God had told them they could return to the Garden.

BEHIND THEM BLOODY GATES

Camps are usually surrounded with barbed wire and entered through guarded gates. Their encirclement is a necessary precaution against sabotage, Fifth Columnists, nosey parkers and nuns with sub-machine-guns up their skirts.

But to the soldier living behind the gates this purpose is often obscured by its secondary object, to prevent his going in or out of camp without permission. In his life he approximates more closely to an undesirable alien than to a civilian of his own nationality. The greatest difference between an army and an internment camp, he feels, is that the soldier has to work.

Civilians cannot imagine the difficulty which soldiers encounter in getting passes, the calculated humiliations imposed by company sergeant-majors who resent others going out while they stay in camp, the hours spent waiting to collect passes which have already been made out, the thought, the intrigue, and even the money spent on obtaining them. Yet the greater the delay, the more important it becomes to get beyond those bloody gates and walk through fields alone, free from the inquisition of military policemen paid four and threepence a day to be offensive, free from the danger of the sudden fatigue, the noise of a barrack room, the sight of Army huts.

Yet, however many passes you get, your life lies behind the gates. Communal living is the ineluctable condition of the soldier. Those who have been to boarding schools think they know communal life. Army life is coarser, more energetic but less brutal than in a boarding school. Our emotions are strong and simple. Sleeping, feeding and working together breeds comradeship. Each man has a mate. You exchange duties, make one another's beds, cover one another's absence. Yours is the alliance of two, within the structure of greater alliances, your platoon against other platoons, your regiment against other regiments, your fellow rankers against N.C.O.s, commissioned officers, coppers and red caps.

But after a time you notice a habit of your mates which irritates you. Maybe he lets his wind with bravado and always says, 'It must have been them beans.' Maybe it is his way of saying 'Them's fighting words, buddy', when he can think of nothing else to say. It makes no difference. Whatever it is becomes focus of your hatred. With a passion you thought had died at five, you wait for him to repeat his offence, and when he does, it is like petrol flung on the fire of your rage. How you flare up! You could kill him, like a boot dragged over the floor and the shattered cockroach gummed to the boards by its white intestines.

We are being trained to kill, you see, and it is amazing how quickly our instinct for murder, disciplined by civilization to lie quiet, gets up, vigorous, at encouragement. It is not so amazing that Jerry, the fellow conscript in another land, is not the only focus for our rifle sights. If bullets solve arguments, the brain ponders, why not dispute in lead with sergeant, C.S.M. and officers? Many old scores are paid on the battlefield.

You don't think like that in Civvy Street. But it comes naturally to us, the boys in battle dress. It's a gift, gift from the W.O., along with our rifles and the bayonets we are trained to stick in stuffed sacks. 'If you see a Jerry, lying wounded on the ground,' says the instructor, 'stick 'im, before you go on. The more dead Jerries there are, the better.'

Don't think we spend all day nursing murder. I just give you this to show how we are different. The annoyance which would pass in a moment becomes the impulse to kill. All emotions are exaggerated in the same way. Our greed, for example. You should see us at table, the knives scooping more than our share of butter, the spoons heaped with marmalade running on to the boards of the table, the bread cut so thick a man has to gnaw at it, like a dog at a knucklebone. We are afraid that we won't get enough, so we take too much; and two out of twelve go short. We believe that pot. brom. is put in our tea to keep our sexual appetites within bounds. But all our passion is directed towards food. Not women haunt our dreams, but eggs and bacon . . .

Our public life is one of strong primary sensations and emotions. There are times of physical suffering when our hands are so numb with cold that fingers feel brittle, or when our feet are blistered on a route march and each step is needles jabbed into the flesh. There are moments of physical ecstasy, the fingers thawing out, fatigue coursing through the relaxed limbs, hot toast before a fire, or lying beyond réveillé on the warmth of a straw palliasse. Moments of delight, as

43

when the order confining ninety per cent of troops to barracks was rescinded, and in thirty seconds the news, 'No more passes, no more passes', ran through the camp. It was like fire across dry grass the speed it spread. 'No more passes!' shouted from barrack spider to spider, across the square, through the canteens and the billiard halls, loud voices and soft, high and low; but the same note in all of joy and sudden relief. We could move without authority from behind the barbed wire into the town. We could walk into a pub. We could see strange faces, look at girls and laugh. There are moments of grief, as when the telegram came that F.'s mother was killed by a bomb, and we fell silent thinking of our own, when B. returned from London at the beginning of the Blitz and fell on his bed, crying, 'They wiped out the East End, they wiped it out,' when the Bren-gun carrier overturned and two men were pinned to death beneath it, or when the popular despatch rider crashed at the crossroads by the R.A.C. box and we collected money for his widow. Moments of happiness, singing and laughing, glad in the warm sun, lying in the grass looking up at the sky, sweating after a run, feeling the strength of our bodies.

The only terms which fit our public life are mystical. These emotions are shared by all of us, but belong to none. They are generated by living together, like the heat of two naked bodies lying together in a bed. And, beneath this corporate life, run our separate private lives, which seldom emerge in the daylight of the barrack room. We exist together, lubricating our contact with jokes and slogans and horseplay. But our minds are commanded by civilian interests, our families and friends, sports, hobbies, and the lore of a former trade. Standing in threes on the parade ground, the thirty men, who act as one, are dreaming like thirty of their homes and the cabbage patch, tallyman and income-tax, the bombs raining on the just and the unjust.

But at night private thoughts come into the open. I often return to camp on a late pass and undress in the dark, by the light of matches or the dying glow of the stove. The air is warm and thick with the stench of feet. The others are asleep. With their battle dress they have slipped off their public lives and meet their private images in dreams. They talk in their sleep. It may be the fierce voice of argument, a childish whimper, the naked horror of nightmare or a trailing vocative of love; but whatever the tone, it appears, as startling as a human face rising to the surface in a quiet pool, and disappears again as the sleeper turns on the iron slats of his bed and falls into a deeper sleep, relieved.

This barrack room is where we live by day. We dress and undress, lie resting on the dirty palliasses between parades, write letters at the trestle table, play rummy, brag, or knock-out whist. We sing and squabble and brush our boots here, laugh and toast cheese and scan the *Daily Mirror* for news of London raids. That is our day life, a busy surface existence like little black beetles skimming on a pond. But sleep and darkness give cover to privy thoughts. They creep out like the mice that eat biscuits in our lockers the moment the watcher nods. The barrack room is like a confessional, when I tiptoe in at midnight and the mice scamper squeaking away, and the men break the foot-heavy air with their abrupt alarms . . .

THE HEROIC ATTITUDE

In the defence forces the heroic attitude persists. Men and women face death with courage, at the Wardens' Post and the Auxiliary Fire sub-station, spotting planes and fires from roofs, treating the wounded in the streets. For Day Lewis, 'peering out for invaders', there is a fine unity in the Home Guard.

Destiny, History, Fortitude, Honour – all
The words of the politicians seem too big or too small
For the ragtag fighters of lane and shadow, the love that has grown
Familiar as working clothes, faithful as bone to bone.

What have they got, the ragtag fighters of lane and shadow, which the conscript army lacks?

Patriotism for us is not Parliament, the Lord Mayor of London, Royal Ascot or the British Empire. It is the house and street we live in, our families and friends, security and freedom of movement. For these we want to fight; we would give our lives to save our wives and children; we would run danger to succour the wounded; we would never let the invader land and live here.

But this is not our certain function. We do what we are told, or else jankers and the glasshouse. We are not the people's army, the ragtag fighters, but members of His Majesty's Forces, who go where they are ordered. It may be Libya, to take a desert from the Italians; or India, to arrest more friends of Mr. Nehru; or Poland, to assist the Poles to wreak vengeance on their oppressors. And the reason why we have not got the heroic attitude is because no one has persuaded us yet that dying on foreign soil is going to help Millie, and Daisy and Lou, back in Bermondsey; or even that it will help our sort of people in Prague, Cracow, Bruges, or Padua. We're willing to be convinced, but it will take more than words to persuade us, more than the lovely promises that didn't fill our fathers' bellies when they were demobbed after the last war. Till we're convinced, we'll carry on the way we are, laughing with the infuriating sceptical laughter of the twice shy.

The officers had a different sort of war and a different view of it.

HOME·FRONT: 1942

Marching in step, the Battery subalterns
Moving along the footpath of the main road,
Chat about minor military concerns;
Bracing their shoulders as to take a load,
Swinging their canes, eyeing each girl that passes,
Feeling distinctly distant from the masses.

Grudgingly sidecapped gunners give salutes,
Murmur obscenities beneath their breath,
Gossiping news and public house disputes:
Tired of the drag of service, tired to death.
Their only thought to catch a bus as far
As the local town hall dance or cinema.

These carry now the future in the heads
Fouled with the daily drug of great events;
Discuss it in their buttockbiting beds
Or argue in the damp despair of tents
While hired wireless sets dictate aloud
The paths which must be followed by the crowd.

Unheeding now through summer days they give
Their drilled attention to the killers' art
Rehearsing in their minds the life they'll live
When some day soon their second life will start,
And ripping, every time they thrust, the drab,
Embittered present with a bayonet jab.

Sitting in the Mess, the Battery Subalterns
Spreading their legs around a firelit hearth,
Distant from Army Orders and returns
Carry their talking down a well trod path.
'When this is finished we'll . . .', is all the theme
Of their age old and never realized dream.

Robert L. Chaloner

OFFICERS' MESS

It's going to be a thick night to-night (and the night before was a
    thick one);
I've just seen the Padre disappearing into 'The Cock and Bull' for a
    quick one.
I don't mind telling you this, old boy, we got the Major drinking –
You probably know the amount of gin he's in the habit of sinking –
And then that new M.O. came in, the Jewish one, awful fellow,
And his wife, a nice little bit of stuff, dressed in a flaming yellow.
Looked a pretty warmish piece, old boy – no, have this one with me –
They were both so blind (and so was the Major) that they could hardly
    see.
She had one of those amazing hats and a kind of silver fox fur
(I wouldn't mind betting several fellows have had a go at her).
She made a bee-line for the Major, bloody funny, old boy,
Asked him a lot about horses and India, you know, terribly coy –
And this M.O. fellow was mopping it up and at last he passed right out
(Some silly fool behind his back put a bottle of gin in his stout).
I've never seen a man go down so quick. Somebody drove him home.
His wife was almost as bad, old boy, said she felt all alone
And nestled up to the Major – it's a great pity you weren't there –
And the Padre was arguing about the order of morning and evening
    prayer.
Never laughed so much in all my life. We went on drinking till three.
And this woman was doing her best to sit on the Major's knee!
Let's have the blackout boards put up and turn on the other light.
Yes, I think you can count on that, old boy – to-night'll be a thick night.

Gavin Ewart

Alun Lewis wrote about the boredom of training.

ALL DAY IT HAS RAINED . . .

All day it has rained, and we on the edge of the moors
Have sprawled in our bell-tents, moody and dull as boors,
Groundsheets and blankets spread on the muddy ground.
And from the first great wakening we have found
No refuge from the skirmishing fine rain
And the wind that made the canvas heave and flap
And the taut wet guy-ropes ravel out and snap.

47

All day the rain has glided, wave and mist and dream,
Drenching the gorse and heather, a gossamer stream
Too light to stir the acorns that suddenly
Snatched from their cups by the wild south-westerly
Pattered against the tent and our upturned dreaming faces.
And we stretched out, unbuttoning our braces,
Smoking a Woodbine, darning dirty socks,
Reading the Sunday papers – I saw a fox
And mentioned it in the note I scribbled home;
And we talked of girls, and dropping bombs on Rome,
And thought of the quiet dead and the loud celebrities
Exhorting us to slaughter, and the herded refugees;
– Yet thought softly, morosely of them, and as indifferently
As of ourselves or those whom we
For years have loved, and will again
Tomorrow maybe love; but now it is the rain
Possesses us entirely, the twilight and the rain.

And I can remember nothing dearer or more to my heart
Than the children I watched in the woods on Saturday
Shaking down burning chestnuts for the schoolyard's merry play,
Or the shaggy patient dog who followed me
By Sheet and Steep and up the wooded scree
To the Shoulder o'Mutton where Edward Thomas brooded long
On death and beauty – till a bullet stopped his song.

*Timothy Corsellis found training in the Air Force too much preparation
for the aerial combat that would kill him.*

WHAT I NEVER SAW

I was ready for death
Ready to give my all in one expansive gesture
For a cause that was worthy of death
I wanted to fear, to watch blood and torture,
To draw my last breath
Amidst a chaos of dramatic thunder.
I dreamt of aeroplanes sweeping the sky,
Gave war her ghastly lure,
Came, ready to fight and to die.

I thought in my mufti
Of brave men marching to battle

And came here to join them,
To share the machine guns' rattle

What I never saw,
Were the weary hours of waiting while the sun rose and set,
The everlasting eye turned upwards to the sky
Watching the weather which said,
'Thou shalt not fly.'

We sat together as we sat at peace
Bound by no ideal of service
But by a common-interest in pornography and a desire to outdrink
    one another.
War was remote:
There was a little trouble in Abyssinia;
Some of us came from Kenya and said,
'Why I was on the spot all the while
And the Italians sprayed the roadsides with mustard gas.'
Theirs were the stories of war.

Then came the queuing, the recurrent line of pungent men
The collar that is cleaner than the shirt
And the inevitable adjectives.

The papers ran out early today,
There was no butter for the bread at breakfast,
Nobody calls us at dawn,
We never strain or sweat,
Nor do they notice when we come in late.

When I was a civilian I hoped high,
Dreamt my future cartwheels in the sky,
Almost forgot to arm myself
Against the boredom and the inefficiency
The petty injustice and the everlasting grudges,
The sacrifice is greater than I ever expected.

Roy Fuller reduced his training in the Navy to a primer and an alphabet.

ABC OF A NAVAL TRAINEE

A is the anger we hide with some danger,
Keeping it down like the twentieth beer.
B is the boredom we feel in this bedlam.
C is the cautious and supervised cheer.

D is the tea dope and E English duping,
Too feeble for folly, too strong for revolt.
F is the adjective near every object,
The chief of desires for both genius and dolt.

G is the gun which can kill at, say, Greenwich
If fired at St Martin's, and H is our hate
Non-existent behind it wherever we wind it.
I is the image of common man's fate.

J is the Joan or the Jill or Joanna,
Appearing in dreams as a just missed train.
K is the kindness like Christmas tree candles,
Unexpected and grateful as poppies in grain.

L is the lung or the limb which in languor
Rests after work and will soon be exposed
To M which is murder, a world rather madder,
Where what we pretend now's as real as your nose.

N is the nightingale's song that we're noting
When the sky is a lucid darkening silk,
When the guns are at rest and the heart is a cancer
And our mouths make O at the moon of milk.

Then we remember, no longer a number,
We think of our duties as poets and men:
Beyond us lie Paris, Quebec, Rome, where diaries
Of millions record the same troubles and pain.

S is the silence for brooding on violence.
T is the toughness imparted to all.
U is the unit that never will clown it
Again as the lonely, the shy or the tall.

V is the vastness: as actor and witness
We doubled our role and stammer at first.

W is war to start off the quarries –
Our everyday hunger and everynight thirst.

X is the kiss or the unknown, the fissure
In misery stretching far back to the ape.
Y is the yearning for Eden returning;
Our ending, our Z and our only escape.

*In the camps, the military men waited for something to happen. A. D.
Bass was killed in action after his long wait.*

'HERE IN A HILLSIDE CAMP'

Here in a hillside camp, preparing for the day
In tiny military world secure, within the wide
And comfortable contours of the Plain
There is the time for curious thought to rush away
Ahead of time –
To peer round the corner of some foreign lane
And jump back terrified –
To look down on a curve of sunlit road
Breathless, exhausted, from a hurried climb
And see below some frightful episode
That will take place in time.

The armed forces were taught how to drill and how to kill.

SQUADDING

The sergeant's roar, interpreted aright
by instinct of fear, dies bouncing on the asphalt.
The squad, grey-denimed in the distinct light
stand-easy, adjust a cap or finger a belt.

Shedding its shell, a crab must feel like this,
lost between two worlds, not so much scared as wary.
They consider the sergeant without prejudice
and accept the insulting candour of his stare.

Why is it when that with arms and legs loosened
out of a random rhythm they are forced to move

in a strange unison? Apart from the nuisance,
there is a buoyancy, even a kind of love.

Yet still, as the clue's emerging, they feel again
that pull of difference splitting each life into two.
More than the sergeant, each stands apart. The brain
is numbed with a semi-defiance. It isn't true.

It isn't true, each insists. It isn't happening.
This is not me. But it is. And you grin to find
the will re-welded, richer. You lose your cap,
feel foolish; and an urgency raps your mind –

tightened, look, in the buckle of belt and sling,
jestingly sealed in each momentous trifle,
stamped now, clamped in the bolt and the bayonet-ring,
fondled and final in the uplifted rifle.

Jack Lindsay

*As Julian Symons found out, the conscripts discovered their own philos-
ophy.*

CONSCRIPT

'O now to train you in a murdering air . . .'
Behind their defensive positions the officers whisper,
The organization of madness proceeds by orders,
These decorous lips are faintly touched with foam.
On the parade ground clerks and electricians
Forget the antique laws by which their lives
Ran in the cooling capitalist groove.
The commando training prepares for death.

This sudden collapse into the real deceives us.
The mind makes pictures and calls them a lasting
Image of what is, what really is. The blinding
Light on the square deceives, we are all deceived,
Trapped in a mechanical country where escape is
A privilege reserved for the unhappy.
We, who were happy, were afraid of action.
Expected leisure always, and loving hands.

But now no longer the bourgeois lives go on.
Something is asked or ordered: the bewildered faces,
Repeating words, cannot believe the passing
Days are extinguishing home and mother.
Few die of grief, the human animal
Adapts itself, our attitudes are casual.
Yet here the naïve are thinking passionately:
Victory for our blood. The road goes on.

How into this to introduce that picture
We call a poem? To give the chaotic
Elements of our lives a single meaning,
The rational correctness of a square?
There is nothing we do not know here, and nothing
That is worth knowing. The rifles, the
Clouds and the marching, precipitate a spectre:
This fascinating, precise and empty earth.

All that remains of the old gestures and wishing
Is: our eyes sparkle and we say 'Tomorrow':
But that is false. Nothing remains. Our agony
Should be farewell, be a prolonged farewell.
Yet still, although the end waits quietly,
Our human thoughts cannot embrace that sea,
Whose murmuring waves will never speak of death
But whisper still of *Love* and *Poetry*.

Paul Scott asked the old soldiers to pass on their expertise to the recruits.

TELL US THE TRICKS

Say, soldier! Tell us the tricks,
    the tackle of your trade;
The passage of your hours;
    the plans that you have made –
Of what do you think – what consider?
Tell us of the slow process,
That gradual change
    from man to soldier –?

And what can I say, what reply?
    There is no answer.
The tale is hidden in the eye.

The soldier's here – the man is not:
Man's voice was lost;
The sex decayed   ·
By the bitter bayonet – the chattering shot
The growth delayed.
The brief days of youth,
And its forgotten past,
Cannot be commanded to appear,
We hope they may at last
   – some other time – some different year.

In learning the art of war, the range was the most important place.

AT THE RANGE

Through windows, as we marched, the distant rooms
Led us a moment back along the road. We saw again
The bureau open, the coloured vase of ferns,
Lilies' unvenomed fangs whose wound could yet cause pain.
Thatched houses stared indifferent to our claim:
And the church clock to stress our trespass there
Kept its own hour eternally at ten. A sudden climb
Turned from the village. Ahead the downs were bare.

Bullets speed towards a future day:
Each rifle cracks our whispering of the past.
The target changes as we fire: men who will die
Fall on the splintered chalk: until the eye sees at last
Only the dull butts and the warning red flag wave.
The acrid powder smells on our fingers. In groups we stand
Tall in this quarry where sun and shadow weave
Patterns of isolation, gulls over desolate sand.

Our minds from scattered journeys, concentrate
Upon the target rings. 'Inner at nine o'clock':
We are not thinking of an enemy, nor trite
Slogans of hate. We wait, loose-limbed, for shock.
The butt is firm, at home against the shoulder.
The bull obscures village and room from sight.
There is only this minute: each wholly a soldier.
I sense the birds above me flying into light.

After cigarettes we collect the flags,
Fold over groundsheets, march back to the 'drome.
Rain driven by April gusts stings against the face.
The village no longer offers an idea of home.
We quicken steps, eager to reach our huts;
Content at first to smoke or talk, as the wind
With envied fury beats against the walls:
Till thoughts of other rooms come back to mind.

H. B. Mallalieu

In Lilliput, *Frank Kelly made fun of the artists at war at the range.*

THE ARTIST

'I can't understand it,' said the C.O.

The Sergeant-major registered an appropriate expression of bewilderment.

The accused said nothing. He was a small man with tragic eyes. He badly needed a hair-cut.

'Let me have the facts again, Sarmajor,' said the C.O. 'You say that this man had spent the entire day painting targets.'

'Yes, sir.'

'They measured four feet by six?'

'That's right, sir.'

'You say he made a very good job of them.'

'A very good job, sir.'

'And when they were complete he invited you to inspect them.'

'He did, sir.'

'You complimented him on his work, Sarmajor?'

'I did, sir.'

'And then what happened?"

The Sergeant-major cleared his throat. 'The accused said – these were his exact words, sir – the accused said, "I am glad you like them. Watch what I am going to do with them."'

The Sergeant-major paused.

'Well, Sarmajor?'

'Then, sir, he picked up a bucket of black paint and sloshed it all over the targets.'

'Extraordinary,' said the C.O. 'Extraordinary. I can't understand it.'

He eyed the accused. 'This is rather serious, you know. It needs an explanation. Have you nothing to say?'

For a moment or two the accused stared down at his feet in silence. He looked very miserable. Then he took a deep breath and raised his head. He had the air of a man about to dispose, once and for all, of a painful business.

'Sir,' he said, and there was dignity in his voice, 'Sir, I have been painting targets, which measure four feet by six, for the past six weeks.'

'Well,' said the C.O.

'I take a great deal of trouble over them, sir.'

'I know that,' said the C.O.

'I put a lot of work into them, sir.'

'Quite,' said the C.O.

'They're big targets, sir, and they take a lot of painting.'

'I know all about that,' said the C.O. testily. 'Knowing that,' he went on, 'I am all the more amazed that on this particular day you should suddenly take it into your head to fling paint all over your work. You have destroyed a dozen targets, to say nothing of messing up the paint shop and wasting valuable Government material.'

The accused, in turn, became impatient.

'Well, sir, don't you see, sir, I spend all my time painting these targets –'

'Yes, yes.'

'I claim, sir, with all modesty, that they are little short of master-pieces. I get them exactly right. The bull is dead in the centre, not a fraction of an inch out. The circles are perfectly symmetrical.'

'Well?'

The accused drew himself up to his full height. He clenched his fists. His tragic eyes flashed.

'And then, sir,' he thundered, in a sudden savage outburst, 'they take them up to the range and shoot hell out of them!'

Bayonet practice was probably the most fearsome training of all. G. S. Fraser used to look up from the Company Office at the bayonet drill out-side.

It was strange, for instance, to look up from my typewriter, to the three gibbets across the grass, where the squads were at bayonet drill. From each gibbet hung a sack stuffed with straw. In threes, brown figures advanced towards the sacks. They advanced at the 'On guard!', took a sudden leap, pointed, withdrew, on guard again, and passed: three paces past, they came to the high port, then turned about, and on guard again. The sacks bled straw. Some movements of bayonet drill were like ballet. One in particular seemed to me to have the beautiful kind of slow-motion inevitability about it of a cinema camera analysing the motions of an athlete. The bayonet is pointed at your heart: with your elbow, you thrust it aside, at the same time stepping forward, and bringing your own bayonet up over your left shoulder your butt smashes in your enemy's face; as he stumbles, you bring your hands forward, and the edge of the blade slashes his skull; and then as he falls your hands continue their uninterrupted movement downwards and the point is at his belly. But if this movement is like ballet, the response to it is like pantomime. As the butt comes thrusting at your face, you drop your own rifle like a red-hot poker, grab your enemy's, and bring your clumpy army boot up to kick him in the crotch . . . War is not an art. It has no unity of tone.

John Gawsworth wrote a poem about the training.

BAYONET INSTRUCTION

Get fierce now; froth; select a vulnerable point.
Go forward at High Port until you see,
Your face asmile with grim ferocity,
Your opening to hamstring or to disjoint.
Turn the blade, to slip in between the ribs.
If you miss parrying, buttstroke, kick his balls.
Your idea is to smash his Nazi ribs
And finish him before the bastard squalls.

Your order is 'No prisoners', my lad.
Now don't you feel you want his blood to spirt?
Why, wash your face in it; get downright mad
And wipe your hands upon your dead man's shirt!
Of course, if the blade sticks, fire in a round.
You'll get release then easy from the wound.

In the end, all those who were training in the camps and waiting for the war to start for them were the people Keith Vaughan called 'Exiles in Khaki'.

from EXILES IN KHAKI

In the village the windows are all tightly shuttered, and only the chinks of light indicate the separate and private existences within. Outside, ceaselessly, to and fro, the jagged iron-clad ring of boots in the darkness. Exiles in khaki, an army in occupation of their own country. Dressed alike, eating alike. Every town and village has its contingent like its cats. Each one of us has his roots, his beginnings and his future, each one belongs somewhere, but not here. The world we have left, the world of childhood and youth, of our tiny triumphs and failures beyond the ring fence of this camp is burnt to ruins. A costly ceremonious cremation of a thing already long dead. The future is everything or nothing behind the smoke. Or perhaps the end is still the beginning.

Night closes impartially over the village and the camp, over the raw tin huts and the mellow steeple of the church, over the gardens of the large houses and the compact roofs of farmsteads and the grey peaked cones of canvas. A moth flies at the flame, singes its wings and drops into the hot wax. A canvas breadth away the moon steers a steady course through the velvet sky and the night's flock of bombers, flying high, turn southward. 'I bet they're giving them hell,' says Don, 'they say it's the biggest battle in the history of the world. More killed in the last few weeks than since the beginning of the war.' He curls his toes, one foot round the other, sitting on his bed and munching chocolate.

'I'd like to see every country in the world,' said Johnnie.

Meaning the world of a fireside, a girl, a radio and a safe job.

The exiles in khaki lived for their leaves and the 48-hour passes which they could spend with their women. Keith Footit was to die in a bombing raid over Germany, and Alun Lewis in Burma.

TWO PAIRS OF SHOES

Draw back the curtains,
Dim the electric light.
Now the stage is set for
Our impromptu first night.

We've had no rehearsals,
We don't need the cues,
And out in the corridor
Are two pairs of shoes.

If I could find the time, dear,
By looking in your eyes,
I'd never find the time for
God and apple pies.

If love was set to music,
And played at Albert Hall,
Man would love his neighbour,
There'd be no war at all.

Whisper, dear, you love me:
That's all you need to say.
To-morrow I must leave my heart
For you to take away.

There's no time to lose, dear,
There's no time to lose.
Already they are polishing
Our two pairs of shoes.

Keith Footit

GOODBYE

So we must say Goodbye, my darling,
And go, as lovers go, for ever,
Tonight remains, to pack and fix on labels
And make an end of lying down together.

I put a final shilling in the gas,
And watch you slip your dress below your knees
And lie so still I hear your rustling comb
Modulate the autumn in the trees.

And all the countless things I shall remember
Lay mummy-cloths of silence round my head;
I fill the carafe with a drink of water;
You say 'We paid a guinea for this bed,'

And then, 'We'll leave some gas, a little warmth
For the next resident, and these dry flowers,'
And turn your face away, afraid to speak
The big word, that Eternity is ours.

Your kisses close my eyes and yet you stare
As though God struck a child with nameless fears;
Perhaps the water glitters and discloses
Time's chalice and its limpid useless tears.

Everything we renounce except our selves;
Selfishness is the last of all to go;
Our sighs are exhalations of the earth,
Our footprints leave a track across the snow.

We made the universe to be our home,
Our nostrils took the wind to be our breath,
Our hearts are massive towers of delight,
We stride across the seven seas of death.

Yet when all's done you'll keep the emerald
I placed upon your finger in the street;
And I will keep the patches that you sewed
On my old battledress tonight, my sweet.

Alun Lewis

For the best short-story writer of the conditions of war, Julian Maclaren-Ross, love at camp was difficult.

A SENTIMENTAL STORY

The first time they met she had dark glasses on and he could not see her eyes. It was in a café and she was a WAAF. What was he writing was it poetry. It was, but at first he would not admit it because of his uniform. For a private soldier it is not easy to admit writing poetry; in our country such an admission is always difficult to make and when you are at the same time a private in the army the difficulty becomes almost insuperable. You can tell yourself that the uniform does not matter that you are the same underneath but it does matter and you are not the same because the attitude of others makes you what you are and of course to a private soldier the attitude of others is entirely different and you yourself are different too. It is like not having money only worse.

So where are the war poets and this was one of them: a private soldier sitting in a café that was a civilian café and where you could have the illusion of being yourself a civilian so long as you paid and spoke to no one. And when she spoke at first he would not and then later did. She was a WAAF who worked in the operations room and had a zigzag of lightning on her sleeve and she herself wrote poetry and had wanted in peacetime to be a psychologist; she had been to Egypt and to Vienna and she spoke french; how old was she, twenty-two.

His uniform did not make any difference to her since she herself had on what was approximately its equivalent and soon they were talking, she had read things of his and liked them and he was flattered because she recognized his name which in the army had been shortened for reasons of convenience. What was he writing and what did she write. He told her about the long one that was to appear in LYRA; the collected poems from Faber at Christmas. She listened and he could not see her eyes. The dark glasses made her face anonymous and inscrutable.

Next time they met she was not wearing the glasses and as she looked up at him and smiled he noticed her eyes and he could feel his face alter as she looked at him.

She had lovely eyes: they were large and light grey with very long lashes and they were luminous and intelligent and they upset him. He had never been susceptible to eyes before and because he knew his face had altered without his wanting it to alter he was angry and when they walked together up the hill where all the trees leaned surrealistically sideways he would not speak or look at her directly.

Later they sat side by side in a cinema and watched Mickey Mouse cavort in colour across the screen. She laughed and he looked sideways at her and her eyes did something to him again and he was silent and resentful. Coming out it was dark; he could not see her eyes and it was all right. They arranged to meet again; her bus left at ten.

Walking downhill towards the town, clambering over and ducking through rusty iron barricades, he saw searchlights swing over the sea; a Jerry plane pulsed through the dark pursued by Ack-Ack fire: tracer bullets spattered a trail of crimson sparks across the sky. He walked slowly back to the billet while flares floated like falling stars above the town. Climbing the three flights of wooden stairs towards the army blankets, the straw palliasse, the room that smelt of socks, he decided not to see her again.

But two nights later he was standing at the top of the hill when her bus came in and this time they were both a little shy and he could not look her in the face at all.

They had not much time together because of the buses and she had not been able to get a pass. They walked between two road blocks and out past a line of shuttered bathing cabins through paths that twisted upwards through trees and overlooking the sea. There were heavy clouds that made the night draw in and nobody about. It started to rain but where they sat on a bench under the overhanging trees they were moderately sheltered; only a few drops came through.

He said to her abruptly: 'I'm being posted to-morrow.'

'Far?'

'No not far. The order came through quite suddenly.'

'So we'll still be able to meet?'

'If you think it's any use.'

'Don't *you* think it's any use?'

'I'm not sure.'

'That's not very nice.'

'No but then I'm not a very nice person.'

'You can be awfully nice.'

'I can be but not tonight.'

'Why not tonight?'

'You should know. You're a psychologist aren't you?'

'There's no need to be quite so nasty.'

'I'm sorry,' he said.

He put out his hand to touch hers. The rain splashed down onto the gravel below, running off the leaves of the trees. It was getting dark and she had taken off her cap and shaken out her hair and she leaned back on the bench quite close to him and her fingers were smooth and cool in his.

She said: 'You like to be alone, don't you?'

'I don't like it but I've got to be.'

'Why?'

'Because where I'm going one has got to be alone or one would never get there.'

'Always?'

'It's better that way.'

'You're very selfish aren't you?'

'I've got to be selfish.'

'You needn't be. And you don't have to be alone either.'

'Yes,' he said, 'yes,' and put his arm around her shoulders. She turned her face to his, cool and smooth and with a faint perfume and the taste of her lipstick in his mouth. As they kissed in the dark he could not see her large luminous eyes that drew something out of him. When he released her she said: 'You see? You're not alone now.'

He didn't speak.

'Are you?' she said.

He didn't speak, he drew her to him and started to kiss her again. He held her tightly to him and forced her head back and her lips open under his kiss. He felt her body recoil a little but he held her tighter; his mind was quite made-up now. He knew that tomorrow he would be sad and disgusted with himself but he knew that he was right: he had got to be alone.

When he began to fumble with the buttons of her tunic she twisted her head sharply away and her body out of his arms.

'Why did you do that?' she said.

'Are you scared?'

'No,' she said, 'I'm not scared.' She had drawn away from him a little on the bench. 'Why did you do it?' she said again.

He laughed. 'Isn't it what every soldier does on the night before he leaves a station?' he said.

She stood up without speaking then. She took up her cap and the folio with the poems of hers that she had wanted to show him and walked quickly away down the path where the rain had now almost ceased. He could hear her shoes crunching the gravel and the rain dripping from the leaves. She left him sitting there in the dark.

3
Blitz

JOURNEY TO LONDON

From the Welsh wick asleep in the globe of winter
I came across England to love and anger,
Came from that mountainous indifference
To where my hopes were, your lips, our danger.

Riding the three ranges, the high midland
Where history piled stone on stone together,
Furnishing from grey stone our politics
And the harsh principles that slay my brother,

Riding the three ranges, I left Malvern
In the flush of sunset and all Oxfordshire
To the veiled glory of its fabled spires,
Came down to darkness and a city's fear.

O London, from the pellucid flame of Wales,
I your citizen and twenty others
Crossed from the Chiltern daylight into darkness,
The night that drowns our enemies and lovers,

Journeyed from grey stone to bombs exploding
Our politics and prayers, to a new anger
Striking from war this poetry. I came
To the heart of love, to the heart of danger.

J. C. Hall

To Graham Greene, the blitz was a fit judgement on society at the time.

from AT HOME

One gets used to anything: that is what one hears on many lips these days, though everybody, I suppose, remembers the sense of shock he felt at the first bombed house he saw. I think of one in Woburn Square neatly sliced in half. With its sideways exposure it looked like a Swiss chalet: there were a pair of skiing sticks hanging in the attic, and in another room a grand piano cocked one leg over the abyss. The combination of music and skiing made one think of the Sanger family and Constant Nymphs dying pathetically of private sorrow to popular applause. In the bathroom the geyser looked odd and twisted seen from the wrong side, and the kitchen impossibly crowded with furniture until one realized one had been given a kind of mouse-eye view from behind the stove and the dresser – all the space where people used to move about with toast and tea-pots was out of sight. But after quite a short time one ceased to look twice at the intimate exposure of interior furnishings, and waking on a cement floor among strangers, one no longer thinks what an odd life this is. 'One gets used to anything.'

But that, I think, is not really the explanation. There are things one never gets used to because they don't connect: sanctity and fidelity and the courage of human beings abandoned to free will: virtues like these belong with old college buildings and cathedrals, relics of a world with faith. Violence comes to us more easily because it was so long expected – not only by the political sense but by the moral sense. The world we lived in could not have ended any other way. The curious waste lands one sometimes saw from trains – the crated ground round Wolverhampton under a cindery sky with a few cottages grouped like stones among the rubbish: those acres of abandoned cars round Slough; the dingy fortune-teller's on the first-floor above the cheap permanent waves in a Brighton back street: they all demanded violence, like the rooms in a dream where one knows that something will presently happen – a door fly open or a window-catch give and let the end in . . .

That, I think, is why one feels at home in London – or in Liverpool or Bristol, or any of the bombed cities – because life there is what it ought to be. If a cracked cup is put in boiling water it breaks, and an old dog-toothed civilization is breaking now. The nightly routine of sirens, barrage, the probing raider, the unmistakable engine ('Where are you? Where are you? Where are you?'), the bomb-bursts moving nearer and then moving away, hold one like a love-charm. We are not quite happy when we take a few days off. There is something just a little unsavoury about a safe area – as if a corpse were to keep alive in some of its members, the fingers fumbling or the tongue seeking to taste. So we go hurrying back to our shelter, to the nightly uneasiness and then the 'All Clear' sounding happily like New Year's bells and the first dawn look at the world to see what has gone; green glass strewn on the pavement (all broken glass seems green) and sometimes flames like a sticky coloured plate from the *Boys' Own Paper* lapping at the early sky. As for the victims, if they have suffered pain it will be nearly over by this time. Life has become just and poetic, and if we believe this is the right end to the muddled thought, the sentimentality and selfishness of generations, we can also believe that justice doesn't end there. The innocent will be given their peace, and the unhappy will know more happiness than they have ever dreamt about, and poor muddled people will be given an answer they have to accept. We needn't feel pity for any of the innocent, and as for the guilty we know in our hearts that they will live just as long as we do and no longer.

Londoners crowded into the Underground or other makeshift shelters from the bombs. Ritchie Calder described the notorious shelter at Tilbury.

from THE LESSONS OF LONDON

When the official shelter was crowded out, those in charge of the other parts allowed the people to use it, on compassionate grounds. The result was unbelievable. Estimates of the numbers using this expropriated shelter varied, but on the wet night when I was there, extra people came in from their domestic shelters which had flooded, and the shelter wardens calculated that in the two halves there were over 14,000 people.

People queued up from midday, waiting for the gates to open at four-thirty in the afternoon. Service men on leave kept places for their families out at work. Unevacuated schoolchildren were 'proxies' for their relatives. Old folks in bathchairs, cripples, children in perambulators, and men and women of every age and condition lined up, oblivious of daylight sirens and even dog-fights overhead, because if they took shelter they lost their places in the queue and their 'option' on their favourite sleeping-spot for the night. When the gates were opened the police linked hands to stem the rush down the slope, but it was like holding back a stampede of buffaloes. Usually a way was made for the aged, and for mothers with perambulators and young children (although the police got wise to the fact that some were getting priority for perambulators which contained not babies, but the family valuables). Sometimes women and children got crushed in the rush.

At night, it presented a scene unequalled by anything west of Suez. One had to pick one's way along the roads between the recumbent bodies. Until the Ministry of Food intervened and had the cartons of margarine and the other food stuffs removed, people slept in the bays, beside or on the food. To begin with there was practically no sanitary provision, and the filth seeped into the blankets or was spread by trampling feet. Cartons filled with margarine were sometimes stacked up to form latrines.

Every race and colour in the world were represented there – Whites, Negroes, Chinese, Hindus, Polynesians, Levantines, East Europeans,

Jews, Gentiles, Moslems, and probably Sun-Worshippers were all piled there in miscellaneous confusion. Seamen came in for a few hours between tides. Prostitutes paraded. Hawkers sold clammy fried fish, which cloyed the fug with greasy sickliness. The police broke up free fights. And children slept.

The atmosphere in the shelters was strange during the long nights.

NIGHT RAID

The sleepers humped down on the benches,
The daft boy was playing rummy with anyone he could get,
And the dancing girl said, 'What I say is,
If there's a bomb made for YOU,
You're going to get it.'
Someone muttered, 'The bees are coming again.'
Someone whispered beside me in the darkness,
'They're coming up from the east.'
Way off the guns muttered distantly.

This was in the small hours, at the ebb.
And the dancing girl clicked her teeth like castanets
And said, 'I don't mind life, believe me.
I like it. If there's any more to come,
I can take it and be glad of it.'
She was shivering and laughing and throwing her head back.
On the pavement men looked up thoughtfully,
Making plausible conjectures. The night sky
Throbbed under the cool bandage of the searchlights.

Desmond Hawkins

Both the sheltered and the raiders were linked together by the terrible rain of the bombs.

RAID

How can they understand, the crouchers
under the earth, the sleepers in the tubes,
the pale woman with the baby at her breast,
the questioning child, the silent wise old man?

How can they understand? Do they feel
the force, the urgency, the necessity of war,
the valour and the glory? Let them lie
in their dim caves under the sleeping sky.

Do *they* understand, the pilots of the air,
those cronies of the stars, destructive gods,
are they heart-whole, mind-whole, who drop
the shrieking bomb upon the unknown target?

But those return who are not destroyed,
salute, report to their superiors, and rest
for the next time. Out of the holes in the ground
the weary people carry their bales at dawn.

Séan Jennett

BOMBED CITY

Walk with me to the silent city
walk with me in the fainting street
where the tramlines of evening
wind around the houses.

The churches lay the sorrow
of their bricks across the pavement
and houses no longer
cut the sky with swords.

Tendrils of silence
have bound the broken faces
the lense of day has caught
the overthrow of houses.

What fury here! what pain of living!
What monuments! what pitiless
enduring violin sounds
the white act of dying.

Woman lies with
city to her breast
crushed by the towers
and pain of mortar.

Child lies with
tourniquet of fear
and on his lips
the milk of death.

Inverted image of his city
reflected in the eye of man
his sorrow turns
and writhes like snakes.

Walk with me to the silent city
walk with me in the fainting street
let the knife of seeing
purify your strength.

Alan Rook

Everybody had a different experience of the bombing. Miles Mordaunt gave his account to Constantine Fitzgibbon.

from THE BLITZ

'The first street I turned into near ours was quite dark, and appeared to be deserted. I walked through to the far end of it, keeping my eye on the rooftops where the flames appeared to be leaping up as if they were very near, though actually they were almost two streets away. One of the burning houses seemed to be a draper's. A lot of debris was sailing up into the air with great stateliness. It was textile material that had taken fire and been reduced to the condition of an old-fashioned gasmantle. While holding its shape, it was in an incandescent glow as it rose steadily into the air. The frocks kept a ridiculous appearance of primness, moving like ladies, coming down with the same ladylike movement, managing to come down without the skirt billowing in any way. The extremely fragile burned textiles held their shape very tenaciously as they came down. As I reached the end of the street, a policeman stepped out of the shadows. He was doing what looked like a weird dance. He was beating out pieces of this smouldering textile material that kept landing on him. While of course his uniform was not in danger of taking fire, it would have made it look very mothy. More tenacious even than the dresses were the stockings, which wriggled down through the air like snakes. Several of these looped round him in a most persistent way. I helped him beat out some of these things on his shoulders, and said goodnight, and went back . . .'

Night by night, during that October, London was vanishing. Down below ground, people might be singing: the nightclubs might be full: above ground, there was only the sound of explosions, of aeroplane engines, of guns, the whispering of fires, the rare shout of a warden, running footsteps, the rattle of shell fragments, an occasional ambulance, fire engine, mortuary van, the rumble of falling brick and stone. And there were still cats. I quote Mr Mordaunt again:

'The familiar London of streets rapidly disappeared and one became used to a nightmare new landscape consisting of sand dunes from burst sandbags, and heaps of rubble where houses had been. When one went to these during the actual Blitz, in the small hours of the morning, when the only light was from incendiary bombs or burning houses, one of the noticeable features reminiscent of the more civilised period were the cats whose homes had been destroyed. They were usually present in force, leaping about madly, occasionally pulling themselves together, and trying to get back to what they knew as home, or people they had known. This characteristic made them useful to us as guides. The newly-made rubble was often very treacherous to move on, and even a dog would have disappeared in it, but the cats seemed to be able to leap and light about on it like birds.'

That was London, in October of 1940, when there seemed no reason why the bombing should not go on for years.

The devastation changed the face of the cities.

LONDON, 1941

Half masonry, half pain; her head
From which the plaster breaks away
Like flesh from the rough bone, is turned
Upon a neck of stones; her eyes
Are lid-less windows of smashed glass,

Each star-shaped pupil
Giving upon a vault so vast
How can the head contain it?

The raw smoke
Is inter-wreathing through the jaggedness
Of her sky-broken panes, and mirror'd
Fires dance like madmen on the splinters.

All else is stillness save the dancing splinters
And the slow inter-wreathing of the smoke.

Her breasts are crumbling brick where the black ivy
Had clung like a fantastic child for succour
And now hangs draggled with long peels of paper,
Fire-crisp, fire-faded awnings of limp paper
Repeating still their ghosted leaf and lily.

Grass for her cold skin's hair, the grass of cities
Wilted and swaying on her plaster brow
From winds that stream along the streets of cities:

Across a world of sudden fear and firelight
She towers erect, the great stones at her throat,
Her rusted ribs like railings round her heart;
A figure of dry wounds – of winter wounds –
O mother of wounds; half masonry, half pain.

Mervyn Peake

STEPNEY 1941

Much as though some one had sung
'House, house, house, house,'
Row after row of times;
And each time one more sprung up
To shiver in the line.
Shall we knock? Shall we get their reactions to the war?
This one will do. But it's empty; no door even
To knock at. And this too; the whole row
And not a soul, all empty and windowless,
With walls standing around regarding one another

74

Naked, as they bear the weight of shocked ceilings.
Let us not speak, for we look into hearts
That are drained and stilled, as though
God had . . . Hell, like a lot of tarts
They are, with their legs cocked, showing the works.
Let's get out of this. Look, there's a cat lurking
In that debris! See, beside that smashed divan.
Here, puss, pretty puss, here. Why, look at it run!
Crazed, and that savage eye, already it has forgotten.

Bertram Warr

Everybody had to be prepared for sudden death and darkness falling from the air.

PUNISHMENT ENOUGH

They say that women, in a bombing-raid,
Retire to sleep in brand-new underwear
Lest they be tumbled out of doors, displayed
In shabby garments to the public stare.

You've often seen a house, sliced like a cheese,
Displaying its poor secrets – peeling walls
And warping cupboards. Of such tragedies
It is the petty scale that most appals.

When you confess your sins before a parson,
You find it no great effort to disclose
Your crimes of murder, bigamy and arson,
But can you tell him that you pick your nose?

If after death you pay for your misdeeds,
Surely the direst and most just requital
Would be to listen while an angel reads
Before a crowd your endless, mean recital:

Golf scorecards faked, thefts from your mother's purse . . .
But why should Doomsday bother with such stuff?
This is the Hell that you already nurse
Within you. You've had punishment enough.

Norman Cameron

Some found a curious freedom and stimulation during the blitz.

from NOTES FROM ANOTHER COUNTRY

A wretched time, people say. I recall it as one of the happiest periods of my life. I have always desired a society in which everything should be impermanent and in which the possession of property and the inheritance of money should be eliminated. It did not disturb me at all to know that the place in which I lived might any day be destroyed, and the routines by which most of us live become meaningless. I know now that I shall never see such a Utopia, but life in London at this time gave a hint of it, as life in Russia must have done in the months after the Revolution. For such a temperament London in those days was in many ways an ideal city. The journey to work was an adventure and an absurdity – twice a bomb fell within a hundred yards of the bus in which I was travelling. Living became a matter of the next meal, the next drink. The way in which people behaved to each other relaxed strangely. Barriers of class and circumstance disappeared, so that London was more nearly an equalitarian city than it has ever been in the last quarter of a century. Was it mere romanticism that discovered 'new styles of architecture, a change of heart' in the bombed places? For a few months we lived in the possibility of a different kind of history. It only just needs saying that the successive pieces of 'bad news' which distressed many people, expressing the consolidation of Nazi power throughout Europe, were to me only an expected proof of an old order breaking up, a new one of perpetual repression and revolt taking its place. The sense of two 'real' worlds, openly repressive and equalitarian, struggling with each other, was exhilarating. This division of society into opposing forces seemed to me as real as the peace of 1945, when it came, was to appear an illusion.

Julian Symons

The burned and disfigured pilot Richard Hillary was in a pub in the East End of London when it was hit by a bomb. He helped to dig survivors out of the rubble nearby.

from THE LAST ENEMY

We dug, or rather we pushed, pulled, heaved, and strained, I somewhat ineffectually because of my hands; I don't know for how long, but I suppose for a short enough while. And yet it seemed endless. From time to time I was aware of figures round me: an A.R.P. warden, his face expressionless under a steel helmet; once a soldier swearing savagely in a quiet monotone; and the taxi-driver, his face pouring sweat.

And so we came to the woman. It was her feet that we saw first, and whereas before we had worked doggedly, now we worked with a sort of frenzy, like prospectors at the first glint of gold. She was not quite buried, and through the gap between two beams we could see that she was still alive. We got the child out first. It was passed back carefully and with an odd sort of reverence by the warden, but it was dead. She must have been holding it to her in the bed when the bomb came.

Finally we made a gap wide enough for the bed to be drawn out. The woman who lay there looked middle-aged. She lay on her back and her eyes were closed. Her face, through the dirt and streaked blood, was the face of a thousand working women; her body under the cotton nightdress was heavy. The nightdress was drawn up to her knees and one leg was twisted under her. There was no dignity about that figure.

Around me I heard voices. 'Where's the ambulance?' 'For Christ's sake don't move her!' 'Let her have some air!'

I was at the head of the bed, and looking down into that tired, blood-streaked, work-worn face I had a sense of complete unreality. I took the brandy flask from my hip pocket and held it to her lips. Most of it ran down her chin but a little flowed between those clenched teeth. She opened her eyes and reached out her arms instinctively for the child. Then she started to weep. Quite soundlessly, and with no sobbing, the tears were running down her cheeks when she lifted her eyes to mine.

'Thank you, sir,' she said, and took my hand in hers. And then, looking at me again, she said after a pause, 'I see they got you too.'

Very carefully I screwed the top on to the brandy flask, unscrewed it once and screwed it on again, for I had caught it on the wrong thread. I put the flask into my hip pocket and did up the button. I pulled across the buckle on my great-coat and noticed that I was dripping with sweat. I pulled the cap down over my eyes and walked out into the street.

Someone caught me by the arm, I think it was the soldier with the girl, and said: 'You'd better take some of that brandy yourself. You don't look too good'; but I shook him off. With difficulty I kept my pace to a walk, forcing myself not to run. For I wanted to run, to run anywhere away from that scene, from myself, from the terror that was inside me, the terror of something that was about to happen and which I had not the power to stop.

It started small, small but insistent deep inside of me, sharp as a needle, then welling up uncontrollable, spurting, flowing over, choking me. I was drowning, helpless in a rage that caught and twisted and hurled me on, mouthing in a blind unthinking frenzy. I heard myself cursing, the words pouring out, shrill, meaningless, and as my mind cleared a little I knew that it was the woman I cursed. Yes, the woman that I reviled, hating her that she should die like that for me to see, loathing that silly bloody twisted face that had said those words: 'I see they got you too.' That she should have spoken to me, why, oh Christ, to me? Could she not have died the next night, ten minutes later, or in the next street? Could she not have died without speaking, without raising those cow eyes to mine?

'I see they got you too.' All humanity had been in those few words, and I had cursed her. Slowly the frenzy died in me, the rage oozed out of me, leaving me cold, shivering, and bitterly ashamed. I had cursed her, cursed her, I realized as I grew calmer, for she had been the one thing that my rage surging uncontrollably had had to fasten on, the one thing to which my mind, overwhelmed by the sense of something so huge and beyond the range of thought, could cling. Her death was unjust, a crime, an outrage, a sin against mankind – weak inadequate words which even as they passed through my mind mocked me with their futility.

A Canadian diplomat saw the sights of the West End of London during the blitz.

from THE SIREN YEARS: UNDIPLOMATIC DIARIES
1937–1945

27 October 1941.

The sights – the long tree-lined avenue in Hyde Park at dusk echoing with the noise of soldiers' boots as they come strolling, swinging, whistling, singing, or alone looking for a girl, and the girls plain – most of them – little working girls in short skirts and sweaters with fancy handkerchiefs around their necks. They know they are wanted – they twist and turn as they walk and break into sudden gusts of giggles and cling to each other's arms. The whole length of the avenue is alive with desires. There are satyrs behind every tree. Silhouetted against the half-light soldiers with their girls sit on the deck-chairs on the grassy stretches that border the avenue. The flicker of a cigarette lighter reveals for a long second – the pose of a head – the movements of hands. Near the park gates the Military Police in their rose-topped caps stand in groups of twos and threes hoping for trouble, longing to exercise summary justice.

In the expensive restaurants at this hour pink, well-scrubbed school-boys masquerading in guards uniforms are drinking bad martinis with girl-friends in short fur caps and Fortnum and Mason shoes, who have spent the day driving generals to the War Office or handing cups of tea and back-chat to soldiers in canteens. Grass widows in black with diamond clips or pearls are finding the conversation of Polish officers refreshingly different from that of English husbands. Ugly vivacious A.T.S. are ordering *vin rosé* at the Coquille. A film actress (making the best of a patriotic part at present) is just going through the swinging door of the Apéritif with David Niven at her elbow. Ageing Edwardian hostesses whose big houses are now shuttered and silent are taking little naps in their hideouts on the third floor ('so much the safest floor, darling') at Claridge's or the Dorchester. Cedric (in a yachtsman's jacket) and Nigel are hipping their way through the crowd of pansies in the Ritz bar (they all have the most madly peculiar jobs in the Ministry of Information or the B.B.C.). At the Travellers' Club Harold Nicolson in his fruity voice is embellishing a story as he settles on the leather sofa. Anne-Marie is sitting on the side of her bed at the Ritz making eyes at herself in the mirror and trumpeting down the telephone in Romanian French. It is a world of hotels and bars and little pubs that have become the fashion overnight – of small drinking clubs run by gangsters who make a nice profit out of prostitutes and the dope racket – packed with R.A.F. pilots, Canadian officers, blondes and slot-machines and perhaps a baccarat table in the upstairs rooms.

And along Piccadilly from the Circus to Hyde Park Corner is an incessant parade of prostitutes, and out of the black-out an acquisitive hand on your arm and 'Feeling lonely, dearie?' 'Hello, my sweet,' (in a Noël Coward voice) or '*Chéri.*' In Berkeley Square the railings are down. An old man is making a bonfire of dead leaves beside the little pavilion in the centre of the garden.

Charles Ritchie

A terrible beauty descended on the devastation of the city, as William Sansom discovered when on duty in the Fire Service.

from WESTMINSTER AT WAR

The weather continued warm, but the nights were lengthening. People looked forward to the winter and the long cold darkness with no relish. The streets emptied now after dusk, and the blackout became largely the property of the wardens and police; though in the West End there persisted a dogged and darkly hurrying crowd of revellers. A City bereft of electric and neon light took on a new beauty – by moonlight the great buildings assumed a remote and classic magnificence, cold, ancient, lunar palaces carved in bone from the moon, and angular overdressed Victorian eccentricities were purified, uncoloured, quietened by the moon's ubiquitous sanity. But on clouded nights and moonless nights it was not so beautiful – in the total blackout nothing could be seen. Torchlight was rationed by a filter of paper, the insides of passing buses glimmered blue, cigarette ends became the means of demonstrating one's passage. A match might not be struck, nor a headlight switched on. A glimmer of 'starlight' filtered down from some street-lamps in the main thoroughfares, the red, green and yellow traffic lights were masked to show only thin crosses of their colour. This darkness flared into sudden relief – in the yellow flash of gunfire, in the whitish-green hiss of incendiaries, in the copper-red reflection of the fires, in the yellow flare of the burning gas main, in the red explosion of the bomb. In such light the gilt tracery of Big Ben's tower flashed into colour, the sombre drab alleys round Covent Garden blazed with a theatrical daylight, the corrugated skylines of Park Lane and Knightsbridge showed black against the deep red sky, the streets of Pimlico and Soho saw the high scarfing columns of a naked gas flame flaring like some giant idealisation of the naphtha flames that through the years had lit their fairs and their stalls.

These were the lights – but there were also dark streets, streets where suddenly a house of blackness collapsed with a roar, shifting down heavily like some bricked elephant lumbering to its knees, thickening the darkness with a poisonous cloud of dust, shrouding the moment after its fall with a fearful empty silence broken only by small sounds, the whispering of broken water pipes, slight shiftings of debris, moans and little cries of the injured; then into the torchlight of the wardens there would stagger those untrapped, lonely figures in the dust-fog bleached grey with powder and streaked and patched with black blood; or – there would be nobody, and not a sound, only a living silence in the knowledge that under a smoking, spawning mass of timber and brick and dust there lay pressed and stifled the bodies of warm people whose minutes were slowly ticking away, whose rescue was absurdly blocked by a mass of intractable weight that angered those standing so few yards above. These are not pleasant memories, but they must be written – otherwise the picture that was essentially one of dirt and anguish becomes too clean. Death and wounding from such explosives was never as neat as a bullet in the head; but the details shall be left to a Barbusse. One of the few consolations was that the explosive force proved in most cases so great as to shock its victim into unconsciousness or at least into a physical incomprehension of what had occurred.

The problem for the writers was to describe the destruction in words that could comprehend the terror and the pity of it all.

MIDNIGHT AIR-RAID

Beyond our factories, like caterpillars curled in a sham death,
Rivers signal their quicksilver treachery, and, in answer,
The guns of midnight pound from roots of earth
Bombarding with their radium mouth and prong of cancer
Eating out the lungs of countries in a bubble of bloody breath.

Sensitive fingers of searchlights pick the pockets of dark.
These are surgeon's pitiless forceps imprisoning in their grip
Anaerobic death, there, in the heart of air, lurking
To burst the harmless tissues of cities. It is an antisepsis
To this blind world of blood, with an unsuspecting child, the dawn,
        forgotten larks.

Now sirens unleash civilian anguish. In a reflex they
Stumble from an underworld of dreams whom abortive desire,
Pillared in moonlit limbs, makes grey;
Freedom's involuntary fighters, knowing no refuge save in fiery
Consciousness, rampant light and the resolution of day.

Night that sealed their visions, drained all thought an hour
Ago, is now their bodyguard; but real defence is an illumination,
Ally of the sun, and fills their brain with staggering power
Where sanity tremors on madness, to beat down explosion
Of wind and the thunder's stupor in a turbulent underground anger.

Here artist and scientist concur to admire
A formal pattern of battle, where herring-bone squadrons

Elude the swaying bars of light, and white fire,
From London's living furnace, flung up like a tilted cauldron,
Splits the atom of doom; yet the poet, in his words,

Knows these mean the end of speech, whose channels are
Mined, and learns to forge his consonants into casings and bolts,
To sew his lines with teeth, like bullets in machine-gun belts,
Filling them all with explosions of wild vowels, and so preparing
For the longer and even more bitter war.

J. F. Hendry

*Those who were despised were those who avoided the bombing by living
and working in a 'safe area'.*

BALLAD OF THE SAFE AREA

A little reading and a little loving
A little eating and a little sleeping
The days went over me half happy
With friends and books and cups of coffee

I watched the trees wave in green gardens
Avoided the police and the air raid wardens
I was delighted when the roses
Showed, like pups, their soft pink noses

Enjoyed the quiet and garrulous evenings
The rhythm of my child's deep breathing
As smoke and faces wove warm patterns
Of home not easily forgotten

I thought of poets lost in barracks
Or crawling about on muddy stomachs
And drank their toasts in beer and whisky
Drank now to Stalin, now to Trotsky

Now to Chamberlain or Churchill
– In fact I wished nobody ill
But loved myself and forgave the devil
And tried, for a time, to live on the level

Lectured each morning to pale students
Taught them intriguing rudiments
Of revolution and laissez-faire
And above all, how to be debonair

So far, so good: the Spring was springing
Through purple heather to brown hills clinging
When over the city the planes came flying
And out I ran with the fear of dying

All night we stood out on the terrace
Watching the glow grow to a furnace
Bombs and shells and whirls of shrapnel
Laid us often on the gravel

Then in the middle of the bombardment
When the whole street was making friends
A landmine fell at the nearest corner
And I thought for a minute I was a goner

Glass flowed like water from all the windows
Black smoke came rushing out in billows
A hundred doors leaped off their hinges
And I said goodbye to books and binges

Then a second landmine dropped just near
At the back of the house where lay my dear
But it didn't explode and I laughed and cried
And cursed as I pulled the family outside

Then along to the bridge where the flats were burning
I didn't look twice but improved my running
With the kid in my arms and the people crying
Past where the dead lay with the dying

But there was nothing for me to do
The wardens don't like you to be a hero
So they pushed me back from the blazing fire
And made me fall over some copper wire

Which made me feel rather a fool.
We all passed the night in a draughty school
And all caught colds, and that is why
Tears are still floating in my eye.

Francis Scarfe

Stephen Spender, who served in the National Fire Service, found a timelessness in fire-fighting.

from *CITIZENS IN WAR – AND AFTER*

Fires are exactly as spectacular as imagination paints them. In fact, like very high mountains, and other elemental things, they are so close to what one imagines that it is difficult to separate the reality from a mental image of a fire which has always been in one's mind. What I remember better than flames pouring out of windows is the hundreds of incendiaries lying in the Kensington streets on our way to the fire, like many workmen's hurricane lamps. In a fire there are violent contrasts of lightness and darkness. A blazing building creates a space of light all round it, like a dramatic city square illuminated by torches for a gala festival. But once outside this square the full darkness of the night may crowd down on one in a side-street. A staircase may be all smothering smoke and darkness, with fires in rooms on either side. One can see the fire faintly through cracks in the doors, as though behind those doors a fairy-tale treasure of golden brightness were locked.

On the second fire to which I went, I recognized the phrase which many firemen use when describing their experiences on a night of blitz: 'Time seemed meaningless.' I had to go up a staircase, through a door into a top room, of which the ceiling and roof were on fire. There were also other rooms on fire and another roof, on the same landing. As the pressure of water required to put out this fire was not very great, I was alone for a lot of this fire. It was, on the whole, a pleasurable sensation. The very closeness of the fire, and the dry, crackling sound of burning timber made me feel very far away from the Blitz, and in so far as there was an enemy in the room, it was one towards which I felt an almost personal feeling, not untinged with friendliness. Here I experienced that loss of time sense which I had heard spoken of. I was alone with an element – fire – as much as if I had been alone in a patch of sunlight by a pool of water in the centre of a forest. In the desert, in the forest, on the ocean, high up in the centre of the sky, time ceases to be a matter of minutes and hours moving along a narrow measured track, or travelling round a clock's dial. It becomes as solitary and enormous as the element itself. One is surrounded by the silence, the loneliness, the space, which seem immeasurable. Time is measured only by the incidents within that spacious changelessness. The ticking of an insect in the forest, the fall of a leaf, the movement of branches, the wrinkling of the waters on the skin of a wave, the paint on a window-sill slowly turning black with heat, these are the things which count as time when one is really alone with an element, and it is impossible to relate them to clocks and routine. So with a fire. In the centre of a great city, the fireman stands alone in a room directing the jet of water from a hose against the wall. Through a door or window the flames are crackling with a secret noise of their own combustion.

Perhaps if you have been a fireman for long you see the causal connection between the water coming from the hose and the flames gradually dying away. Myself, I am always astonished when the fire subsides, and in place of a powerful glowing interior like lit alabaster, there is water, hissing steam, and charred wood.

William Sansom wrote the best account of fighting blazes during the blitz in the National Fire Service anthology, Fire and Water, *illustrated by Leonard Rosoman and other artists.*

THE WALL

It was our third job that night. Until this thing happened, work had been without incident. There had been shrapnel, a few inquiring bombs and some huge fires; but these were unremarkable and have since merged without identity into the neutral maze of fire and noise and water and night, without date and without hour, with neither time nor form, that lowers mistily at the back of my mind as a picture of the air-raid season.

I suppose we were worn down and shivering. Three a.m. is a mean-spirited hour. I suppose we were drenched, with the cold hose water trickling in at our collars and settling down at the tails of our shirts. Without doubt the heavy brass couplings felt moulded from metal-ice. Probably the open roar of the pumps drowned the petulant buzz of the raiders above, and certainly the ubiquitous fire-glow made an orange stage-set of the streets. Black water would have puddled the City alleys, and I suppose our hands and our faces were black as the water, black with hacking about among the burnt-up rafters. These things were an every-night nonentity. They happened and they were not forgotten because they were never even remembered.

But I do remember it was our third job. And there we were – Len, Lofty, Verno and myself – playing a fifty-foot jet up the face of a tall City warehouse and thinking of nothing at all. You don't think of anything after the first few hours. You just watch the white pole of water lose itself in the fire, and you think of nothing. Sometimes you move the jet over to another window. Sometimes the orange dims to black – but you only ease your grip on the ice-cold nozzle and continue pouring careless gallons through the window. You know the fire will fester for hours yet. However, that night the blank, indefinite hours of waiting were sharply interrupted by an unusual sound. Very suddenly a long, rattling crack of bursting brick and mortar perforated the moment. And then the upper half of that five-storey building heaved over towards us. It hung there, poised for a timeless second before rumbling down at us. I was thinking of nothing at all and then I was thinking of everything in the world.

In that simple second my brain digested every detail of the scene. New eyes opened at the sides of my head so that, from within, I photographed a hemispherical panorama bounded by the huge length of the building in front of me and the narrow lane on either side.

Blocking us on the left was the squat trailer pump, roaring and quivering with effort. Water throbbed from its overflow valves and from leakages in the hose and couplings. A ceaseless stream spewed down its grey sides into the gutter. But nevertheless a fat iron exhaust-pipe glowed red-hot in the middle of the wet engine. I had to look past Lofty's face. Lofty was staring at the controls, hands tucked into his armpits for warmth. Lofty was thinking of nothing. He had a black diamond of soot over one eye, like the White-eyed Kaffir in negative.

To the other side of me was a free run up the alley. Overhead swung a sign – 'Catto and Henley'. I wondered what in hell they sold. Old stamps? The alley was quite free. A couple of lengths of dead, deflated hose wound over the darkly glistening pavement. Charred flotsam dammed up one of the gutters. A needle of water fountained from a hole in a live hose-length. Beneath a blue shelter light lay a shattered coping stone. The next shop along was a tobacconist's, windowless, with fake display cartons torn open for anybody to see. The alley was quite free.

Behind me, Len and Verno shared the weight of the hose. They heaved up against the strong backward drag of water-pressure. All I had to do was yell, 'Drop it!' – and then run. We could risk the live hose snaking up at us. We could run to the right down the free alley – Len, Verno and me. But I never moved. I never said, 'Drop it!' or

86

anything else. That long second held me hypnotized, rubber boots cemented to the pavement. Ton upon ton of red-hot brick hovering in the air above us numbed all initiative. I could only think. I couldn't move.

Six yards in front stood the blazing building. A minute before I would never have distinguished it from any other drab Victorian atrocity happily on fire. Now I was immediately certain of every minute detail. The building was five storeys high. The top four storeys were fiercely alight. The rooms inside were alive with red fire. The black outside walls remained untouched. And thus, like the lighted carriage of a night express, there appeared alternating rectangles of black and red that emphasized vividly the extreme symmetry of the window spacing: each oblong window shape posed as a vermilion panel set in perfect order upon the dark face of the wall. There were ten windows to each floor, making forty windows in all. In rigid rows of ten, one row placed precisely above the other, with strong contrasts of black and red, the blazing windows stood to attention in strict formation – the oblong building, the oblong windows, the oblong spacing. Orange-red colour seemed to *bulge* from the black framework, assumed tactile values like boiling jelly that expanded inside a thick black-squared grille.

Three of the storeys, thirty blazing windows and their huge frame of black brick, a hundred solid tons of hard, deep Victorian wall, pivoted over towards us and hung flatly over the alley. Whether the descending wall actually paused in its fall I can never know. Probably it never did. Probably it only seemed to hang there. Probably my eyes digested its action at an early period of momentum, so that I saw it 'off true' but before it had gathered speed.

The night grew darker as the great mass hung over us. Through smoke-fogged fire-glow the moonlight had hitherto penetrated to the pit of our alley through declivities in the skyline. Now some of the moonlight was being shut out as the wall hung ever further over us. The wall shaded the moonlight like an inverted awning. Now the pathway of light above had been squeezed to a thin line. That was the only silver lining I ever believed in. It shone out – a ray of hope. But it was a declining hope, for although at this time the entire hemispherical scene appeared static, an imminence of movement could be sensed throughout – presumably because the scene was actually moving. Even the speed of the shutter which closed the photograph on my mind was powerless to exclude this motion from a deeper consciousness. The picture appeared static to the limited surface senses, the eyes and the material brain, but beyond that there was hidden movement.

The second was timeless. I had leisure to remark many things. For instance, that an iron derrick, slightly to the left, would not hit me.

This derrick stuck out from the building, and I could feel its sharpness and hardness as clearly as if I had run my body intimately over its contour. I had time to notice that it carried a foot-long hook, a chain with three-inch rings, two girder supports and a wheel more than twice as large as my head.

A wall will fall in many ways. It may sway over to the one side or the other. It may crumble at the very beginning of its fall. It may remain intact and fall flat. This wall fell as flat as a pancake. It clung to its shape through ninety degrees to the horizontal. Then it detached itself from the pivot and slammed down on top of us.

The last resistance of bricks and mortar at the pivot point cracked off like automatic gunfire. The violent sound both deafened and brought us to our senses. We dropped the hose and crouched. Afterwards Verno said that I knelt slowly on one knee with bowed head, like a man about to be knighted. Well, I got my knighting. There was an incredible noise – a thunderclap condensed into the space of an eardrum – and then the bricks and the mortar came tearing and burning into the flesh of my face.

Lofty, away by the pump, was killed. Len, Verno and myself they dug out. There was very little brick on top of us. We had been lucky. We had been framed by one of those symmetrical, oblong window spaces.

And Dylan Thomas wrote one of his finer poems about a child who died by fire.

A REFUSAL TO MOURN THE DEATH, BY FIRE, OF A CHILD IN LONDON

Never until the mankind making
Bird beast and flower
Fathering and all humbling darkness
Tells with silence the last light breaking
And the still hour
Is come of the sea tumbling in harness

And I must enter again the round
Zion of the water bead
And the synagogue of the ear of corn
Shall I let pray the shadow of a sound
Or sow my salt seed
In the last valley of sackcloth to mourn

The majesty and burning of the child's death.
I shall not murder
The mankind of her going with a grave truth
Nor blaspheme down the stations of the breath
With any further
Elegy of innocence and youth.

Deep with the first dead lies London's daughter,
Robed in the long friends,
The grains beyond age, the dark veins of her mother,
Secret by the unmourning water
Of the riding Thames.
After the first death, there is no other.

Cecil Day Lewis used to speak about how one of his poems grew from seeing a child with her doll in a shelter.

About 'IN THE SHELTER'

One night in London, during the blitzes, I popped into an air-raid shelter. The Luftwaffe was getting a bit too close for my liking. It wasn't at all a deep shelter. There were a lot of grown-up people there, and we were all quite a bit frightened and pretending we weren't – making jokes and so on. One old man, I remember, was sitting on a bunk and shaking, shaking, shaking like an aspen leaf. Every bomb that fell seemed to start another rivet in me, and a bit more fear leaked in. Then a small girl entered the shelter. She must have been about seven or eight years old: a pretty little girl carrying a doll half as big as herself. Her grandmother – some old woman anyway – came in behind her. The little girl sat down on a broken-backed chair in the middle of the shelter, still nursing the doll, her long black hair falling over it. A stick of bombs fell close. The shelter seemed to rock and settle back again. I was watching the little girl. She bent closer over the doll as the bombs shrieked down; she was murmuring to it, comforting it. She seemed extraordinarily alone there, in the midst of the crowded shelter. Alone, but not lonely. The shelter was whitewashed glaring white, lit by naked electric bulbs. But this small girl seemed to me to be shining too, glowing, like a storm-lantern or a night-light. She looked absolutely self-possessed, self-contained she and her doll. I simply couldn't take my eyes off her. And after a bit, the raid ended.

And I realised that ever since this girl, this little night-light had come in and I'd begun to watch her, I'd forgotten to be frightened, I really had hardly heard the bombs and the barrage. There was she, absorbed in her doll; and there was I, intent on her, on the almost unearthly beauty of her face and her pose as she comforted her doll . . .

> Dear sheltering child, if again misgivings grieve me
> That love is only a respite, an opal bloom
> Upon our snow-set fields, come back to revive me
> Cradling your spark through blizzard, drift and tomb.

John Singer pointed out that the cities would not die.

CITIES ARE PEOPLE

> You can't dismiss cities with an idealist cry,
> With a sigh; you may bomb them, smash them.
> But cities don't easily die.
>
> Houses, people and parks, buildings and shops,
> Spire and steeple, and the simple satisfying sun,
> Are real; are remembered like good crops.
>
> Are thought about deep down, are part of those born there.
> The ordinary people whose sweat made the very bricks.
> Even the unlucky ones, even those forlorn there.
>
> Love of birthplace isn't jingo, isn't worldly, isn't witty.
> The countryman wants quiet lanes, the townsman loves his city
> And his roots in it go deeper than your makeshifts and your pity.

Putting on uniform and the loss of all possessions could mean a kind of liberation.

SOLDIERS AND CIVILIANS

It was not until I stood in front of No. 24, where I had lived for many a year, that I realised the extent of the disaster. It wasn't a direct hit: the bomb had dropped on No. 23, tearing No. 24 from No. 25, with the result that my house, though still standing, was suspended in the air, obliquely, like a nightmare version of the Tower of Pisa.

My things which were stored in the basement when I left for the Army were flooded as the water-main burst, and all my belongings were ruined. I just took a good look at the scene and left, realising that any attempt at salvage would be but waste of time. As a member of the Pioneer Corps clearing away the débris in the East End, I had seen plenty of places like this one. The scene was familiar enough. Yet this was my own home: I had my personal belongings there, my books, my manuscripts, my notes on the 'Early Mystics'. I saw some of the latter floating in the stagnant murkiness of the flood water that gave the basement the aspect of a malarial bog. I touched nothing and walked away; there was nothing else to do.

At first, I did not think. Intellectually, the loss of my property did not affect me; in fact, I was hardly aware of it. A little later, when I found myself walking slowly along Oxford Street, I was little by little overcome by a queer feeling of lostness and sentimental stress, which seemed to emerge from my subconscious; waves of emotions, impossible to formulate, assailed me from within, with my heart the centre of the target area, as it were. My brain was in a muddle. I failed to follow the drift of my own confused thoughts and feelings. I made an effort to shake myself out of this bizarre lethargy, and slowly my mind became clearer, focussing at last upon reality.

I had joined up, simply because I wanted to contribute to the common war effort; without even being quite sure of having the makings of a soldier; and certainly without the least spectacular *arrière-pensée* of becoming a hero. Thus, at the age of 44, I became a soldier, about a year ago.

But up to now, I was still a soldier attached to my past, civilian life by my personal belongings, my clothes, books, pipes, souvenirs, letters, manuscripts, etc. And from that past life, I now suddenly found myself brutally severed: I felt as though some invisible, psycho-umbilical cord had been cut: and out of the warm and cosy womb of civilian life I suddenly emerged, in the middle of Oxford Street, a newly-born entity, a baby soldier. A somewhat bewildering experience for a grown-up man, walking in broad daylight through the main artery of the Borough of St. Marylebone.

In a shop window, my eyes caught a reflection of myself, in battledress, and suddenly it occurred to me that this battledress was now my unique suit of clothes. Never before had I thought of my battledress in terms of a suit of clothes. For one thing, it wasn't mine, but Government property; and somehow one doesn't associate a uniform with its civilian equivalent. In a way, the uniform can hardly be described as wearing apparel. The suit clothes a man, the uniform simply renders him undistinguishable. Just as a forage cap can never take the place of a hat; or a pair of 'ammunition boots' the place of shoes.

It is rather difficult to define the definition: the suit expresses the individual, the uniform an organisation. The uniform cuts the man off from one mode of living, and subjects him to another: it lends to the soldier an air of discreet anonymity. No tailor, from Savile Row to Commercial Road, can achieve the same effect. Just from looking at a soldier, it is difficult to say, unless the traits are very marked, whether the man is intelligent or an imbecile; sensitive or a brute; a millionaire or a pauper; an artist or a stockbroker; a writer or a bookkeeper; a gentleman or a factory hand. One can hardly say whether he is a good soldier or a bad one.

The civilian, on the other hand, reveals much more of his status and individuality, no matter how inconspicuously he chooses to dress. It is a perfectly true saying that the man can be judged by his clothes; he can never be judged by his uniform. An old, filthy, threadbare, battle-worn uniform gives you no more clue to the man's personality as a brand-new battledress just issued from the Quartermaster's stores.

One often recognises a man, his character and whole outlook upon life, by his hat hanging on a peg. But there is no such thing as a forage cap with a personality. The hat tells a life-story, the peak-cap is always non-committal. A pair of shoes may have character; ammunition boots are merely things which perform 30-inch regulation steps.

The uniform takes all the gestures away from the man, all his habits, hobbies and peculiarities. The soldier appeals to the emotions, just as the civilian appeals to the intellect. Hence, I should say, the women's susceptibility of being attracted by uniformed men. The civilian cannot help displaying his background, education, likes and dislikes, profession, tastes, state of mind – even his bank balance. The soldier, on the other hand, is fundamentally anonymous; under his uniform he is as enigmatic as any sphynx. We know nothing about his vices and virtues, his human qualities and defects. No one can tell what the soldier has eaten; the civilian's physiognomy will often reflect the menu of his dinner. The soldier may be in love, but no one, not even his section sergeant, will be aware of it; the civilian, if only slightly infatuated, is recognisable as such at first sight.

One might almost say that the uniform absorbs the man's feelings, thoughts, attitude, creed and sex, like blotting paper. To be sure, closer observation will reveal the man under his uniform. But then he automatically regains, at least in the eyes of the observer, his civilian status. You don't refer to a member of the Forces known to you as a soldier: he is a husband, a brother, a father or a sweetheart; or your landlord; or someone who owes you money, or vice versa. The mystery of the uniform is a most profound one. The soldier who wants to reveal his personality has to take off his tunic, metaphorically speaking, anyway.

And the battledress I was wearing strolling along Oxford Street protected me with its khaki anonymity from all curiosity, malevolent and benevolent. Only I knew that I had just lost all my terrestrial goods. It did not matter. After all, I had lost nothing essential. As a matter of fact, all I had lost was essentially inessential. Out of a sudden, I realised that all one possibly can lose must needs be inessential.

My sadness and strange feeling of lostness of a moment ago suddenly gave way to a sensation of immense exultation. Yes, I had lost everything, and I felt insanely happy and exuberant. As light as a bird. Unchained to any material possessions. For the first time in my life, I had the feeling of being *inwardly* a free man. *Vive la liberté*. To hell with my clothes! I shouted almost at the top of my voice. Haven't I still got a governmental battledress? Do I need silken things and fancy ties, dressing-gowns, dinner jackets and dress suits? All those things were just so much weight, they weigh you down, reducing your life to the sedentariness of a cliché existence. Why in hell did I ever buy all that stuff?

All my books gone. Good riddance! Those of the books I hadn't read were just dead weight, anyhow. And what's the use of keeping the others? I might as well have conserved a collection of squeezed-out lemons.

True enough, there were my notes on the 'Early Mystics', which had taken me nearly a year to compile at the British Museum. A year's work wasted, there's no way of getting around that. But then, the war had come in between. Would I be likely to take up the same book again after the war when everything, including myself, will be changed? There will be an entirely new world to be approached from an entirely new angle. So to hell with the 'Early Mystics''!

In a state of unbelievable elation, I walked into a pub and ordered a triple whisky and soda. 'Heil Hitler!' I almost shouted aloud, thankful to world's enemy No. 1 for having taken the load off my hands, mind and heart. *Vive la liberté*!

Alfred Perles

4
Love of Weapons, Fear of Death

"Now 'ere you 'ave a more or less perfect example of what 'appens to a feller what's never troubled to master the art of unarmed combat"

The Royal Air Force won the Battle of Britain in the skies. John Pudney was its leading poet and collected the verses written by the airmen.

COMBAT REPORT

Just then I saw the bloody Hun.
You saw the Hun? You, light and easy,
Carving the soundless daylight. *I was breezy*
When I saw that Hun. Oh wonder
Pattern of stress, of nerve poise, flyer,
Overtaking time. *He came out under*
Nine-tenths cloud, but I was higher.
Did Michelangelo aspire,
Painting the laughing cumulus, to ride
The majesty of air. *He was a trier*
I'll give him that, the Hun. So you convert
Ultimate sky to air speed, drift, and cover:
Sure with the tricky tools of God and lover.
I let him have a sharp four-second squirt,
Closing to fifty yards. He went on fire.
Your deadly petals painted, you exert
A simple stature. Man-high, without pride,
You pick your way through heaven and the dirt.
He burnt out in the air: that's how the poor sod died.

Olivia Fitzroy saw a figher pilot in a pub.

FLEET FIGHTER

'Good show!' he said, leaned his head back and laughed.
'They're wizard types!' he said, and held his beer
Steadily, looked at it and gulped it down
Out of its jam-jar, took a cigarette
And blew a neat smoke ring into the air.
'After this morning's prang I've got the twitch;
I thought I'd had it in the teased-out kite.'
His eyes were blue, and older than his face,
His single stripe had known a lonely war
But all his talk and movements showed his age.
His whole life was the air and his machine,

He had no thought but of the latest 'mod',
His jargon was of aircraft or of beer.
'And what will you do afterwards?' I said,
Then saw his puzzled face, and caught my breath.
There was no afterwards for him, but death.

Some pilots such as David Bourne, who was to die, never wanted to come to earth.

PARACHUTE DESCENT

Snap back the canopy,
Pull out the oxygen tube,
Flick the harness pin
And slap out into the air
Clear of the machine.

Did you ever dream when you were young
Of floating through the air, hung
Between the clouds and the gay
Be-blossomed land?
Did you ever stand and say,
'To sit and think and be alone
In the middle of the sky
Is my one most perfect wish'?

That was a fore-knowing;
You knew that some day
To satiate an inward crave
You must play with the wave
Of a cloud. And shout aloud
In the clean air,
The untouched-by-worldly-things-and-mean air,
With exhilarated living.

You knew that you must float
From the sun above the clouds
To the gloom beneath, from a world
Of rarefied splendour to one
Of cheapened dirt, close-knit
In its effort to encompass man
In death.

So you can stay in the clouds, boy,
You can let your soul go onwards,
You have no ties on earth,
You could never have accomplished
Anything. Your ideas and ideals
Were too high. So you can stay
In the sky, boy, and have no fear.

But Bourne's duty was to shoot down the enemy and return to base if he could.

FIGHTER BY NIGHT

Twelve jets and spume of flame
Stumble and leap into the blackness,
To be held there for an instant.
Then away and up, stuttering Firefly of revenge.

Then it is for me and my machine
To turn along the line of flares;
Thumbs up and a pulse beating louder,
Louder into a roar:
A surging, with swift rivulets of ground
Bumping, jerking me into the abyss of blackness –
Blackness of brief, brief uncertainty.

Never has a man been more alone
Than when he is alone above the night –
The night you knew before.
Never has so much rested
On the inconstant constancy of mind
And will to do just one thing only
At a time – there is no other.
A concentrate of action, and yet wait –
Wait for the dim black shape
On moonlight clouds.
Jet of exhaust again, the foe
Below and alone.
One thing now, the shape resolved
Into an aeroplane, distinctive tail
(Never blink your eyes but stay them there,
There: See? Stay them there)

Then a spurt of bullets – and –
A pattern of flame from the bomber's belly,
(Passing through your belly, too)
A flash that blinds you momentarily . . .
And we're off to see the wizard
The wonderful wizard of Oz –
Lost? No. Motherdrome will see you home
So we gallop back merrily singing,
(Carefully, carelessness now would spoil.)
Below leap the flares,
But high we glide,
To the sagging weight until the bounce;
Now joyful (now no sinking hearts for this)
To the taxi-in triumphant.

Killing was an art in the sky.

AVIATOR

So carefully
The eye glances along the sights,
The instinctive mind calculates familiar data;
Ease forward, control the fall.
A white blur of face
Storms sickeningly up, confused among dark wings
And the steel-jawed chatter of bullets.
Staring eyes framed in glass
Flash to the brain the absurd question.
Grace of limb and hand
Jerked and twisted into idiot futility
And helplessness.
To what end rests this power,
Leashed behind some dim corner of thought,
Within the soul to provoke
This slow black surge of blood?

In the throes of it
The done cannot be undone;
So fierce is no fire to weld
The snapped spirit and flesh cold.

E. Denyer Cox

The fighters were mainly defensive weapons, but the bombers flew away to spread destruction from the air over Germany. One pilot who was to die on an air raid remembered the example of the Greeks at Troy.

RAIDERS OVER TROY

Then we set course for Troy, and it was done.
We moved above the city, dark, where fire was to run
and saw the crawling target. Fingers tensed to guide
steel on the winds, the flames
that lit our thunder dance in the streets.
And now Troy answered, fury scarred the air
and our dark squadrons saw wings, star-spangled, fail,
while through a gale-churned foam of flame there burst
stars thunderborn, where the darkest corners of masonry tossed
ruinous fountains: so we left Troy burning, and returned.

M. Macnaughton-Smith

Some of the missions set out joyfully.

DAYLIGHT OPERATIONS

They waved. He climbed the ladder, crawled
along the catwalk to his glittering turret:
with armour plate and perspex his world was walled,
but in the excitement none could cage his spirit,
that dared, defied, and laughed at every danger.
Crouched, he felt the bouncing tail: the hangar
slid away. He was aloof, alone,
poised in a throbbing day bright with sky and colour.
Below, the earth fell sharply like a stone,
and hill dropped to a level as up rose the valley.
The laughter left him giddy, the handwaving
along the way, the nods and friendly voices.
He had not realized till now that he'd be leaving
England for the bitter east. The faint noises
of people talking haunted him: but now they were
drowned in the air and voices of the Lancaster.

He recalled the cheering and again,
turning his turret, the colour and the laughter.
No fear oppressed him: his spirit lifted,
singing above the white clouds that had no rain.

Herbert Corby

Patric Dickinson, who remained in England during the war, would reflect upon the bombers on their going out on their missions.

BOMBERS: EVENING

The sun was nearly home
When the clouds broke and the sky
Unveiled its infinite dome
Like the eyelid from an eye.

I watch the bombers come
Beating upon the air
The dolorous slow drum
Of the executioner.

The sun below the hill
Was hidden from my sight;
But these, though sunlit still,
Put on the mask of night.

And as I watch and count
The fair impassive wings
I see the victims mount
Self-willed their scaffoldings.

And now the sun has set.
Thoughts jostle and peer and call:
The drums have ceased to beat:
The heads must fall, must fall.

O from that dreadful show,
For all its justice, may
We each in secret know
One thought that turns away.

Some of the aeroplanes were reported missing.

REPORTED MISSING

With broken wing they limped across the sky
caught in late sunlight, with their gunner dead,
one engine gone – the type was out-of-date –
blood on the fuselage turning brown from red:
knew it was finished, looking at the sea
which shone back patterns in kaleidoscope,
knew that their shadow would meet them by the way,
close and catch at them, drown their single hope:
sat in this tattered scarecrow of the sky
hearing it cough, the great plane catching
now the first dark clouds upon her wing-base
patching the great tear, in evening mockery;
so two men waited, saw the third dead face,
and wondered when the wind would let them die.

John Bayliss

MISSING

They told me, when they cut the ready wheat
the hares are suddenly homeless and afraid,
and aimlessly run the stubble with scared feet
finding no homes in sunlight or in shade.
– It's morning, and the Hampdens have returned,
the crews are home, have stretched and laughed and gone:
whence the planes came and the bright neon burned
the sun has ridden the sky and made the dawn.
He walks distraught, circling the landing ground,
waiting the last one in that won't come back,
and like those hares, he wanders round and round,
lost and desolate on the close-cropped track.

Herbert Corby

MISSING

Less said the better.
The bill unpaid, the dead letter,
No roses at the end
Of Smith, my friend.

Last words don't matter,
And there are none to flatter.
Words will not fill the post
Of Smith, the ghost.

For Smith, our brother,
Only son of loving mother,
The ocean lifted, stirred,
Leaving no word.

John Pudney

NO ANSWER

They found the corridor of wind, and sank
   in trancelike staggerings, down the long clear sky:
   the wings were dying slowly, with a sigh,
drawn to where breakers shimmered, rank on rank.
They shrugged: and if they'd had it now, no blame
   or guilt would tinge the quietly dying mind.
   One tried with desperate thoroughness to find
the radio answer: but it never came.

The earphones crackle; her hands upon her lap
   curl like decaying roses, her careless head
lolls against the red and yellow map.
   – But in the icy dawn the crew were dead,
no rescue boat had come: a coldness seeps
through this bleak traitorous room: but still she sleeps.

Herbert Corby

Before his own death, Rollo Woolley wrote a story about searching for the missing.

THE SEARCH

On the map of the island the sea is marked in pale wintry blue, whereas all lochs and rivers are coloured deep blue, with the purpose perhaps of emphasising their position as landmarks in the green and brown contours of the land. Often during a flight when I have opened a map in the cockpit I have half expected to find this contrast of blues repeated in the country below – dark blue waters forcing their way into a pallid sea. But how falsely the map reads! It is the ocean that has thrust blue fingers up the island's valleys, carving a rocky way through the island's mountains; thirstily it demands the fresh rushing torrents that the rivers yield to the salt tides.

That was the impression I had on this morning as our two planes climbed out of the shadows, over the hills, towards the sea. We were flying in close formation at first, wing-tip to wing-tip, but when we started the search we opened out to a distance of some several hundred yards, for the search demanded all our attention.

What did we expect to find? I was not sure. Maybe a débris of wood and torn fabric that might have belonged to a wing or a tailplane, splinters of wood that had shrieked its way into the uncut corn, or dashing against a cliff head had fallen and scattered on the sands below. Perhaps only a wound in the earth, a burning of green grass. Or perhaps a patch of brown oil on the sea, a glassy surface sliding from one wave to another.

But we found nothing. We flew on long parallel courses beginning over the land and turning further and further out to sea. On top of the cliffs clouds still covered some of the higher hills. Often a hill or a fragment of white cloud separated me from the other plane, and afterwards I would see it again half a mile ahead, so that I would have to push open the throttle for a moment to catch up. As we came low over the hills we saw children run out of the doorways of the whitewashed cottages to see us; two horses raced up and down their field excitedly; some men and women digging paused in their work and looked up; someone waved. But we were intruders in their morning; what could they understand of our search? Down on the land it was very cool and still, with the stillness of early morning. I could feel this stillness in every sign of the disturbance we made, the frightened horses and the faces looking upwards. In spite of the noise of the engine I could sense this stillness as closely as if I was with them on the ground. There was no débris to be seen, no black wound in the earth; and for the moment I forgot what we were searching for – it might have been a castle or a village, or even something very small and precious, a rare flower, say, or a lost ring.

'Spread out a bit more, Black Two,' said Ronnie's voice over the R.T.

'Okay, Black One,' I said.

'Turning now, Black Two.'

Over the sea we could fly lower, about two hundred feet, and we kept on a course from the mouth of the loch to the black rocks off the western shore of the island, turning out to sea each time. The sea was very calm. Only off the rocks were there white wave crests, the waves dancing and jostling with each other for room where a shore current crossed the tide. There were no boats off this part of the coast. I think the war had stopped most of the island's fishing. But far out to sea a long line of ships was sailing in convoy, and they took no notice of us when we approached them. I felt angry at their complete unconcern for our search. Then I wished that we had been looking for a lost schooner which we might have found drifting helplessly with broken masts, and its position would be reported and everything would be all right. (Was it after all a schooner which we were seeking?) We continued to look ceaselessly over the glittering water surface, our eyes became sore with the sea's brightness. And each time I came across a dark patch I would circle round carefully, until I recognised it as a mass of seaweed or an abandoned barrel rocking on the waves . . .

Then we were recalled. 'Return to base, Black section,' said the voice from the land. Soon we were back at the aerodrome again, taxiing round the perimeter track to dispersal.

'No luck?' asked the flight riggers, pushing the plane back into its bay.

'Did you see anything?' people asked us over the telephone.

What did they expect us to find? No, we had seen nothing. All our lives we had been searching and had found nothing. Only the whitewashed cottages and some strands of seaweed. Only some fragments of cloud and the blueness of the sea. Only the blueness of the empty glittering waves. I felt too weary to remember the original object of our search. Certainly it had been quite clear a little while ago: a plane was missing: one of our pilots had not returned. But that was only the previous night, and surely we had been searching for longer than that? Ages and ages before we had begun the search, and now an accident had happened to remind us that we must continue to look. We had even merited this new loss because we had become too indolent or ill-directed in our searching. And to-morrow or the next day, or maybe much later, we would have to set out anew.

The convention and the necessity was to be laconic about dying. It could happen to anyone on any mission. Gavin Ewart wrote about a Beaufighter crashing into the sea.

WHEN A BEAU GOES IN

When a Beau goes in,
Into the drink,
It makes you think,
Because, you see, they always sink
But nobody says 'Poor lad'
Or goes about looking sad
Because, you see, it's war,
It's the unalterable law.

Although it's perfectly certain
The pilot's gone for a Burton
And the observer too
It's nothing to do with you
And if they both should go
To a land where falls no rain nor hail nor driven snow –
Here, there or anywhere,
Do you suppose *they* care?

You shouldn't cry
Or say a prayer or sigh
In the cold sea, in the dark,
It isn't a lark
But it isn't Original Sin –
It's just a Beau going in.

C. R. Sanderson wrote of two of the airmen who died.

TO PETER

Quietly, efficiently, he did his work,
And that was bombing Germany.
It didn't give him any pleasure
Normally, he wouldn't kill a spider:
The danger, the uncertainty,
And constant fear.
He didn't flinch from – outwardly –
Off duty, he would wander
Round, or sit quietly half-drunk,
His senses not disagreeably dulled.
He says he may go mad.

When it's all over,
Or perhaps be killed,
Or again, that he'll survive
In disillusioned apathy.
No one can act too long
Against his beliefs.
He was doing nothing else,
With a sort of disillusioned heroism.

POEM

The engine cut on take-off . . .
To think it had to be Dick,
There weren't many like him.
I never knew him stop trying,
Not that he really liked it:
He felt he had to do it
Or let everyone down.
He was quite inscrutable
And quietly gallant. . .
The engine cut on take-off.

In the film of The Way to the Stars, *Michael Redgrave spoke a poem by John Pudney as a consolation for a war widow.*

FOR JOHNNY

Do not despair
For Johnny-head-in-air;
He sleeps as sound
As Johnny underground.

Fetch out no shroud
For Johnny-in-the-cloud;
And keep your tears
For him in after years.

Better by far
For Johnny-the-bright-star,
To keep your head,
And see his children fed.

John Pudney

Bertram Warr answered for the bereft woman.

WAR WIDOW

I can have no speech with them
When they grope at me with softness
Of lip motions thudding against thick glass.
Tears, they are born from torn places;
There is no pain, for I have tried to cry.

He is with me still.
The years have cast up and drifted out again;
And the memories, dried on the shore,
Have been bundled and stored
For this time,
For this quiet while that I am alone.

Timothy Corsellis regretted the death of a friend.

IN MEMORIAM – A.N.C.W.

I knew Nigel Weir
Slightly so
He stood upright and still
With an uncertain smile playing
Swaying, across his lips.
Straight he stood as a poker
His neck ran into his head
And his chin was close to his throat.
When he spoke
His words came kindly, softly clear
Lisping but meticulously formed
Each syllable was of kindness.

I knew Nigel Weir
Sometimes he spoke to me
When I was scarcely nice to know
Spoke kindly and wisely
The man was polite –
Oh ugly word, polite –
Where others did not care.

He and I fenced each other
His was the greater grace
His foot was swifter sure
His hands knew more.

I knew Nigel Weir
Even saw his soul
In his few verses
More able and more lovely
Then my own wild words
He and I felt together
But he always excelled
In his feelings, his actions
And his pliant expression.

I read his poems
But only once I wondered
At Nigel Weir
Until I saw him
Moving among the Spitfires
Remembered his swift arms
And his sensitive eyes
And I pitied the German sons
And I pitied his troubled soul.

I knew Nigel Weir
And the strange contradiction
Of his coarse hands.
Heard he had won him a victim
Envied his arm and
Pitied his mind.

Then I took to the sky
And forgot the man Weir.

Periodically I saw his brother.

And he died
With the frustration
Of a ribbon for valour
Sewn on his chest,
Cruel mean joke,

This jeering compensation.
I remembered the words of another
> *"Just as the flower of life seemed set to bloom,*
> *And the sun had pierced a frigid sky,*
> *You chose the solemn, unrelenting tomb*
> *You chose to die."*

I joined them to your name, Nigel –
Strange, that this should be the first time
I've ever called you "Nigel" –

I knew Nigel Weir
Vaguely so
He was always one step ahead of me
And he was of greater promise.
O world, it's Weir that's dead.

Even those who did not return from the air raids had little to say. Brian Allwood was another of the young pilots who were killed in action.

PILOT

The airman has nothing to say about this.
The moon is rising and she is not his,
Or wings are caking with malignant ice.

Distant the point where different language speaks.
The hours are minutes and the years are weeks.
The slow gulls wander; and the tracer streaks.

Has nothing to say, and this is done.
At night the long youth of the flaring gun;
Against the great raiders, the great sun.

Returning now the dawn lets him be safe:
No one has really asked him for his life,
Eating eggs and bacon with a fork and knife.

Brian Allwood

The NAAFI canteen was a consolation for the pilots.

NAAFI AT THE DROME

Flushed faces of the young
like miniatures hung
upon grey walls of silence,
the smoke of myraid cigarettes
weaves through the hushed regrets
and lulls the violence.

The piano tinkles out its trite
reminders of their night
of dreams, with muffled glee
they sip their cup of bitter tea
at tables that are stained
as finally as their lives.

When they have gone, the room
retains its temperature of doom,
the smell of waste;
of stubbed out fags, stale tea
and that sharp memory
of the flushed faces of the young
hung, for ever, hung.

Bruce Bain

At the canteen, the survivors sang songs. One of the favourites was 'Far Away':

FAR AWAY

Around her leg she wore a purple garter,
  She wore it in the springtime and in the month of May.
And if you asked her why the hell she wore it,
  She wore it for an airman who is far, far away.

Chorus: Far away, far away, far away, far away,
    She wore it for an airman who is far, far away.

Around the block she pushed a baby carriage,
  She pushed it in the springtime and in the month of May,
And if you asked her why the hell she pushed it,
  She pushed it for an airman who is far, far away.

Far away, far away, far away, far away,
She pushed it for an airman who is far, far away.

Behind the door her father kept a shotgun,
    He kept it in the springtime and in the month of May,
And if you asked him why the hell he kept it,
    He kept it for an airman who is far, far away.

        Far away, far away, far away, far away,
        He kept it for an airman who is far, far away.

Upon his grave she placed a bunch of flowers,
    She placed it in the springtime and in the month of May,
And if you asked her why the hell she placed it,
    She placed it for an airman who is *six feet down*.

        Six feet down, six feet down, six feet down, six
            feet down,
        She placed it for an airman who is six feet down.

*In one poem, James Monahan spoke of the dead who haunted those who
still flew and lived.*

GHOSTS

(Three years after the Battle of Britain)

Night bomber pilot, just a fraction drunk:
    I tell you there are ghosts –
    new ones between, say, Brighton and the stars.
    I tell you. (*And he struck the shiny bar,
    making the glasses splash.*) Oh, I have met them
    above where the hops would be
or where the downs
are rashed with bungalows towards the sea . . .
That night . . .
all much the same it seemed, the Ruhr a white
carpet of agony,
for us the tight
instants of Junkers, when you think – like sharks
they're smelling your blood across that dreadful sky.
And all that flak and, as I say, the Ruhr

bright on our faces like the mask of hell.
Oh, it was bad enough – mind you, no worse
than other nights, not so to make you mad
and hear things . . .

                Well, the Ruhr was far behind
and we towards home, all checked for damage done
and not much found;
so thinking silently about the ground
and food there. Well – you know the Intercom? –
it started to talk. That's what it was. Just that.
First crackly fragments, things like a flight of Spits
correcting formation as they took the air,
then laughs from 'Dick' to 'Rabbit', 'Johnny' joining
the quips for a moment – 'What the devil's this?'
I called each one of them, the six, my crew,
'Do you hear what I hear? And which of you
is talking this lunatic stuff?' They all had heard.
And no one had said a word.
But Bill said 'Listen' –
and there is was again, jokes, then a warning
'Dorniers starboard, low'; a silence after,
stretching and stretching to a single call,
once, twice, three times and then a fourth time – 'Rabbit,
you O.K., Rabbit?' There was no reply.
'You O.K., Rabbit?' 'Oh my God,' said Bill,
'I knew that chap. That chap's been dead three years.
Spit caught by five great Huns near Beachy Head.
Remember,' he said, 'that day the East-end docks
first got it bad? We got a hundred down.
But they got Rabbit.' Bill said, 'Oh my God,
it was three years ago this very day.'
And down the Intercom his voice had risen
high to a jangling shout. It snapped off short
to the queerest quiet through the engines' roar.
And not a sound
from me or the rest or Bill. And no more voices.
But all the night around
was busy with the wings of the three-year-dead
and we through their territory riding
like wanderers returned to yesterday . . .
No . . . their voice did come again,
their voice but big as the wind,
their voice but it was desperately sad,

'Ah, we were proud, were proud,' then like a sigh,
'Do they remember us?' . . . Far, dwindling, lost,
'They say, they say they do . . .'

On the ground, the gunners felt a link with the enemy airmen in their high machines.

UNSEEN FIRE – Second Sonnet

This is a damned unnatural sort of war;
The pilot sits among the clouds, quite sure
About the values he is fighting for;
He cannot hear beyond his veil of sound,

He cannot see the people on the ground;
He only knows that on the sloping map
Of sea-fringed town and country people creep
Like ants – and who cares if ants laugh or weep?

To us he is no more than a machine
Shown on an instrument; what can he mean
In human terms? – a man, somebody's son,
Proud of his skill; compact of flesh and bone
Fragile as Icarus – and our desire
To see that damned machine come down on fire.

R. N. Currey

The anti-aircraft gun was appreciated by its gunners as the aeroplane was by its pilots.

ACK ACK SAID THE INSTRUCTOR

Ack Ack said the instructor
bofors tommy gun lewis gun
(which has 156 different parts –
EACH THE GRANDEST BRIGHTEST BESTEST
EACH THE ONLY GOD–DAMN THING
ON THE MARKET
GUARANTEED WARRANTEED MONEY BACK IF NOT SATISFIED)
and this thing here's called the cruciform

(didn't any of you bastards
ever go to church?)
as you can see it's shaped like a cross

Yes said the instructor
blow his bloody brains out with
(our recognized brands the best that are made)
he's trying to blow your bloody brains out with
(OUR RECOGNIZED BRANDS THE BEST THAT ARE MADE).

Brian Allwood

THE BOFORS A.A. GUN

Such marvellous ways to kill a man!
An 'instrument of precision', a beauty,
The well-oiled shining marvel of our day
Points an accusing finger at the sky.
– But suddenly, traversing, elevating madly
It plunges into action, more than eager
For the steel blood of those romantic birds
That threaten all the towns and roads.
O, that man's ingenuity, in this so subtle,
In such harmonious synchronization of parts,
Should against man be turned and be complaisant,
The pheasant-shooter be himself the pheasant!

Gavin Ewart

*Because of the instruments and the distances, often the killers were
separated from the killed.*

RADAR

Distance is swept by the smooth
Rotations of power, its staring
Feelers multiplying our eyes for us,
Marking objects' range and bearing.

Linked to them, guns rehearse
Calculated obedience; echoes of light

Trigger the shadowing needle, determine
The arrest of night.

Control is remote; feelings, like hands,
Gloved by space. Responsibility is shared, too.
And destroying the enemy by radar
We never see what we do.

Alan Ross

UNSEEN FIRE – First Sonnet

This is a damned inhuman sort of war.
I have been fighting in a dressing-gown
Most of the night; I cannot see the guns,
The sweating gun-detachments or the planes;

I sweat down here before a symbol thrown
Upon a screen, sift facts, initiate
Swift calculations and swift orders; wait
For the precise split-second to order fire.

We chant our ritual words; beyond the phones
A ghost repeats the orders to the guns:
One Fire . . . Two Fire . . . ghosts answer: the guns roar
Abruptly; and an aircraft waging war
Inhumanly from nearly five miles height
Meets our bouquet of death – and turns sharp right.

R. N. Currey

Francis Scarfe appreciated the anti-tank gun and the grenade.

25-POUNDER

O little dragon
Best seen from behind,
You have no paragon
In dragon-kind,
For you can kill
Wherever you will
Without the bother
Of climbing a hill.

This much you have
In common with love.

GRENADE

As a full fruit, ripe,
I hold you in my palm
As a child holds an apple,
The fingers curling,
Glad of the weight,
Till it grows warm
And ready for tasting.

May they who take you
Into their flesh,
Whose ears are split
By your mad laughter,
Not know how long
I weighed your evil
And flung for shame.

*Three more poems showed an admiration of the rifle and the tommy-gun
and the Bren-gun.*

BOY WITH A RIFLE

Pacifist must find an answer,
League of Nations, Super-State,
Every pattern of New Order:

Rifle-virgin, dedicate
To this yard of metal, slender
Strange and lovely as a mate,

Trigger gravely-curved and tender
As a lover's lips, a rod
And a thimbleful of thunder

Carrying life-and-death, and shod
With the speed of instancy,
Exquisitely just as God

Neat as trigonometry;
Mortal flesh to an immortal
Element swears constancy,

Cheek pressed closely to the fatal
Beauty, and the quivering shy
Finger on the tender petal

Of release, the ecstasy
And agony of consummation,
Cardboard iris, human eye

Checked in slightly-swaying motion
Their brief unity to put
On record. How but by this weapon

Or the million-spawn irate
Machine-gun or the Rabelaisian
Cannon can we sublimate

Youthful energy and passion?
Find an answer, victor-nation.

R. N. Currey

CAMOUFLAGE

Because the paint is not the spread of branches
But dies like a fish on the concrete in the sun's glare,
Leaving the mechanical outline bare
To fool only the plane's mechanical glances.

Because this bonhomie is a skinny false
Mask on the iron skeleton of constraint
And freedom in newsprint only a smear of paint
Across the ancient menace, 'Believe, or else . . .'

Therefore if I must choose I prefer to sing
The tommy-gun, the clean, functional thing,
The single-hander, deadly to the rigid line,
Good at a job it doesn't attempt to conceal.

Give me time only to teach this hate of mine
The patience and integrity of the steel.

John Manifold

DEFENSIVE POSITION

Cupping her chin and lying there, the Bren
Watches us make her bed the way a queen
Might watch her slaves. The eyes of a machine,
Like those of certain women, now and then

Put an unsettling influence on men
Making them suddenly feel how they are seen:
Full too many purposes, hung between
Impulse and impulse like a child of ten.

The careless challenge, issued so off-handed,
Seems like to go unanswered by default –
A strong position, small but not commanded
By other heights, compels direct assault.

The gunner twitches, and unreprimanded
Eases two tensions, running home the bolt.

John Manifold

Field-glasses gave to the watcher a perspective on war.

FIELD-GLASSES

Though buds still speak in hints
And frozen ground has set the flints
As fast as precious stones
And birds perch on the boughs, silent as cones,

Suddenly waked from sloth
Young trees put on a ten years' growth
And stones double their size,
Drawn nearer through my glasses' greater eyes.

Why I borrow their sight
Is not to give small birds a fright
Creeping up close by inches;
I make the trees come, bringing tits and finches.

I lift a field itself
As lightly as I might a shelf,
And the rooks do not rage
Caught for a moment in my crystal cage.

And while I stand and look,
Their private lives an open book,
I feel so privileged
My shoulders prick, as though they were half-fledged.

Andrew Young

*A trilogy of poems by Henry Reed was a masterpiece of war poetry. His
voice grew silent in the peace and was a loss to the language.*

THE LESSONS OF WAR

*Vixi duellis nuper idoneus
Et militavi non sine gloria*

1

NAMING OF PARTS

Today we have naming of parts. Yesterday,
We had daily cleaning. And to-morrow morning,
We shall have what to do after firing. But to-day,
To-day we have naming of parts. Japonica
Glistens like coral in all of the neighbouring gardens
      And today we have naming of parts.

This is the lower sling swivel. And this
Is the upper sling swivel, whose use you will see
When you are given your slings. And this is the piling swivel,
Which in your case you have not got. The branches
Hold in the gardens their silent, eloquent gestures,
      Which in our case we have not got.

This is the safety-catch, which is always released
With an easy flick of the thumb. And please do not let me
See anyone using his finger. You can do it quite easy
If you have any strength in your thumb. The blossoms
Are fragile and motionless, never letting anyone see
    Any of them using their finger.

And this you can see is the bolt. The purpose of this
Is to open the breech, as you see. We can slide it
Rapidly backwards and forwards; we call this
Easing the spring. And rapidly backwards and forwards
The early bees are assaulting and fumbling the flowers:
    They call it easing the Spring.

They call it easing the Spring; it is perfectly easy
If you have any strength in your thumb: like the bolt,
And the breech, and the cocking-piece, and the point of
    balance,
Which in our case we have not got; and the almond-blossom
Silent in all of the gardens and the bees going backwards and
    forwards,
    For today we have naming of parts.

2

JUDGING DISTANCES

Not only how far away, but the way that you say it
Is very important. Perhaps you may never get
The knack of judging a distance, but at least you know
How to report on a landscape; the central sector,
The right of arc and that, which we had last Tuesday,
    And at least you know

That maps are of time, not place, as far as the army
Happens to be concerned – the reason being,
Is one which need not delay us. Again, you know
There are three kinds of tree, three only, the fir and the poplar,
And those which have bushy tops to; and lastly
    That things only seem to be things.

A barn is not called a barn, to put it more plainly,
Or a field in the distance, where sheep may be safely grazing.

You must never be over-sure. You must say, when reporting:
At five o'clock in the central sector is a dozen
Of what appear to be animals; whatever you do,
  Don't call the bleeders *sheep*.

I am sure that's quite clear; and suppose, for the sake of ex-
ample,
  The one at the end, asleep, endeavours to tell us
What he sees over there to the west, and how far away,
After first having come to attention. There to the west
On the fields of summer the sun and the shadows bestow
  Vestments of purple and gold.

The still white dwellings are like a mirage in the heat,
And under the swaying elms a man and a woman
Lie gently together. Which is, perhaps, only to say
That there is a row of houses to the left of arc,
And that under some poplars a pair of what appear to be
humans
  Appear to be loving.

Well, that for an answer, is what we might rightly call
Moderately satisfactory only, the reason being,
Is that two things have been omitted, and those are important.
The human beings, now: in what direction are they,
And how far away, would you say? And do not forget
  There may be dead ground in between.

There may be dead ground in between: and I may not have got
The knack of judging a distance; I will only venture
A guess that perhaps between me and the apparent lovers,
(Who, incidentally, appear by now to have finished,)
At seven o'clock from the houses, is roughly a distance
  Of about one year and a half.

3

UNARMED COMBAT

In due course of course you will all be issued with
Your proper issue; but until tomorrow,

You can hardly be said to need it; and until that time,
We shall have unarmed combat. I shall teach you.
The various holds and rolls and throws and breakfalls
    Which you may sometimes meet.

And the various holds and rolls and throws and breakfalls
Do not depend on any sort of weapon,
But only on what I might coin a phrase and call
The ever-important question of human balance,
And the ever-important need to be in a strong
    Position at the start.

There are many kinds of weakness about the body,
Where you would least expect, like the ball of the foot.
But the various holds and rolls and throws and breakfalls
Will always come in useful. And never be frightened
To tackle from behind: it may not be clean to do so,
    But this is global war.

So give them all you have, and always give them
As good as you get; it will always get you somewhere.
(You may not know it, but you can tie a Jerry
Up without rope; it is one of the things I shall teach you.)
Nothing will matter if only you are ready for him.
    The readiness is all.

The readiness is all. How can I help but feel
I have been here before? But somehow then,
I was the tied-up one. How to get out
Was always then my problem. And even if I had
A piece of rope I was always the sort of person
    Who threw the rope aside.

And in my time I have given them all I had,
Which was never as good as I got, and it got me nowhere.
And the various holds and rolls and throws and breakfalls
Somehow or other I always seemed to put
In the wrong place. And as for war, my wars
    Were global from the start.

Bernard Gutteridge remembered how it was with his platoon.

MY PLATOON

Marching at ease against the fanning dust
Pleased with themselves and happy, whistle and sing
Their bawdy and their sentimental songs.

How thirty of them can, acting together,
Become one person, a Lancashire lad.
'– Oh she likes a little bit in the morning –'

Then break up for their intimate moments;
Listening to Vera Lynn, reading their letters.
'– I'll be with you in apple blossom time –'

Alone on sentry in the bomb smashed docks,
The movement in the ruined shadows beyond –
When you visit that silhouette against the phosphorescent sea
You get so near and get so very fond.

War changed the nature of the soldier, as Alun Lewis pointed out.

from LANCE JACK

The soldier doesn't bother. He is a migrant, an Arab, taking his belongings with him, needing surprisingly little of the world's goods. He leaves his violin and his Cézanne and his garden behind. His wife, too, and his children, as time passes. Hitler's soldiers have been taught two simple things: Obey Commands; Forget Home. In the long run these two rules are easier to learn than to resist. That is the danger. That is why I say: to women, feel less; to men, feel more. I may be exaggerating this danger. Certainly the soldier's heart leaps for leave. But when I go home on leave I feel vaguely 'out of it'. The new carpet doesn't thrill me as it should; the troubles and little quarrels with neighbours are no longer my troubles; they are the preoccupations of strangers. I feel sympathetic, I listen and suggest. But I don't interfere, I don't trespass on them. And perhaps they think I don't talk much, don't open up, don't confide. Until one of them divines the reason, and knows me as a stranger, and takes me in as a stranger, into her lonely arms. We talk quietly of strangenesses, night marches, bivouacs, odd and far-off incidents, Europe. Till our loneliness is complete, and we are united in loneliness, just the two of us, as it used to be when first we sought each other, losing and finding each other, never quite giving in, never quite defeated.

The soldier says: 'Life is a series of meetings with strangers. We are all strange, to ourselves as well.'

That is true. But it is dangerous, like cynicism. For sometimes when he is utterly alone, utterly impersonal, on guard in the night at some outpost, somewhere, he can only envisage the human past, the great centrifugal force of the heart which draws into its orbit and unites in love all differences of people, mother and sweetheart, friend and pauper, employer and baby daughter, I say he can only envisage this great power of life as a swarming of bees on a bough, of flies on a fallen damson, a noisy, slightly indecent congress. A complex, if you prefer.

And if you ask why a man appears to prefer what is casual, rough, hazardous, and incomplete to what is warm and personal and loving, I suggest you read Edward Thomas's poems again. It is, if you like, curious that the idealist should live casually with regard to himself and the preservation of himself, that he should find the haversack, the trench, the journeying most suited to the pursuit of high ends. Christ had no home. Women dislike, even hate, this quality in their men. It is the overturning of all that was so hard and slow to win, the gradual building up of friendship, love, mutual knowledge, home, children, the rooted beauty of flowers, budding and opening in petal and colour and curve *in one place*. But it is a fine quality, in the best man. And there is always, it seems, some suffering. There is Beethoven as well as the nine symphonies. Man or woman, each must discover the balance of forces. And now that the women are being bombed in their homes while the men are untouched in their trenches and tents, perhaps there will be less hatred among the women that their men should leave them to follow something else. It is a new way of *life*.

When the men were called to the war, they had to leave the women and lead their different lives.

TO CERTAIN LADIES, ON GOING TO THE WARS

Goodbye ladies, O ladies sweet, goodbye,
No more the gentle flowers,
Another life I'll try.
No more the scented evenings,

The tussles in the hay,
It's time that I was leaving
To live another way.

O, there'll be blood, my ladies
(And not all mine, I hope),
And damp beds under hedges
And washing without soap.
Black lice will bite the body
That knew your friendly limbs;
In barrack-blocks I'll envy
Your silken-sheeted rooms.

But goodbye ladies, O ladies don't complain,
It's time I learnt to shoot straight
Or fly an aeroplane.
So many lads I knew once
Are rotting under sods:
I owe them this one journey –
So farewell, pretty birds.

Henry Treece

There were ways out of the war – and different sorts of courage.

THE HIGH JUMP

This bloke, Old Brownie, was determined to get off the draft.

He wasn't windy, mind; it was his missus. His missus swore blind she'd do herself in if he went overseas; when he went home on embarkation leave she even picked up the carving knife to prove it. Got all hysterical, she did. My opinion, it'd have been a good thing for old Brownie if she'd used the knife, but course he couldn't see it that way.

So as I say he'd made up his mind he'd dodge the draft, come what may. He thought up all sorts of stunts, he even wanted old Dusty Miller, in the M.T., to run him over one time. Offered him a packet of fags for doing it.

'Run you over?' old Dusty said. 'No bloody fear. I ain't swinging for nobody's murder, not me.'

'Murder?' old Brownie said, 'Don't be daft. Nobody mentioned nothing about murder. Just my leg.'

'Your leg?'

'That's it. I go and lay in the road, see, and all you got to do is run your truck over my leg. Simple.'

'Which leg?' old Dusty said.

'Doesn't matter. Either one.'

'Nothing doing,' old Dusty said. 'Not a chance.'

'I'll make it forty fags,' old Brownie said.

'Wouldn't do it for fifty,' old Dusty told him. 'Not for a hundred, neither.'

So old Brownie had to give that idea up, in the finish. He tried getting hold of some poison next, only nobody'd give him any. He tried the M.I. Room, everywhere. No good. Then he tried drinking a bottle of Bluebell, but all it did was make him spew. Reckon his guts'd got used to anything swilling that Naffy beer. What with that and the tea. Anyhow, old Brownie was at his wit's end.

Then one night I was in the canteen and he come up to me. 'Thought of a new way out,' he said.

'What's it this time?' I asked him.

'I'm going to jump off the Spotting Tower,' he told me.

'You're crazy,' I told him. 'You'll break your bleeding neck jumping off that. It's too high.' The Spotting Tower was what we used to do guards on, watching out for Jerry planes, see? I don't rightly know how high it was, but too high for any fancy jumps, take it from me.

But old Brownie shook his head. 'Fall soft,' he said. 'Sand all around it. Break a leg, not more. Nice little spell in dock. Just you watch.'

'When're you going to do it?' I asked him.

'To-night,' he told me. 'Ten o'clock.'

'Why ten?'

'My lucky number,' he told me.

'It'll be your unlucky number if you break your neck,' I told him.

Well, naturally, I never thought he'd do it. I thought he was having me on. But he did do it.

When the canteen closed, ten o'clock, we went along with him to the Tower, quite a crowd of us that he'd told what he was going to do.

'How're you going to get past the sentry?' we asked him.

'I'll just tell him I want to cadge a smoke from one of the guard,' old Brownie said.

Well that was nothing new, with him, and it worked a treat. He went off up the steps and pretty soon we saw him show up right on the top of the Tower.

'Good old Brownie,' we yelled at him, and he waved his hand at us and then he jumped. Just like that. The sand went up all around him as he landed.

We all started to run at that. We reckoned he'd broke his neck for sure, but no, when we got to him there he was picking his self up out of the sand and swearing blue murder.

'Too soft,' he said. 'Have to have another go.'

'You're never going up there again?' we said to him.

'Bleeding am,' he said.

And he did. The guard tried to stop him this time, knowing what he aimed to do, but he got through 'em somehow and slung his self over. And this time he didn't get up, he just lay there groaning with one leg doubled under him.

'Okay,' he said. 'I done it proper. Get the M.O. quick.'

So someone phoned up the M.I. Room and they sent an ambulance down and off went old Brownie to the Sick Bay.

He went on the draft just the same, though. It got put back, see, and by the time it went, old Brownie was out of dock with his leg mended all right, and they got him again.

You must have seen his photo in the papers day or two back: got the V.C. for some screwy thing he did out there. He was that kind of a bloke, old Brownie. Stands to reason, bloke who'd jump twice off that Tower ain't going to be scared of a few bleeding Jerries.

As for his missus, she didn't do herself in after all. Course not. She's living with another bloke now. I always knew that bitch was no bleeding good. I could've told him.

Julian Maclaren-Ross

The soldiers came from all stations during the war.

SIGNALS SECTION

Be pleasant with these men,
Some are oldtime soldiers; some
Are raw from families, and smart
At every khaki clatter on their heart.
A few welcome the company, after the crumb
They knew as friendliness in towns
Where banged the bleating pinstripe clowns
Upon their Commerce kettledrum.

Then, there was always work without end,
Though work to fools is its own end,
And Finance, that's too cut-throat for a friend,

Jumped on the youngsters, pick-a-back,
And took them from this corner into that
From nine till six, or seven until eight,
From slight of sun till black.

And some grouse, saturnine,
Wrestle what's unfair and miss the fine,
Or sit upon an ill-admitting spine
To wait discomfort; rub their sores in brine.

Yet, if I hold them up, I show you but yourselves
Haphazardly; we khaki toys
Are you removed from graded shelves
And have your mannerisms, make your noise:
Are timid Pucks turned murderous elves
Our civil world employs.

Lawrence Little

The war was still more watching and waiting than fighting.

STAND-TO

The sea at dawn is grey, sombre as metal,
With dull unburnished strength.
The light expands till the horizon,
Once more defined, encircles our day.
In the tufted grass and the sea-pinks
Our rifles lie, clean, with bolts oiled,
Our pouches hard with rounds.
A metal world of rifle, sea and sky.

The cramped limb moves; the eyes stare outwards.
Only behind is life where the fields stretch
And new smoke lifts from silent houses.

We forget the pre-vigil days
The time of fretting and proposition
Of clamorous words and fear be-devilled plans.
Perhaps we were wrong then,
And all the holy words
Were cried in a madman's dream.

Peace and freedom
Dwelled in the clarity of delirium;
The scales of justice balanced neatly
Not now, but in the future of a mirage.

We have returned to faith
For the argument did not reach its conclusion.
The words were buried by bullets, and the guns drowned our
   songs.
Here, leaning on the side of the weapon-pit,
A trickle of sand on our boots
There is only the tense eye and the tired mind
That does not plead or suffer but has learned patience.

Neil McCallum

The soldiers waited and waited. Patience was all.

HALE, Y.M.C.A.

(Written on returning from Christmas leave)

The piano vaguely strums old tunes,
Across the smoke and talk recalls
A moment, multiplies a memory, dies and falls
Then changes partners, leaves Atlantis in our arms,
And all for nothing. I thought here is Freud and Adler,
Here the unrehearsed familiarity of soldiers
Grows, thickens, develops an eternity, becomes
Important, a parcel of the afternoon.
Here the welcome of cigarettes and tea,
The firm handshake of hearty laughter,
The familiarity of things we understand.

Outside the exiled wind grumbles round the door
And winter's edge sharpens the corners
Of the evening, bitterly but honestly;
Inside we take the edge off life itself,
Do nothing, think, gaze at the past, endure
Ourselves, suffer our neighbours,
Let jealousy grow dangerous fingers,
Eat, do everything, commit adultery by proxy –
(The shawl has fallen from her shoulders

131

And she slips into her bed) –
All this before the afternoon is dead,
All this and more, while one man fumbles
For his matches, and another yawns.

Last week's Christmas hung across the room,
Drooping from the ceiling, dispirited,
Reminds us another Christmas is gone
And what have we achieved, what done?
They go on, the smoke and the talk,
The piano and the soldiers,
The soldiers let the piano take them for a walk,
But what will be achieved or won?

Kenneth Neal

And, in the end, life could be hard on the soldier who had had so little life.

SIXTY CUBIC FEET

He was the fourth his mother bore
    The room was ten by twelve
His share was sixty cubic feet
    In which to build himself.

He sat and learned his letters
    With forty in a room
And sixty cubic feet of draught
    The Council lent to him.

At fourteen he must earn a wage
    He went to pit from school
In sixty feet of dust and gas
    He lay and hacked the coal.

At twenty-two they told him
    His freedom was at stake
He left his sixty cubic feet
    A soldier for to make

He slept with seven others
    The tent was pitch on clay
The rain ran down the hillside
    And drenched them night and day.

He lay and coughed his heart out
  In sixty feet of damp
At last when he could hardly stand
  They marched him out of camp

They bought him from the hospital
They brought him home alone
In sixty cubic feet of deal
  That he could call his own.

Randall Swingler

The troops travelled from city to camp. Alun Lewis wrote a story about the train from London.

NIGHT JOURNEY

An hour before the midnight train left Paddington all the seats were full, the blinds all drawn, the corridor full of kitbags and suitcases and the burning ends of cigarettes. Several Welsh soldiers were singing Cwmrhondda and Aberystwyth and the more maudlin hymns of the Evan Roberts Revival. Every compartment was hooded and blue with smoke. Just before the train started a young captain with the badge of an infantry regiment on his black beret opened the door of one compartment, a third-class one, and was about to make his way through into the corridor when a private soldier sitting in the corner said, 'Here you are, sir, squeeze in here.' He said, 'Thanks a lot,' and sat down. He was perspiring and dead white, he had no luggage, not even a respirator. He looked done in.

The crowded compartment looked at him with the same reserved inquisitiveness as the inmates of a small boarding house covertly examine a new resident at his first meal. There were two WAAF's. The bespectacled one simply wondered why he wasn't travelling first and thought he looked distressed. The one with lipstick, who had been interrupted in her tale of her boy friend Bob, a pilot who didn't give a damn and was wizard with a kite, patted her set waves self-consciously and looked at him with wide filmstar eyes. The tank corps sergeant-major, a young sandy-haired man with facile features and the cocksure glance of the too successful, raised his fair eyebrows knowingly, discerning some irregularity. 'Good evening, sir,' he said politely. 'Good evening, sergeant-major,' the officer replied. Finally the R.A.F. corporal and his companion, a blonde civilian girl cuddled close under his shoulder, disturbed themselves sufficiently to crane forward a moment before reposing again. The officer wiped his face with a dirty handkerchief, and then noticed that an aircraftsman was standing up in the compartment.

'I'm very sorry,' the officer said. 'You were here before me. I've taken your seat.' He stood up, deferentially.

'That's all right, sir,' the corporal said, craning forward again, the hooded light full on his bryl-creamed curls. 'He's a prisoner. I'm escorting him to detention barracks, sir. He don't sit down.'

'Oh, surely, that's not fair,' the officer insisted, still offering his seat.

'He's standing up on my orders, sir,' the corporal retorted.

The officer shrugged his shoulders.

The train slid a little, imperceptibly beginning its long journey, then jerked forward with a puff.

'My God,' said the WAAF with lipstick. 'It's actually moving. Well, as I was saying, when I asked Bob to take me up, he said, "If you were fat and ugly I wouldn't mind risking it. But you – no, I won't risk you," he said. Sweet of him, I thought.'

'Maybe he just wanted something for nothing,' the sergeant-major said with a naughty gallantry.

'You men,' countered the WAAF, very haughtily. 'Your thoughts never rise any higher than your manners. Well, Bob isn't that sort, thank you.' She wanted to assert her value; she wasn't going to let him knock her price down; she sulked and considered what was best. The other WAAF was reading a Penguin.

'Got a penknife, sir?' the private asked. 'I've lost my corkscrew.' He had a bottle of liqueur whisky between his knees; he was evidently a man of importance in the compartment. They all looked at him, for the first time really; he'd only been a private soldier before. Now he had a bottle of liqueur whisky. The sergeant-major was the first to produce a knife.

'Here you are,' he said with alacrity.

'Thanks, major,' the private replied. He was a tall groomed man, with smooth hair, a big chin blue with shaving, a clever surface-smartness in his nodding glance. He scraped away at the cork, smiling to himself. The WAAF hadn't considered him before. She looked interestedly at him now. After all, she hadn't actually *cut* him before.

'Would you ladies like a little chocolate while I'm opening this,' he asked, passing a box of chocolates round. The WAAF fell on it with little girlish cries of delight.

'Now, gentlemen, a toast to us all,' he continued, lifting the bottle to the light. 'You, sir, first.'

They all demurred; he reassured them. Sure, he had two more such bottles in his respirator, and 500 Players. They were welcome. Go on, sir. Sorry there's no wine-glasses. Nice drink, isn't it? Got connections, see, sergeant-major. Go on, drink it up. My connections wouldn't give me poor stuff, don't you worry. Come on, lady, drink to that pilot boy of yours. Come on, corporal, sweeten your breath. What? Not allowed to drink on escort? What a sense of duty. Blimey. Well, what about the prisoner. Come on, prisoner. Sweet as your mother's milk it is. Take a good swig now. I won't be calling round in the morning, you know. Oh, come on, corp, let the poor sod have a drink. Being alive isn't much fun for him. Yeh, why not?'

'If the prisoner's going to have one I don't see why I should go without,' the corporal said, anxious as a man who has bought a shirt too big for him and hurries back to the shop, blustering and dubious, to revoke the deal.

'Sure, that's the spirit, that's swell,' the soldier pattered.

'Now that's how I like it. We're all social now.'

'Or do you mean socialist?' the officer asked.

'Oh no, sir, begging your pardon, we're not socialist. Here's the capital here, sir, here' – he patted the golden bottle – 'and wherever you find capital you find the black market, and wherever you find the black market you find yours truly, sir. I'm not proud of being a capitalist, sir. It's just an inescapable fact, that's all, sir. Calls for another drink, I think, sir.'

Here's a case, the sergeant-major's grin seemed to say, I'd like to get him on a fatigue, by God, I'd shake him. He took a second draught with a friendly and local condescension.

'What shall I drink to?' the WAAF said coquettishly.

'You don't need to drink to anything,' the soldier said. 'You just want to drink, that's all, lady. However, drink to the rebuilding of Stalingrad, if you want to.'

'Why in particular Stalingrad?' the officer asked. 'Why not London?'

'Sure, London if you like. I don't mind. Every city's a job of work to me. I'm an internationalist. Paid by America, Dupont of America, via the Chase National Bank – heard of it, sir? – no income tax on my salary, two thousand a year I get, sir. Before the war I put half the machinery into the Red October factory in Stalingrad, and I'll go and put it back there after this little shake is over. I built factories in Magnitogorsk, too. Hitler won't see them, sir.'

'Say, you're talking big,' said the sergeant-major.

'Not particular big, major. I'm small fry. Only I get around, you know.'

'And you're only a private, eh?'

'That's right, sir. I'm not ambitious. I'm all right. I've got connections in the Army. Got a living-out pass, got a suite of rooms in the Swan in Dorchester and a taxi to take me to camp every morning. I'm sitting the same course for the fourth time. Usually they send you back to your unit if you fail it once, but they're letting me stay on because I'm keen to get through, you know, real keen. Very comfortable down there. Course I volunteered for the Army, you know. Only I'm not ambitious, not like you sir, or you, major.'

'Are you married, soldier?' the WAAF asked clumsily.

'Married, lady? What, me? I've got only the best wife in the world, that's all. Look, here she is.' He fished a wallet out of his trousers and hunted among the white five-pound notes for a couple of photographs. 'There she is, lady. That was taken in Shepheards Hotel, Cairo. Here we are, both of us again, in the garden of the Grand, in Bucharest.'

'You look much nicer in tails than you do in battledress,' she said.

'My battledress wasn't made in Saville Row, lady,' he laughed. 'How d'you like my wife?' (She was a beautiful voluptuous woman in a glittering evening gown). 'She's a fine wife. Sends me 600 Players a week, and I love her like I'd just married her, though I got a son of seventeen. He's in the States, he is, apprenticed to Henry Ford. Good kid he is, too.'

The stuffy compartment, overheated with the breath and talk and whisky, swaying a little with the advance of sleepiness and the unreality of the big names he flung out like attracting stars leaving their proper orbit, rocking with the gathering motion of the train, played a cartoonist's trick on them all. How absurd and how amiable they seemed, these little people with long and short noses, with vanities and illusions and daydreams, with their fatigues and desires and routines, their religion and bewilderment and pettiness! There was a gradual relaxation in them all, a common impulse to stretch their limbs and loose their guard. The WAAF leaned up against the sergeant-major; he took her hand; her regulation underwear crinkled the tight blue skirt against her thighs. He took her at his own valuation, pilot or no pilot. O.K., big boy. O.K., baby. The bespectacled girl let her Penguin lapse. She looked at the officer, dreamily, disinterestedly, as though there was something there that distressed her and wouldn't let her alone. Only the prisoner stood like a great dull bull, holding on to the strap, dark and swaying. His great sullen head and shoulders were in the shadow, overpowering. He was a miserable devil. The whisky didn't seem to improve him at all.

'I'm an internationalist,' the private soldier said. 'I don't agree with wars between one country and another. I don't believe it. I got nothing against Russia. I worked there. Nothing against Germany. They're a smart lot. I take my hat off to them. America's the best of the bunch for a living. England's the salt of the earth. I didn't make this war, and I'm not fighting it. Ever had your fortune told, lady? I'll tell it for you with this pack of cards. O.K.?'

'I believe you're a Fifth Columnist,' the WAAF said lazily, snug in the sergeant-major's arms. She shuffled uneasily, paused, sat up, looked at him with a frown, puzzling over him. Certainty dawned in her silly eyes. She pointed a hand at him, hard and splenetic. 'That's what you are, you're a fifth columnist. I know you are.' Her hard grasping voice had the high pitch of hysteria. 'You can't fool me,' she jeered. 'You dirty fifth columnist. And they'll get you.'

'Aw, shut up,' he said. 'I never had no education but I don't make a fool of myself in public like you, lady. Ever been in the Ritz?'

'What do I want with the Ritz?' she shouted, screaming with laughter. In the unreality of the moment the dark prisoner moved towards the corridor. The door was open into the corridor.

She was laughing uncontrollably.

'The fifth column dine in the Ritz,' she shouted, waving her arms and body from the waist upwards like a snake.

'Look here, lady, I never been insulted like this before. Look here, I got Commander Anthony Kimmins's autograph here, see? He gave it to me when we was playing billiards after lunch in the Ritz.'

'He's a liar,' she shouted, terrible tears in her eyes. 'They're all liars. Bob took me to the Ritz for a week-end, and I'm going to have a baby now, I'm going to have a baby,' she was weeping now, 'and he got himself posted to another squadron, he did.'

'Your prisoner's gone, corporal,' the sergeant-major said with the coolness of a man in the thick of mechanized battle.

'Christ,' the corporal gasped, suddenly white, his enjoyment of the scene sucked out of him. He jerked himself to his feet, pulling out his revolver. 'I'll get the swine.'

The officer pulled him back by the neck of his jacket.

'Put it back you fool,' he said quietly, and slipped past the corporal into the corridor.

The Welsh soldiers were singing their national anthem in harmony, softly and most tenderly, alto and tenor and bass moving back and forth like searchlights over the range of sound. The prisoner was leaning by an open window, looking at the misty moonlit fields.

'Hallo, prisoner,' the officer said. 'They've just missed you.'

'I was born just over them fields, sir,' the prisoner said, heavily, slowly, peaceably. 'See that level crossing there? Used to go over that to school every day.'

'Never mind,' said the officer. 'We'd better go back now. Both of us.' Both men sighed, and turned away from the misty white fields and returned.

Julian Maclaren-Ross wrote another story about a man who managed to get out of the war.

HE DIED FOR HIS COUNTRY

I didn't know he was dead at first. He didn't look dead to me.

Big, strapping bloke, hat on the back of his head, leaning against the pub counter drinking a pint. What's more, he'd just bought me one.

'What're you having, mate?' he said, and pulled out a wallet fairly bulging with quid notes. 'Another pint, miss. Always glad to buy a drink for anyone in the Army. Ex-soldier meself.'

'Get your ticket?' I asked him.

'In a manner of speaking,' he said, bending confidentially forward.

'Do you know what?' he said. 'You're talking to a dead man.'

'A dead man?' I said.

'Straight up,' he said. 'Honest truth.'

'How long have you been dead?' I asked him.

'Ever since Dunkirk,' he told me. 'That's where I got killed – Dunkirk.'

'Were you blown up or just shot?'

'That I couldn't rightly say, mate. Got killed in action, that's all I know. Tell you how it happened. I gets back from Dunkirk, see? Goes to a big kind o' rest camp first of all. Officer there pays me out four quid and gives me a seven-day pass. Off I goes back home to the missus. "I'm home for keeps," I tells her. "I ain't a-going back." "What you going to do?" she says. "Get work," I says. "What about identity?" she says, "you can't get work without you have identity. You only got your Army book," she says. "I ain't got that," I tells her, "chucked it down the bleeding drain. I'm through with the Army, I am. Civvy from now on." "You're crackers, Bert," she tells me.

'Anyhow, couple o' days later I'm going through one of me old civvy suits and I comes acrost me identity card. I can't have give it up when I went in the Army, see! So off I goes with it to a big munition factory where they needs blokes. They don't arst me no questions, I don't tell 'em no lies. I gets signed on, seven pound a week. Dead cushy.'

'Didn't they come after you?'

'They did not. Course, arter I been absent couple o' weeks I expected 'em to. I says to the missus, "Ethel," I says, "I best get digs out, they'll be calling round here right shortly." "Right you are, Bert," she says. So I gets digs close to me work.

'But I ain't been there two days afore the missus come over in the hell of a dooda. "Here, Bert," she says, "look what I got," and she waves a War Office telegram at me. "Your husband reported missing, believed killed," it says. "Stone a crow," I says. "Make a muck of anything they would in the Army," I says. "I'm minded to go right back there and chew 'em up about it." "Don't you be so foolish, Bert," she says. "Can't you see? If they think you're dead you won't never have to go back." "There's something in that," I says. So I stays put, and by and by letter from Records come through saying they're sorry I'm dead. Killed in action. Dunkirk.

' "Well, that's legal," I says to the missus, "they can't get round that. I'm dead right enough," and the missus gets herself all decked out in black straight off. "We'll get a pension now, Bert," she says: "just you keep under cover till it comes through. Widow's pension, see?" And sure enough she did. Extra quid a week for damn all.

'And that's where the trouble starts. She moved out when the pension started coming. "Ain't safe to stay around here with everyone thinking you're dead," she says to me. And she goes and gets digs elsewhere.

'Well, she don't come over to see me for going on a fortnight. And what d'you think? She's got another bloke meantime. "Get out," she tells me, "we don't want no dead men around here." Well, I gave it her proper, then. "Corpse, eh!' I says. "And me that died for my country, too." And I gives her a black eye. Then this bloke she got now came out, ruddy civvy, reserved occupation, never done his bit. I didn't 'arf lay into him. Knocked him for six.

'Then out I goes to the pub and gets proper cut. I'd put away a good few pints and I comes out closing time and bumps bang into an M.P. arresting an absentee. Well, as I say, I'm always ready to help a soldier, so I hauls this M.P. off. "You let that bloke go," I says to him. "Who the hell are you?" he says. "Never you mind," I says. "I do mind," he says. "Let's see your identity card," he says. "I'm dead," I tells him, "you can't do nothing to a dead man." "What d'you mean, dead?" he says. So I pulls out the letter from Records and shows it him. "There you are," I says, "black and white, official."

'Up comes another M.P. "What's the row?" he says. Anyhow, in the finish they run me in, dead man or no dead man. In the morning I wakes up. I thinks, "that's caused it. Anyhow, they'll stop the wife's ruddy pension, that's one comfort," I says to meself.

'By and by an escort from me old mob comes to fetch me. Down to Depot. No one I knew there. "Who're you?" they say. "I'm dead," I say. "All right then, you don't want no ruddy grub," they say. "Don't I, by heck," I says. In the end they give me some bread and cheese. I go before the M.O. "Dead, eh!" he says. "Well, I can't do nothing for you." I come up before the Old Man. He says, "Dead, are you? Get the hell outa here."

'So they give me a railway warrant and the letter from Records saying I'm dead, and off I goes back to me job.

'Have another pint? Loan of a quid? Sure, take it. Always ready to help anyone in the blinking Army.

'Oh, and what d'you think? A proper laugh. Copper come round checking up at my digs yesterday. Summonsed me, he did, for having an identity card belonging to a dead man. Got to come up before the beak Monday. Much I care. Nothing they can do, see? Anyhow, I'm not worrying. Why worry? Dog's don't.'

Unless the convoys had crossed the oceans, Britain would have starved.

CONVOY

Together, keeping in line, slow as if hypnotised
Across the blackboard sea in sombre echelon
The food-ships draw their wakes. No Euclid could have devised
Neater means to a more essential end –
Unless the chalk breaks off, the convoy is surprised.

The cranks go up and down, the smoke-trails tendril out,
The precious cargoes creak, the signals clack,
All is under control and nobody need shout,
We are steady as we go, and on our flanks
The little whippet warships romp and scurry about.

This is a bit like us: the individual sets
A course for all his soul's more basic needs
Of love and pride-of-life, but sometimes he forgets
How much their voyage home depends upon pragmatic
And ruthless attitudes – destroyers and corvettes.

Louis MacNeice

The merchant ships were defended by destroyers and corvettes.

CORVETTE

Dully she shudders at the solid water,
A pause, and spray stings angrily over.
She plunges, and the noisy foam leaps widely
Marbling the moon-grey sea. Loud in the shrouds
Untrammelled winds roar songs of liberty.
Free as the petrels hovering astern
Her long lithe body answers to the swell.

Pardon if all the cleanness and the beauty
Brave rhythm and the immemorial sea
Ensnare us sometimes with their siren song,
Forgetful of our murderous intentions.
Through our uneasy peacetime carnival
Cold sweat of death rained on us like a dew;
Even this grey machinery of murder
Holds beauty and the promise of a future.

Norman Hampson

NIGHT PATROL

No moon tonight. Nor cloud to hide
That sparkling, silv'ry spray of stars
Splashed carelessly upon the wide,
Black-marbled dome we know as night.
Ashore, the wigwammed searchlights trace
The path of hostile aircraft bent
On murder; while some other place
Is canopied by bursting shell.
A winking buoy-light speeds us on
Our course. The lightship watch
Responds to greetings. Once there shone
A guiding beam . . . Now there is none.

We turn, two trawlers hand-in-hand . . .
Untiring waves give way to our
Proud bows, assaulting as they stand
The guns' crew. This a damp rebuke
For having been disturbèd so.

John Wedge

NIGHT PATROL

We sail at dusk, the red moon
Like a paper lantern setting fire
To our wake. Headlands disappear,
Muffled in their own velvet.

Docks dwindle, rubbed out by mists,
Their cranes, like drunks, askew
Over jetties. Coal is unloaded
Under blue arc-lights.

Turning south, the mapped moon
Swings between masts, our aerials
Swollen and lurching. The bag
Of sea squirts black and sooty.

Flashes of gunfire, perhaps lightning,
Straddle our progress, a convoy
Of hearses. The bow-waves of gunboats
Sew us together, helplessly idling.

The watch changes, and changes
Again. We edge through a minefield,
Real or imaginary. The speed of a convoy
Is the speed of the slowest ship.

No one speaks, it might be a funeral.
Altering course, the moon congeals
On a new bearing. The telegraph rings,
And, at speed now, clouds grow visible.

We're on our own, making for harbour.
In tangerine light we sniff greenness,
Tremble like racehorses. Soon minesweepers
Pass us, continuing our business.

Alan Ross

The ships were attacked by submarines and German aircraft.

WHEN THE PLANE DIVED

When the plane dived and the machine-gun spattered
The deck, in his numb clutch the tugging wheel
Bucked madly as he strove to keep the keel
Zig-zagging through the steep and choppy sea –
To keep zig-zagging, that was all that mattered . . .
To keep the ship zig-zagging endlessly,
Dodging that diving devil. Now again
The bullets spattered like a squall of rain
About him; and again with desperate grip
He tugged, to port the helm . . . to keep the ship
Zig-zagging . . . zig-zagging through eternity;
To keep the ship . . . A sudden scalding pain
Shot through his shoulder and the whole sky shattered
About him in red fire; and yet his grip
Tightened upon the wheel . . . To keep the ship . . .
Zig . . . zig . . . zig-zagging, that was all that mattered.

Wilfred Gibson

ACTION STATIONS

'Action stations.' Tin hats and apprehension;
Rush to guns and hoses, engine room
And wireless office. Air of tension.
Eyes uplifted and some seawards gazing.
Ears are straining for a distant 'boom,'
Or roar of engines. Lips are phrasing
Prayers, maybe, or curse upon the hun.
Friendly aircraft in the distance loom
And are gone. Minutes pass . . . 'Carry On.'

John Wedge

TO A YOUNG SAILOR

If you are cynical and wise,
    When you are twenty-one,
What will you have to smile at
    When this war is done?

143

You cheer through the smoke-blast
    The crash of the doomed flier
That rips the night with shrapnel,
    And you laugh with the answering fire:

'There's one in the eye for Hitler!
    The score is eighty-five!'
Bringing down ruddy Jerries
    Is the reason for being alive!

Yes. I agree it is shameful
    When happy countries fall;
But spoiling the eager edge of life
    Is the greatest crime of all.

Ken Etheridge

Yet the seamen spent much of their time below.

MESSDECK

The bulkhead sweating, and under naked bulbs
Men writing letters, playing ludo. The light
Cuts their arms off at the wrist, only the dice
Lives. Hammocks swing, nuzzling in tight
Like foals into flanks of mares. Bare shoulders
Glisten with oil, tattoo-marks rippling their scales on
Mermaids or girls' thighs as dice are shaken, cards played.
We reach for sleep like a gas, randy for oblivion.
But, laid out on lockers, some get waylaid;
And lie stiff, running off films in the mind's dark-room.
The air soupy, yet still cold; a beam sea rattles
Cups smelling of stale tea, knocks over a broom.
The light is watery, like the light of the sea-bed.
Marooned in it, stealthy as fishes, we may even be dead.

Alan Ross

Some died, such as the gunner on Charles Causley's ship, HMS *Glory.*

SONG OF THE DYING GUNNER

Oh mother my mouth is full of stars
As cartridges in the tray
My blood is a twin-branched scarlet tree
And it runs all runs away.

Oh *Cooks to the Galley* is sounded off
And the lads are down in the mess
But I lie done by the forrard gun
With a bullet in my breast.

Don't send me a parcel at Christmas time
Of socks and nutty and wine
And don't depend on a long weekend
By the Great Western Railway line.

Farewell, Aggie Weston, the Barracks at Guz,
Hang my tiddley suit on the door
I'm sewn up neat in a canvas sheet
And I shan't be home no more.

But the best narrative poem of naval action was written by Alan Ross,
who served on a destroyer when the convoy it was escorting to Russia
encountered a German battle-fleet.

from J. W. 51B

A CONVOY

And if you had brought
To the attention of Dinwiddy,
A three-badge A.B., notorious
For the kindness of his soul,
The foulness of his language,
His captain's intuitive appreciation
Of a situation fraught with ambiguity,
Six enemy destroyers off the starboard quarter,
A pocket battleship and a heavy cruiser
Approaching on the port bow,
And the necessity of drawing fire
Away from the convoy, yet not deserting it,
His head would have reeled,
His tongue licked out obscenities,

His heart hardened, though even as
He blasphemed, simulating fear,
And voicing the popular opinion
That for a destroyer to engage
An eight-inch cruiser was a form
Of insanity credible only
In one wanting a double layer
Of scrambled egg on his cap,
He would have grown most
Marvellously cool and unfussed,
As loyal to the concepts
Of sacrifice and duty
As to his often, and fastidiously expressed,
Devotion to his own self-interests.

For the ears, the thud of gunfire,
The thunderous shudder of impact,
The hissing of charred wood,
The clanging of steel doors;
And the faint voice of the Gunnery Officer,
Relayed over earphones,
'Short' – 'Over' – 'Straddle',
The thin bird-cry of a man
Pinioned under shells, and the endless
Injections of the surgeon.
For the nose, smell of burning,
Clove sweetness of anaesthetic, the acrid
Odour of cordite.

For the eyes, smoke
Stinging, disarrangements
Of the familiar, Rita Hayworth
Stripped from a locker lid, dice
Rattling in a tea cup, and Reid's
Severed arm cuddling a hammock.
The slow grey heave of waters
A Focke-Wulfe cruising,
Predatory as a shark.

The cold seen almost as a colour
– Ice-grey, gelatinous, glass-edged –
And that rose-shaped explosion of fire,
Booming over bruised sea,

Which those on deck or bridge
Saw as either doom or rescue
And had to guess which.
Enemy withdrawn, and convoy
Proceeding to Kola. This night
Of New Year, sea moderating,
Darkness scattered its largesse,
Though the close escort, not
Knowing the enemy's movements,
Had small feeling of escape,
Merely of being afloat.
Of inching forward into dawn,
Eastward round the North Cape.

But the conclusion of the war was finally death.

IN CONCLUSION

It will be small loss, never to return.

The summer-house will be cobwebbed,
The plaster flaked;
The nets over the unpruned fruit-bushes
Holed and torn.

Wild grasses dropping seeds on the sundials
And the penny-farthing and the saddlery
Grown dusty in the stables,
And mildewed the embroidered
Dressing-up clothes in the chest,
The artificial lake stagnant and undrained,
The hedges unclipped, the boarding rotten,
The lawn rough-floored under the cedar-trees,

And the pigeon-cot stairs will be broken,
The swing hanging broken.
The engine in the boiler-house will have ceased its beating,
The known voices will no longer be heard about the house.
There will be weeds and crumbling and desolation only.

We should be sorry we returned.

David Graves

SOLDIER'S SONG

O death, be kind to the swaddie
  The man with a load of bull –
Be kind to the muscled body,
  Thumbs-up and belly-full.

Browned-off with the bints and boozing,
  Sweating on news from home,
Bomb-happy, and scared of losing
  This tent of flesh and bone –

These prized, unique possessions:
  Quick hand and practised eye,
The senses at action-stations,
  Alert to perceive or die;

Gun-proud and proud of body,
  With stripped and easy mind:
O Death be kind to the swaddie,
  In whom our world shall find

Its seed and fierce begetting:
  The future and shining land
Sprung from our dark sun's setting –
  A harvest, bird in hand.

                              Jocelyn Brooke

CONVERSATION

I sat by a sailor to learn of the sea,
But he swore as he drank,
Then he said to me:
'Leave it alone, lad, the sea's a bitch.
    All smells and bells
    And bosun's yells.
    The stokehole a stinkhole,
    The galley a hell-hole.
And we're carrying carrion into Cadiz.'
    'But what of the flying fish,
    White moon and mermen?

What of the islands –
Your tropical trips?'
But the sailor swore and laughed as he said,
'The sea would be fine if there weren't any ships.'

I sat by a soldier to learn of the wars,
But he swore as he drank,
Then he said to me:
'Leave it alone, lad, the army's a sod.
    Attention, detention
    And brasshat pretension,
    You spit and you polish,
    You fight and they promise.
And maybe you'll find yourself bound for Cadiz.'
    'But what of the glory,
    The trumpets and singing?
    What of the friendship –
    The nation's applause?'
But the soldier swore and laughed as he said,
'Life would be fine if there weren't any wars.'

I sat by an airman to learn of the sky,
But he sighed as he drank,
Then he said to me:
'Leave it alone, lad, the sky's a witch.
    All zooming and booming
    And gunning and bombing,
    The pranging and slanging,
    All drinking, no thinking.
Forgetting the massacre – was it Cadiz?'
    'But what of the power,
    The freedom and stillness?
    How lovely to fly
    High over the town . . .'
But the airman drank and swore as he said,
'To fly would be fine if you never came down.'

Elizabeth Berridge

LADY IN BLACK

Lady in black,
I knew your son.
Death was our enemy
Death and his gun.

Death had a trench
And he blazed away.
We took that trench
By the end of the day.

Lady in black
Your son was shot.
He was my mate
And he got it hot.

Death's a bastard
Keeps hitting back.
But a war's a war
Lady in black

Birth hurt bad
But you didn't mind.
Well maybe Death
Can be just as kind.

So take it quiet
The same as your son.
Death's only a vicar
Armed with a gun.

And one day Death
Will give it back
And then you can speak to him tidy
Lady in black.

Alun Lewis

L.R.D.G.

He threw his cigarette in silence, then he said:

You can't predict in war;
It's a matter of luck, nothing less, nothing more.
Now here's an instance. Darnley copped it in the head
His third day up the blue although he'd seen the lot
In Dunkerque, Greece and Crete –
The sort that went in tidy and came out neat;
He copped it when the going wasn't even hot.
And there was little Pansy Flowers,
Machine-gunned through the guts; he bled
(And not a murmur from him) for hours
Before he jagged it in.
                And you remember Bowers?
Bowers got fragmentation in the lungs and thigh;
We couldn't do a thing: the moon was high
And a hell of a bright
On that particular night.
Poor sod, he won't kip in a civvy bed.

It's queer . . . I've even laughed
When blokes have chucked it in and gone daft.
I remember one that scarpered bollock-nude
One midnight, out across the dunes, calling for Mum;
You'd have thought him blewed.
He wasn't seen again – not this side of Kingdom Come.

One job that I really funked
Was when Fat Riley bunked
From a Jerry leaguer on a getaway.
We found him blind, with both hands gone.
When we got him back inside the lines
He'd only say,
Over and over, 'the mines, the mines, the mines'.
It's the lucky ones get dead:
He's still alive. I wonder if his wife understands
How you can't even shoot yourself without your hands.

J. G. Meddemmen

SIMPLIFY ME WHEN I'M DEAD

Remember me when I am dead
and simplify me when I'm dead.

As the processes of earth
strip off the colour and the skin:
take the brown hair and blue eye

and leave me simpler than at birth,
when hairless I came howling in
as the moon entered the cold sky.

Of my skeleton perhaps,
so stripped, a learned man will say
'He was of such a type and intelligence', no more.

Thus when in a year collapse
particular memories, you may
deduce, from the long pain I bore

the opinions I held, who was my foe
and what I left, even my appearance
but incidents will be no guide.

Time's wrong-way telescope will show
a minute man ten years hence
and by distance simplified.

Through that lens see if I seem
substance or nothing: of the world
deserving mention or charitable oblivion,

not by momentary spleen
or love into decision hurled,
leisurely arrived at an opinion.

Remember me when I am dead
and simplify me when I'm dead.

Keith Douglas

5
The Home Front:
Country and Factory

Refugees could never escape the war.

ESCAPE

The roads of Europe are running away from the war,
Running fast over the mined bridges and past the men
Waiting there, with watch, ready to maim and arrest them,
And strong overhead the long snorings of the planes' tracks
Are stretching like rafters from end to end of their power.
Turn back, you who want to escape or want to forget
The ruin of all your regards. You will be more free
At the thoughtless centre of slaughter than you would be
Standing chained to the telephone-end while the world cracks.

W. R. Rodgers

STATELESS PERSONS

They carry no shadow, the past like a slate
Rubbed out by a future that arrived too late.

Visaless and visionary, they travel to discover
Contiguous ruins that are all like each other.

New smells, new ghettos, reflect on their eyes,
But self-pity demolishes, conditions surprise.

Nothing is relevant, important or true. The message
Was too long delayed. They are part of their passage.

Alan Ross

Children were evacuated from the cities for fear of the bombing. The cartoonist Mel Calman remembered his flight.

I have this image of a small boy with a label tied round his neck.
The boy has no features and is crying.
He is carrying a cardboard box, which contains his gasmask.

I remember that labels with our names on were pinned to our clothes
before we left London. I think I felt that I had no identity and was a

155

parcel being posted to the country. The labels frightened me as much as the idea of leaving my parents. A child of seven, if lost, can tell people his name. A label assumes that he does not know his name, or worse, has no name and is given one at random from a list of names.

Perhaps the gasmask felt like a second face, a mask that would replace my own face as soon as I left London. I remember that the gasmask looked inhuman with its celluloid eyeshield and metal snout. I remember that it smelt of rubber and that I could not breathe properly inside it. The shield misted over with condensation and it felt warm and suffocating inside this second face.

I know that we rehearsed the evacuation every morning for a week. Each morning my sister and I would leave home with our packed sandwiches and clothes. We would say goodbye to our parents. Our labels were pinned on and I felt sick. We were not told the date of the real departure in case the Germans bombed the train. That seems hard to believe now, but at that time people seemed to find spies under their beds every night. So we had to leave home without knowing if we would return that day or not. We went through this awful ritual of goodbye every morning for a week. Every morning I felt sick and kissed my parents and felt I was leaving my name and identity with them.

Even nowadays whenever I travel anywhere and have to say goodbye to my own children, I identify with that small boy. I remember the label and the gasmask and feel anxiety gripping my bowels. I write my name on the luggage labels and hope I do not return to find my home bombed to ruins and my identity lost somewhere underneath the rubble.

The very countryside seemed at war.

SEPTEMBER HOLIDAY

All Nature's agents image war to me,
Even that butterfly above the ditch
Flutters with sinister intent; a bee,
Heavy with honey, drones at bomber's pitch.
The distant tractor furrows for attack
Trenches meticulous as a general's plan.
Those corn-shocks rest like rifles in a stack;

That sheaf ungathered is a fallen man . . .
Nothing is simple now, nothing immune
From war's contagion, time's conspiracy.
Throughout the sunny Cotswold afternoon
All Nature's agents image death to me.

Clive Sansom

THE ARMOURED VALLEY

Across the armoured valley trenched with light
Cuckoos pump forth their salvoes at the lark,
And blackbirds loud with nervous song and flight
Shudder beneath the hawk's reconnaissance:
Spring is upon us, and our hopes are dark.

For as the petal, and the painted cheek
Issue their tactless beauties to the hour,
We must ignore the budding sun and seek
To camouflage compassion and ourselves
Against the wretched icicles of war.

No festival of love will turn our bones
To flutes of frolic in this month of May,
But tools of hate shall make them into guns
And bore them for the piercing bullet's snout
And through their pipes drain all our blood away.

Yet though by sullen violence we are torn
From violet couches as the air grows sweet,
And by the brutal bugles of retreat
Recalled to snows of death, yet Spring repeat
Your annual attack, pour through the breach
Of some new heart your future victories.

Laurie Lee

COUNTRY TOWN IN WAR-TIME

Red-tiled Sunday is spotted with moss,
Bulging houses topple across
Streets full of straw and dry manure
Trod by the feet of the Sabbath pure;
Air is solid with war and thunder –
The seamless sky will not always endure
Its angry scab, will crack asunder
In livid blue, and everywhere under
Will sag and quail in the threshing rain;
But to-day the world's uneasy peace
Worships a jauntily-angled cross,
And tells its broken beads again.

Vic Turner

The country towns could also be bombed.

BOMBS ON MY TOWN

The farmers I spoke of that night
In London, drive into High Street
A roundabout way,
Their stunted, aggressive features
More death-vacant than ever,
Since yesterday.

Quiet, an empty dray
Only to mark for this scooped-hollow
Yeomanry, its past proud chatter,
Its market clatter
Of carriage and horse,
Now a sad echo,
An exhumed decay.

The tradesmen I've known for years
Bow with civic ponderosity
Over smashed pavements, to collect
Their stock, swept, with their integrity,
Beneath the quick stroke
Of an uncaring raider,

Whose fifth-rate dentistry tore
Our houses from the long, gaping maw
Of High Street.

To see your small, damaged town
Where each stone
Holds a history of its own,
Evokes a wild pity
Deeper than being
With strange folk; seeing
The devastation
Of their city . . .

Charles Hamblett

The landscape was disfigured by the ravages of war.

from THE FACE OF ENGLAND

The onset of war has enormously accelerated the process of beauty's destruction. All over the country, lanes are being turned into roads, trees and hedges are being cut down, turf is being gashed by lorries, margins and verges destroyed by tanks, fields converted into seas of mud, covered with concrete or asphalt, stacked with dumps or littered with rubbish. Great tracts are studded with concrete posts or bound with barbed wire. Meanwhile barracks, camps, Ack-Ack battalions, searchlight units, aerodromes, air fields, munition works, and all their attachments and appendages in the way of hutments, shacks, rubble, barbed wire, latrines, tents and rubbish dumps, are bidding fair to turn England into a devastated area. It has long been known that with the possible exception of poultry, soldiers create more ugliness, destroy more beauty, and do these things more rapidly, than any other form of living organism. 'It is no use,' said a friend of mine in the Army, referring to the mess that has been made of Box Hill, 'expecting us to do any different. Wherever we go we shall destroy trees, cut up the grass, make mud, leave tins, stick up wire, and generally make a mess.'

C. E. M. Joad

Yet the countryside would still endure.

LIVES

You cannot cage a field.
You cannot wire it, as you wire a summer's roses
To sell in towns; you cannot cage it
Or kill it utterly. All you can do is to force
Year after year from the stream to the cold woods
The heavy glitter of wheat, till its body tires
And the yield grows weaker and dies. But the field never dies,
Though you build on it, burn it black, or domicile
A thousand prisoners upon its empty features.
You cannot kill a field. A field will reach
Right under the streams to touch the limbs of its brothers.

But you can cage the woods.
You can throw up fences, as round a recalcitrant heart
Spring up remonstrances. You can always cage the woods,
Hold them completely. Confine them to hill or valley,
You can alter their face, their shape; uprooting their outer
    saplings.
You can even alter their wants, and their smallest longings
Press to your own desires. The woods succumb
To the paths made through their life, withdraw the trees,
Betake themselves where you tell them, and acquiesce.
The woods retreat; their protest of leaves whirls
Pitifully to the cooling heavens, like dead or dying prayers.

But what can you do with a stream?
You can widen it here, or deepen it there, but even
If you alter its course entirely it gives the impression
That this is what it always wanted. Moorhens return
To nest or hide in the reeds which quickly grow up there,
The fishes breed in it, stone settles on to stone.
The stream announces its places where the water will bubble
Daily and unconcerned, contentedly ruffling and scuffling
With the drifting sky or the leaf. Whatever you do,
A stream has rights, for a stream is always water;
To cross it you have to bridge it; and it will not flow uphill.

Henry Reed

POEM

The evening, the heather,
the unsecretive cuckoo
and butterflies in their disorder;
not a word of war as we lie,
our mouths in a hot nest
and the flowers advancing.

Does a hill defend itself,
does a river run to earth
to hide its quaint neutrality?
A boy is shot with England in his brain,
but she lies brazen yet beneath the sun,
she has no honour and she has no fear.

Laurie Lee

The woods could be an escape for the soldiers in the camps.

THE NAKED BOY AND THE BRIGADIER

Every Sunday afternoon throughout the whole of the summer he had crept out of camp, across the surrounding fields and through the forest to his own particular little spot miles from anywhere. And he had taken off his uniform and his harsh shirt and cotton underclothes and binding boots and stiff socks and stretched his young body gratefully in the sun and air.

Every Sunday afternoon; that brief end-of-week recreation had kept him going throughout his recruit training period. At first he had only taken his shirt and vest off; then he had noticed that his body looked funny when he was under the showers with the other lads – two-coloured, the top half rich brown and the rest horribly white. So he had begun to take all his clothes off half-way through the summer and now he was all brown and glistening, like copper.

Every Sunday afternoon; he could be himself and forget his uniform for a while and just sprawl out on the grass and think about things.

The sun seemed to cleanse him and heal all the little worries and anxieties; he could drowse and sleepily solve his problems.

At twenty, his problems seemed terribly urgent sometimes; but on Sunday afternoons he could map out his decisions and make what he mentally called his 'plans for the future.' He had a wonderful future –

a magnificent, terrific, breath-taking future. And it wasn't just a wishful sort of thing; all week he studied in every moment of his spare time – maths, English, geography and French; there were examinations to be completed as soon as he got back home; they were all part and parcel of his future.

What had happened in the past was over – forcibly put out of his mind; disappointments and one tragedy – the sort of tragedy that people who have very little money and no influential friends all encounter sooner or later.

But time, and his Sunday afternoons, had helped him to reconstruct and alter his plans.

Harold Grant, twenty, C. of E.; height 5.11; weight 160. Fresh complexion, grey eyes. No distinguishing marks. That was his official paybook description, briefly, perfectly filled in by the recruiting station M.O.

He probably weighed a little less after his six months in the army. Exercise and less food; and transplantation.

The sun was going in, but it was still quite warm; gently, quietly, the hum of the forest and the whisper of leaves and scurrying busy-body birds lulled him to sleep; every Sunday afternoon they combined to give him the same service as if they had accepted his brown, long boy's body as part of the forest itself.

The Brigadier was one of those veterans who in some magic manner have kept in touch with the rank and file despite their own promotion over a period of years and lifetimes; bad tempered, a bit too old physically for his job, but young enough mentally, he was secretly sick and tired of wars; he had fought in three, to say nothing of a couple of revolutions.

As he tramped through the forest he cursed under his breath every time he stumbled. But all the time he was measuring distances, noting gulleys and taking thorough stock; to-morrow the forest would be cleared and trenches dug; to-morrow, Sappers would sweat and grouse – and clear the forest and dig the trenches. Local defence scheme; at one time he would have been thrilled at the idea of being responsible for planning the job; but not now. Bally waste of time; but as far as the Brigade went, an excellent scheme, of course.

He almost walked on Harold before seeing him.

The sun's last rays were dazzling in the clearing after the dimness of the forest.

He stopped short.

'What's this, dammit. Out of bounds and stripped to the buff, man; what are you playing at, eh?'

The boy did not stir.

The Brigadier raised his stick to prod him, and, as he did so, the boy rolled over onto his side and wriggled himself more comfortably into the hollows of the ground

Something twisted in the Brigadier's belly and rose to his throat, and he saw processions of other boys, boys in all sorts of uniforms, boys as naked as this one, boys in other wars.

His own two were there, laughing, bronzed and fit in their first officer's uniforms. Young and just as vital as the sleeping boy sprawled with such unconcious grace on the grass.

'Here, dammit. You! me lad.'

Harold's waking impression was terrifyingly full of gold braid and pips and crowns and scarlet, and a huge old man glaring at him ferociously.

He sprang to his feet – to attention.

'What in hell do you mean by it?'

Words froze and coldness ran through his body. His hair was ruffled and one side was patterned from shoulder to knee from the impression of grass and leaves.

'Well, man, what are you standing there for, dammit. Answer my question.'

'I was sunbathing, sir.' His voice sounded unreal and tiny in his own ears.

'Sunbathing? Out of bounds, indecently dressed, or undressed, and you say you're sunbathing, as if that explains everything. What are you, a ruddy Inca or something?'

'No, sir. I just like to get my clothes off; it seems to do me good.'

'Why, don't you like your uniform, me lad?'

'Yes, sir; I volunteered to wear it.'

The slight impertinence went home.

'Report to your Sergeant-Major when you get back to camp. Tell him to see me in the morning. I shall make a bally example of you.'

He saw the boy go white and saw also the tremor that flickered up his thighs and down again to his knees. He saw the boy, still standing to attention, beautiful and nakedly clothed in his own beauty.

The procession of other boys came back and invaded his mind.

Suddenly he felt old and finished.

'Now get your clothes on and get back to camp, you young fool,' he bellowed at the frightened boy. And as his words struck he turned quickly and crashed his way back through the forest.

Once he paused; he wanted to go back and tell the kid not to take any notice of what he had said.

The procession had become a parade, and they were all waiting to see what he would do. Deathlessly stretching back across the years, and his own boyhood was there this time.

A great pain was in him and he hated the boy and his armour of youth. He hated him.

And his hate was so great that he raised his stick and smashed it on a tree trunk and wished it was the world and all young things and himself.

He walked on with sightless eyes and plucked, one by one, the words of his resignation from his old-soldier's heart.

Jack Aistrop

People in the country watched and waited for an invasion that did not come.

THE STAND-TO

Autumn met me today as I walked over Castle Hill.
The wind that had set our corn by the ears was blowing still:
Autumn, who takes the leaves and the long days, crisped the air
With a tang of action, a taste of death; and the wind blew fair

From the east for men and barges massed on the other side-
Men maddened by numbers or stolid by nature, they have their
        pride
As we in work and children, but now a contracting will
Crumples their meek petitions and holds them poised to kill.

Last night a Stand-To was ordered. Thirty men of us here
Came out to guard the star-lit village – my men who wear
Unwitting the season's beauty, the received truth of the spade –
Roadmen, farm labourers, masons, turned to another trade.

A dog barked over the fields, the candle stars put a sheen
On the rifles ready, the sandbags fronded with evergreen:
The dawn wind blew, the stars winked out on the posts where
        we lay
The order came, Stand Down, and thirty went away.

Since a cold wind from Europe blows back the words in my teeth,
Since autumn shortens the days and the odds against our death,
And the harvest moon is waxing and high tides threaten harm,
Since last night may be the last night all thirty men go home.

I write this verse to record the men who have watched with me–
Spot who is good at darts, Squibby at repartee,
Mark and Cyril, the dead shots, Ralph with a ploughman's gait,
Gibson, Harris and Long, old hands for the barricade,

Whiller the lorry-driver, Francis and Rattlesnake,
Fred and Charl and Stan – these nights I have lain awake
And thought of my thirty men and the autumn wind that blows
The apples down too early and shatters the autumn rose.

Destiny, History, Duty, Fortitude, Honour – all
The words of the politicians seem too big or too small
For the ragtag fighters of lane and shadow, the love that has grown
Familiar as working-clothes, faithful as bone to bone.

Blow, autumn wind, upon orchard and rose! Blow leaves along
Our lanes, but sing through me for the lives that are worth a song!
Narrowing days have darkened the vistas that hurt my eyes,
But pinned to the heart of darkness a tattered fire-flag flies.

Cecil Day Lewis

The villages also sent out their young to die. The poet Frank Thompson was himself to be killed.

ALLOTRIAS DIAI GYNAIKOS

Between the dartboard and the empty fire-place
They are talking of the boys the village has lost;
Tom, our best bowler all last season,
Died clean and swift when his plane went reeling;
Bill, who drank beer and laughed, is now asleep
Behind Dunkerque, helped others to escape;
And Dave went down on that aircraft carrier,
Dave, whom nobody minded
But who played the flute rather well, I remember.

'These boys died bravely. We'll always be proud of them,
They've given old Adolf something to set him thinking.'
That was the loudest, the driving wave of opinion.
But in the corners hear the eddies singing –
'They died in a war of others' making.

'Helen the Fair went over the water
With Paris your friend, one of your gang
Whom we never trusted, but you feasted
For years with fawning, let your lands go hang.
We warned you. You could have stopped it . . .
But now we have sent our sons from the cornfields.
War, like a grocer, weighs and sends us back
Ashes for men, and all our year goes black.

'Yes. They died well, but not to suit your purpose,
Not so that you could go hunting with two horses,
While their sons touched their caps, opening gates for pennies.
Perhaps we shall take a hand, write our own ending.'
Soft, but the Titan heard it waking.

For the first time in the history of democracy, Britain conscripted women for service in the factory and on the farm as well as in the armed services. More than five million women worked in industry, and there were a hundred thousand land girls.

THE LIFE OF A LAND GIRL

6.30 a.m.
Awakened by alarm. Switch off swiftly and turn over.
6.45 a.m.
Wake again and lie in comfortable stupor. Turn on light and look at time. Stagger out of bed to find atmosphere remarkably chilly. Huddle on clothes and take hasty wash.
7.0 a.m.
Creak downstairs in dark to kitchen, hoping that house is still asleep and unpunctuality will pass unnoticed. Put on kettle. Don gumboots and overalls.
7.10 a.m.
Gulp down scalding cup of tea and feel slightly more human.
7.15 a.m.
Grope way to dairy in pitch darkness. Fill bucket with warm water for cows' ablutions. Stagger with bucket and milk pails over to shippon. Find Charles already at work doling out crushed oats to cows. Exchange greetings. Charles has been up all night on wind-swept hill top on duty for Observer Corps. Looks fresh as a daisy.

Says bomb dropped three miles away about 4 a.m., was I frightened? Sheepishly admit have slept like log.

7.20 a.m.

Wash cows' udders and scrub backsides. Start milking. Lena waits until pail half full and delivers accurate kick. Collapse in undignified manner and milk is spilt. Restrain language unfit for Charles' ears with difficulty.

7.45 a.m.

Take milk over to dairy, and measure out for house and men's cans. Pour rest into separator. Turn handle.

7.50 a.m.

Pour cream into steen – big stone jar. Take skimmed milk to pig tub in feeding shed.

7.55 a.m.

Dismantle separator and wash first in cold then hot water. Swab down dairy floor. Prepare bread and milk for ferrets.

8.30 a.m.

Welcome cry of breakfast from house. Peel off outer garments and rush to table with mouth watering. Family in flutter over bomb. Breakfast spent in discussion of striking phenomena – e.g. rattling doors, shaking glass, farmyard cries, etc. – and personal reactions. Admission that I have heard nothing received with scorn.

9.00 a.m.

Make bed, i.e. turn back bedclothes in sluttish manner. Take food out to ferrets. Largest buries teeth in my thumb. In middle of invective Tim appears, to whom I recount outrage. He remarks, 'They'm too fat. What they needs is exercise. Course when they see what looks like a bit of meat they puts a tooth in it!' Feel scarcely flattered but dissemble. Tim takes offender by scruff of neck and beats it on head. 'Needs civilisin'.' Discuss Bomb and Air Raids. Cap each other's stories with one more Fearful.

9.15 a.m.

Feed and water hens. Four eggs.

9.20 a.m.

Go to help Charles 'muck out' shippon and attend meal of youngest calf. Cynthia, her foster-mother, behaves in traditional fairytale manner and maltreats her. Cynthia's own child died in early youth. Sad example of unsublimated maternal yearnings. Calf receives kick on nose and retires disheartened.

9.35 a.m.

Turn out cows. Discover Dora lame. Go into consultation with Charles. Dora sags to ground wearing expression of interesting invalid. We pinch her leg and foot with energy and determination. She merely chews cud with smug expression. Charles says it must be the Hard Ground and Massage is the Thing.

9.45 a.m.

'Muck out' shippon. Scatter litter and leave Charles and the patient together with 'Black Heal All, the Wonder Cattle Oil.'

10.15 a.m.

Prepare for butter making. Rinse churn, wash 'hands', draining board, butter worker, etc., and heat up cream. Temperature in dairy positively arctic. Knowing perverse habits of butter which before now has kept me churning for three hours, don two pairs of socks, extra pullover, thick scarf and woollen gloves. Secretly peruse family bookshelf and extract *The Clutching Claw*.

10.40 a.m.

Pour cream into churn. Place cork mat underfoot, open *The Clutching Claw* at Chapter 1 and begin to churn.

11.15 a.m.

To intense disgust just as body discovered in Lord Trex's bed, claw marks at throat, rattle emanates from churn and butter elects 'to come'. Drain buttermilk. Rinse butter four times in water. Collect scales, salt and greaseproof paper from kitchen. Inadvertently leave door open and find dairy inundated by cats, George Snodsbury with head in milk jug. Administer Tim's method of 'civilisation'.

11.40 a.m.

Mix brine and leave butter to soak in it. Clear up general mess.

12.40 a.m.

Make up butter into half-pound blocks. Joined by dear little girl of seven, staying in house who proffers help. This consists of trailing long curls in butter, trampling greaseproof paper underfoot and letting in cats.

12.40 p.m.

Finish last and twentieth block of butter. Wash utensils.

1.0 p.m.

Lunch. The boss is out, having gone shooting. Rest of family – Mother, Stella, eighteen, Mary, fifteen – and dear little visitor, express intention of going to view Bomb Crater. Will I please feed cats and prepare dogs' food?

1.45 p.m.

Help clear away and wash up.

2.10 p.m.

Family and three dogs depart shrilling and yapping in car.

2.15 p.m.

Retire to outhouse with carving knife for ordeal of cutting up strong-smelling lumps of horsemeat for cats' benefit. Feel rather like heathen priestess preparing sacrifice. Cats in full voice press against door. Distribute food. Cats very finicky. Boxing Gloves insists on own plate on wall and Tweets will only feed on granary steps. Take roll-call and find only eleven. Horror, tortoiseshell, and Miss Lamb, white Persian, missing. Miss Lamb discovered on front door mat. As she is deaf unheedful of repeated summons.

2.25 p.m.

'Bowl' wood – laborious process which consists of loading logs from pile which Tim is sawing on wheelbarrow and 'bowling' to wood shed. Logs wet and ice-cold.

3.15 p.m.

Feed hens. Discover recalcitrant Horror – obviously frustrated subject suffering from Freudian inhibitions. She is sitting on three eggs in nesting box. Distressed by Awful Effect of Thwarted Maternal Instincts on Dumb Animals. Remove her.

3.25 p.m.

Go to fetch in cows. Waste considerable time in playful game of hide and seek round haystacks. Eventually persuade cows into yard and to take places in shippon. Find Dora lolling sumptuously on straw luxuriating in massage.

3.40 p.m.

Milk. Cows obviously sulky and resentful of Dora's interesting complaint. Charles gives vivid account of decease of aged cow who died of heart failure in sleep and had to be removed from shippon by tractor.

4.15 p.m.

Take milk to dairy. Separate.

4.30 p.m.

Tea. Find family in state of excitement and laden with bomb splinters after visit to Crater.

5.0 p.m.

Wash up separator and swab dairy floor.

5.20 p.m.

Shut up hens.

5.30 p.m.

Settle down for perusal of paper. Discouraged on reading horoscope by advice to take More Fresh Air.

6.30 p.m.

Wallow in delicious hot bath.

7.15 p.m.

Dinner. Find I am unpopular for taking all hot water. Boss returned with brace of pheasants.

8.0 p.m.

Help clear away and wash up.

8.15 p.m.
    Retrieve *The Clutching Claw* from dairy. Settle in armchair.
9.45 p.m.
    Retire to bed.
10.30 p.m.
    The jealous parlourmaid was murderess after all.

Frances Buckland

Many were also conscripted to work down the pits or in the munitions factories.

CLEATOR MOOR

From one shaft at Cleator Moor
They mined for coal and iron ore.
This harvest below ground could show
Black and red currants on one tree.

In furnaces they burnt the coal,
The ore was smelted into steel,
And railway lines from end to end
Corseted the bulging land.

Pylons sprouted on the fells,
Stakes were driven in like nails,
And the ploughed fields of Devonshire
Were sliced with the steel of Cleator Moor.

The land waxed fat and greedy too,
It would not share the fruits it grew.
And coal and ore, as sloe and plum,
Lay black and red for jamming time.

The pylons rusted on the fells,
The gutters leaked beside the walls,
And women searched the ebb-tide tracks
For knobs of coal or broken sticks.

But now the pits are wick with men,
Digging like dogs dig for a bone:
For food and life *we* dig the earth –
In Cleator Moor they dig for death.

Every waggon of cold coal
Is fire to drive a turbine wheel;
Every knuckle of soft ore
A bullet in a soldier's ear.

The miner at the rockface stands,
With his segged and bleeding hands
Heaps on his head the fiery coal,
And feels the iron in his soul.

Norman Nicholson

MORNING SHIFT

I wrap the morning round me like a muffler,
And bind my hair with the icy ribbon of wind,
Leaving you quiet, my smooth and sleepy lover
Till the yellow winter sunlight wakes your window.

The moon is fading over Edmonton,
The stars like tired workers end their shift.
We, with our torches, arrive in the breaking dawn
Bringing to the still night the noise of morning laughter.

The train shouts energy with defiant puffs,
Breathing determined smoke into the cold,
And we in echo whistle, talk and cough,
Tramping in different steps yet shoulder to shoulder.

Like the beginnings of a planless city
The hulks of factories sprawl in the fog,
Warehouses and scrapheaps and black chimneys
Bulging as we stride nearer, blacker, bigger.

We come with the morning, faltering but certain
Steeled to the buffet of the wind that sings,

The planless city we'll yet shape to our purpose
As we gauge to-morrow's purpose with our brains and fingers.

Honor Arundel

SHELLS

All day like an automaton
She fits the shells into the gauge,
Hour after hour, to earn the wage
To keep her and her little son:
All day, hour after hour, she stands
Handling cold death with calloused hands.

She dare not think, she dare not feel
What happens to the shells that she
Handles and checks so carefully,
Or what, within each case of steel
Is packed as, hour by hour she stands
Handling cold death with calloused hands.

Wilfred Gibson

SWING-SONG

I'm only a wartime working girl,
The machine shop makes me deaf,
I have no prospects after the war
And *my* young man is in the R.A.F.
    K for Kitty calling P for Prue . . .
    Bomb Doors Open . . .
    Over to You.

Night after night as he passes by
I wonder what he's gone to bomb
And I fancy in the jabber of the mad machines
That I hear him talking on the intercomm.
    K for Kitty calling P for Prue . . .
    Bomb Doors Open . . .
    Over to You.

So there's no one in the world, I sometimes think,
Such a wall flower as I
For I must talk to myself on the ground
While he is talking to his friends in the sky:
    K for Kitty calling P for Prue . . .
    Bomb Doors Open . . .
    Over to You.

Louis MacNeice

ARMAMENTS WORKER

Mechanic dark with grease wearing your work
standing among machines in a shaking factory
turning the valve drawing the lever over your breast
lying in the noonhour flat on your back to rest –

and quietly on concrete amongst great machines
forging the weapons to reclaim a landscape,
whose green again will be a people's corn
when guns uncover evening –

work here in cities only half awake,
quicken the anger and increase the pace,
look hard as comrade in your human strength
and soft as love on iron and its peace.

Patrick Anderson

MACHINE SHOP NIGHTSHIFT

The night roars in these walls
And screams in steel,
For we are midwives of a queer nativity
While in the quiet night outside
Hear our winged children drone across the moon.

Death is our child; yet more than death; we've known
These walls stand gaunt against the burning city,
We have crouched down, the pounding of our hearts
Drowned in the hate of slaves of the machine.
We stood again. Our hate was born of pity.

Yet you must know, with us, that ultimately
Machines are our servants. Now our child
Grows big and overdue; our liberty
Moans in this metal, aches for action's day,
Ready to leap, full armed, into the fray.

Maurice Carpenter

Some left the factories for the fighting abroad.

I WAS A LABOURER IN THE SMOKY VALLEY

I was a labourer in the smoky valley,
within the high walls, the tall dark walls of the mills,
where the hills go up to the wild moor.
I am a dog of the dales, broad is my speech,
and my ways are not the smooth ways of the south,
but hard, and used to keener weather.
All week I worked among the looms
while the cloth slacked out and the shuttles clacked
swiftly, as the woof was shot through the warp
and through my brain dim with the webs of years.
All week I was the servant of the loom,
chained to the steel for the promise of meagre coin,
six days a week, but Sunday comes
soon, and I am my master for the waking day
that found me with my whippet on the moor.
O my faithful lass! Soft was her fell;
her eyes were like deep pools stained with peat,
shafted with light; and intelligent.
She was long in the body, but strong of limb and rib,
and her muscles moved under the skin
like currents in a bay of the river.
She was swift as the wind or as the summer swallow,
and I would pit her with the local dogs,
backing her swiftness with my sweaty coin
and many a shilling have I won with her
to spend on some wet evening in a pub
or buy the tickets at the picture palace
when I took out the girl I meant to marry –
but that is all forgotten with the flesh.

I was a labourer in the smoky valley:
I am a brittle bone projecting from the sand.

Séan Jennett

Yet the people's entertainments went on, the music-hall and the pub.
There was still some relaxation in the war.

MUSIC-HALL

Tobacco smoke is heavy stealing
To the dim, baroque, curved ceiling,
Slashed by sword of spotlight-beam,
Shot by fiddle's quickening scream.

Decorous, dark-clad, archly bland
With wink, or twist of head or hand,
The master points his well-worn tale,
The theme is old, its new guise, frail,
But it comes from the basic slag of life,
Of debtor, or lodger, or faithless wife,
And the satisfied laughter surges back
As he deftly shifts to another tack
And sings in voice untrained but strong,
An age-old sentimental song.
Two encores then and the curtain calls.
The star is gone, the tension falls.

As the acrobats swerve and swoop and soar
The circle-bar fills up once more,
Where Hilda the barmaid, peroxide fair,
Dextrously serves and with queenly air
(Adjusting her curls with a petulant twist
That jangles her bangles from elbow to wrist).

They play The King as the curtain falls,
The lights shine harsh from the painted walls
On peeling pillars and threadbare seats.
The crowd shuffles out to the night-drenched streets.
The sudden chill, the horns of cars,
Beer and gin in the down-town bars,
Then home in tram to pay-night meals
Of fish-and-chips or jellied eels.

175

Impatient commissionaire, peevish, swearing,
Giving the house its nightly airing,
Drives out the very breath of earth,
Colour, liquor, music, mirth.

John Arlott

PUB

The glasses are raised, the voices drift into laughter,
The clock hands have stopped, the beer in the hands of the soldiers
Is blond, the faces are calm and the fingers can feel
The wet touch of glasses, the glasses print rings on the table,
The smoke rings curl and go up and dissolve near the ceiling,
   This moment exists and is real.

What is reality? Do not ask that. At this moment
Look at the butterfly eyes of the girls, watch the barmaid's
Precision in pouring a Scotch, and remember this day,
This day at this moment you were no longer an island,
People were friendly, the clock in the hands of the soldiers
   For this moment had nothing to say.

And nothing to say and the glasses are raised, we are happy
Drinking through time, and a world that is gentle and helpless
Survives in the pub and goes up in the smoke of our breath,
The regulars doze in the corner, the talkers are fluent;
Look now in the faces of those you love and remember
   That you are not thinking of death.

But thinking of death as the lights go out and the glasses
Are lowered, the people go out and the evening
Goes out, ah, goes out like a light and leaves you alone,
As the heart goes out, the door opens out into darkness,
The foot takes a step, and the moment, the moment of falling
   Is here, you go down like a stone,

Are you able to meet the disaster, able to meet the
Cold air of the street and the touch of corruption, the rotting
Fingers that murder your own in the grip of love?
Can you bear to find hateful the faces you once thought were lovely,

Can you bear to find comfort alone in the evil and stunted,
        Can you bear to abandon the dove?

The houses are shut and the people go home, we are left in
Our islands of pain, the clocks start to move and the powerful
To act, there is nothing now, nothing at all
To be done: for the trouble is real: and the verdict is final
Against us. The clocks go round faster and faster. And fast as
        confetti
        The days are beginning to fall.

                                        Julian Symons

PALAIS DE DANSE

Can you not see within that small
And callow head, a brightness far
From this dance hall?
Her evening-dress
Is splitting like the chrysalis,
And when she stirs
A caterpillar moves.

Can you not see through her twin panes
Of coloured glass
That dusky room within
Her house of powder'd clay?
O stranger, stay,
Do you not see
A barbarous glory?

Observe her, one of that bright million
Wherever the blood roars and the limbs sing:
Unknown to her
One foot is tap-tap-tapping on the floor:
Her neck supports a brittle
And thoughtless miracle
Deadened with chalky pollen.
A cigarette
Like a white stamen with a burning anther
Is drooping from the flower tropical

177

That has two petals
Of dead, wet scarlet.

The sons of swingtime with their feet tap-tapping
The hollow platform wait the millionth moment
When to let loose on us the tinsel tiger.
Arise the fag-end boys from the tin-tables,
And slide into the hollow of the rhythm.
The crimson jazz is bouncing on the boards!

Where is she now?
She glides,
She comes
With a small shiny man,
And rides
Into the marrow of the Congo drums.

Mervyn Peake

6
Home and Away

Before the soldiers were shipped abroad, they were granted a special leave.

EMBARKATION LEAVE

For each brief embarkation leave
in the changing war that is never over
while we have lives,
we have the need to state our need.

We've both known love as a wound's fever;
known, too, the words 'it isn't loaded'
that are suicide;
and there's plenty left of childhood's greed;

So this loving's possible, and no other:
bodies' delight in beating death –
no fool hope's growth,
none of the waiting, the futile grieving.

We need the sunlight's unhurried loving
that pauses for laughter, or for breath,
but takes no oath.
It is impossible? So is our living.

Tom Wintringham

The troopships herded the men together.

TROOP SHIP

The bunks are crowded:
      khaki is turning in.
Not a fag that glows in the dusk;
War-time forbids it
      and war
Says not to much else.
             There's a rag
Of a sky on the sea, and the waves will not speak tonight.
There are lights
      feverdim
        shining on blanket and bunk.

Overhead
> the funnel mourns
> and a tunnel
Of black creeps in from the west.
There is laughter from a cabin
> and just after a song,
A night song, good night to all,
> from the messroom piano,
And a uniform leaning on rails
> that hears not the laughter or song.

Stephen Fenlaugh

*Some of the troopships were sunk. Roy Campbell wrote of one lost passing
the Cape of Good Hope.*

ONE TRANSPORT LOST

Where, packed as tight as space can fit them
The soldiers retch, and snore, and stink,
It was no bunch of flowers that hit them
And woke them up, that night, to drink.

Dashing the bulkheads red with slaughter,
In the steep wash that swept the hold,
Men, corpses, kitbags, blood, and water,
Colliding and commingling rolled.

Some clung, like flies, in fear and wonder,
Clutched to the crossbeams, out of reach,
Till sprayed from thence by jets of thunder
That spouted rumbling from the breach.

In this new world of blast and suction,
The bulk-head tilted to a roof;
Friend aided friend – but to destruction,
And valour seemed its own reproof.

Forced by the pent explosive airs
In the huge death-gasp of its shell,
Or sucked, like Jonah, by their prayers
From forth that spiracle of Hell –

The ones that catapulted from it
Saw the whole hull reverse its dome,
Then ram the depths, like some huge comet,
Flood-lit with phosphorus and foam.

The shark and grampus might reprieve,
After their jaunt upon a raft,
The few that got Survivor's Leave –
But those who perished would have laughed!

Their fiercest thirst they've quenched and cupped,
And smashed the glass (this life of slaves!);
No hectoring Redcaps interrupt
Their fornication with the waves.

For us, this world of Joad and Julian,
The dithering of abortive schemes;
For them, the infinite, cerulean
Suspension of desires and dreams.

So save your Bait, you Bards and Thinkers!
For us who daren't refuse to chew
Hook, line, and swivel, trace and sinkers,
And rod and all, and like it too!

For them, the wave, the melancholy
Chant of the wind that tells no lies;
The breakers roll their funeral volley
To which the thundering cliff replies.

The black cape-hens in decent crêpe
Will mourn them till the Last Event;
The roaring headlands of the Cape
Are lions on their monument.

The soldiers were shipped out to life in desert or plain, jungle or mountain.

TENT-PITCHERS

This is the third day of the Khamsin,
The fierce monotonous insistence
Of hot dry blast, silting up eyes and hair,
Taut-straining the frayed guy-ropes of resistance,
Heat thick enough to cut. Wind but no air.

Two Swaddies pitching tent in the full sun,
Tugging the bellying canvas down,
Stripped to the waist, hair matted, eyes back chest
Caked in a sweaty plaster, shake their heads.
'Well, Bill? Yer glad yer came out East?'
'Ho, yuss! I wouldn't have missed this for quids!'

Oh England! Oh my lovely casual country!
These are your lads. English as blackthorn-flower,
Bearing your freshness with them, facing each hour,
Desert or death, with the same free unstudied
Serenity of meadowland in April –
Carelessly littered with fritillaries,
Ladysmock, kingcups, cowslips, and wild apple!

Frank Thompson

F. T. Prince saw soldiers in the sea in Egypt.

SOLDIER'S BATHING

The sea at evening moves across the sand.
Under a reddening sky I watch the freedom of a band
Of soldiers who belong to me. Stripped bare
For bathing inm the sea, they shout and run in the warm air;
Their flesh worn by the trade of war, revives
And my mind towards the meaning of it strives.

All's pathos now. The body that was gross,
Rank, ravenous, disgusting in the act or in repose,
All fever, filth and sweat, its bestial strength
And bestial decay, by pain and labour grows at length

Fragile and luminous. 'Poor bare forked animal,'
Conscious of his desires and needs and flesh that rise and fall,
Stands in the soft air, tasting after toil
The sweetness of his nakedness: letting the sea-waves coil
Their frothy tongues about his feet, forgets
His hatred of the war, its terrible pressure that begets
A machinery of death and slavery,
Each being a slave and making slaves of others: finds that he
Remembers his old freedom in a game
Mocking himself, and comically mimics fear and shame.

He plays with death and animality;
And reading in the shadows of his pallid flesh, I see
The idea of Michelangelo's cartoon
Of soldiers bathing, breaking off before they were half done
At some sortie of the enemy, an episode
Of the Pisan wars with Florence. I remember how he showed
Their muscular limbs that clamber from the water,
And heads that turn across the shoulder, eager for the slaughter,
Forgetful of their bodies that are bare,
And hot to buckle on and use the weapons lying there.
– And I think too of the theme another found
When, shadowing men's bodies on a sinister red ground,
Another Florentine, Pollaiuolo,
Painted a naked battle: warriors, straddled, hacked the foe,
Dug their bare toes into the ground and slew
The brother-naked man who lay between their feet and drew
His lips back from his teeth in a grimace.

They were Italians who knew war's sorrow and disgrace
And showed the thing suspended, stripped: a theme
Born out of the experience of war's horrible extreme
Beneath a sky where even the air flows
With lacrimae Christi. For that rage, that bitterness, those
      blows,
That hatred of the slain, what could they be
But indirectly or directly a commentary
On the Crucifixion? And the picture burns
With indignation and pity and despair by turns,
Because it is the obverse of the scene
Where Christ hangs murdered, stripped, upon the Cross.
      I mean,
That is the explanation of its rage.

And we too have our bitterness and pity that engage
Blood, spirit, in this war. But night begins,
Night of the mind: who nowadays is conscious of our sins?
Though every human deed concerns our blood,
And even we must know, what nobody has understood,
That some great love is over all we do,
And that is what has driven us to this fury, for so few
Can suffer all the terror of that love:
The terror of that love has set us spinning in this groove
Greased with our blood.

                          These dry themselves and dress,
Combing their hair, forget the fear and shame of nakedness.
Because to love is frightening we prefer
The freedom of our crimes. Yet, as I drink the dusky air,
I feel a strange delight that fills me full,
Strange gratitude, as if evil itself were beautiful,
And kiss the wound in thought, while in the west
I watch a streak of red that might have issued from Christ's
      breast.

*The first British victory against General Rommel was at El Alamein.
John Jarmain went back to the battleground there.*

El ALAMEIN

There are flowers now, they say, at Alamein;
Yes, flowers in the minefields now.
So those that come to view that vacant scene,
Where death remains and agony has been
Will find the lilies grow –
Flowers, and nothing that we know.

So they rang the bells for us and Alamein,
Bells which we could not hear.
And to those that heard the bells what could it mean,
The name of loss and pride, El Alamein?
– Not the murk and harm of war,
But their hope, their own warm prayer.

It will become a staid historic name,
That crazy sea of sand!
Like Troy or Agincourt its single fame

Will be the garland for our brow, our claim,
On us a fleck of glory to the end;
And there our dead will keep their holy ground.

But this is not the place that we recall,
The crowded desert crossed with foaming tracks,
The one blotched building, lacking half a wall,
The grey-faced men, sand-powdered over all;
The tanks, the guns, the trucks,
The black, dark-smoking wrecks.

So be it; none but us has known that land:
El Alamein will still be only ours
And those ten days of chaos in the sand.
Others will come who cannot understand,
Will halt beside the rusty minefield wires
And find there, flowers.

Keith Douglas left a post behind the lines to fight with his tank squadron at El Alamein and afterwards.

from *ALAMEIN TO ZEM ZEM*

From the first appearance of the enemy, a Crusader troop leader, well out in front of the regiment, sees and hears the whole action, almost as if it were a pageant prepared for his entertainment: for hours on end it may continue to be exciting in quite an impersonal way. He sees a suspicious blob on the horizon; halts his squat turret almost level with a ridge and scrutinises the blob through his glasses. Pressing the switch of his microphone, releasing it a moment to see if someone else is talking, and pressing it again, he says: 'King 2. Something that looks like a tank to my front, about three miles, I'm on your right. Over.' 'King 2. O.K. off to you. King, did you hear King 2's message?' 'King, yes. Let him keep bumming on. But be cautious. Off,' says Piccadilly Jim to Edward. 'King 1,' says Edward, calling the squadron, 'slow down a bit and have a good look from hull down before you go swanning over ridges. Over.' '2 O.K. off, 3 O.K. off. 4 O.K. off.' 'King 2, 3, 4, O.K. off to you. King 5, did you get my last message?' 'King 5. Yes. Over.' 'King 5, well bloody well wake up and acknowledge. Off.' 'Off' caps the rebuke, like a telephone receiver being hung up. We have two main sources of allusion, horses and cricket. 'Uncle Tom what's the going like over this next bit? Can we bring the, er,

187

unshod horses over it?' 'Uncle Tom, I'm *just* going over Beecher's myself, you want to hold 'em in a bit and go carefully, but after that it's good going for the whole field.' 'King 2 Ack,' says someone who has broken a track. 'I shall need the farrier, I've cast a shoe.' Someone else is 'having trouble with my horses insides. Could I have the Vet?' Metaphor changes: 'King 2, someone is throwing stones. I can't see where from yet. Over,' and a little later Piccadilly Jim asks: 'King 2, now that that chap has retired to the pavilion, how many short of a full team are you?' As the action goes on, metaphors, direct speech, codes, sequences of messages are intermingled, until a good deal of concentration is needed to disentangle them. 'King 2. There are a couple of 88's on that grey ridge to my right. One is near the brew up, and the other to the left of it, about two degrees. Over.' 'King 2. O.K. off to you. Orange Pip, can you see those 88's of King 2's? Over.' 'George 4, is that a vehicle moving on your right front? Over.' 'Orange Pip, yes. Getting gunfire on now. Over.' 'George 4. Yes, I reported it just now. Over.' 'George 4, can you bring fire on to it?' 'King, have you anything to report? Over.' 'George, one of your children came up in the middle of my transmission then, when I was trying to talk to King. It's most difficult and annoying, and I won't have it . . . Tell him to bloody well keep off the air when I'm trying to fight a battle. Off . . . er, to you. King, King, have you anything to report? Over.' 'King, King, Signals. Over.' 'King 2, I think one of those guns is being towed away. Over. 'King 2 or whoever that is, GET OFF THE BLOODY AIR when I'm trying to talk to somebody. Off . . . King, King, signals over.' 'King, strength NINER. I'm sorry, I was talking to my jockey. Could you say again? Over.' And so on.

From the conversation it emerges that the Crusaders are held up, that the regiment on the right is under heavy and destructive fire, that there are some of our own armoured cars working forward on our left, which we mustn't fire at. The heavy tanks are engaging targets on the ridge in front of us, behind which we can see the tops of telegraph poles. Every turn of events is recorded on the air. Someone asks for 'the little fat man' – this means they are hopelessly broken down and want the technical adjutant, known officially over the wireless as 'Tock Ack,' to arrange their recovery. The regiment on our right asks for 'our bald-headed friend' on such occasions. It is these individual peculiarities which an enemy listening officer will note. The armoured cars in front, 'Our red friends on ponies, the Cherry Ps,' wheel away towards the regiment on our right – 'Uncle Gordon's boys.' Now and then an awkward, hesitating transmission creates a short silence – 'Nuts three calling. We 'ave, er, 'ad a misfortune. The horse 'as fallen, driver is no more. Can we 'ave Monkey Orange?' The gunner of a tank which has been hit, shaken by the impact of the shell, the sight of one of his friends beheaded, and another bleeding from a great wound, has forgotten his wireless procedure, if he ever knew it. If the M.O. is not already attending to someone, he will try to reach the tank in a scout car. Meanwhile, the gunner must try to get the unconscious corporal out, because the tank is burning, and bandage him roughly, because he is bleeding to death.

Before being killed in action in France, Keith Douglas proved to be one of the best young poets of the war, a good soldier and a compassionate man.

HOW TO KILL

Under the parabola of a ball,
a child turning into a man,
I looked into the air too long.
The ball fell in my hand, it sang
in the closed fist: *Open Open
Behold a gift designed to kill.*

Now in my dial of glass appears
the soldier who is going to die.
He smiles, and moves about in ways
his mother knows, habits of his.
The wires touch his face: I cry
NOW. Death, like a familiar, hears

and look, has made a man of dust
of a man of flesh. This sorcery
I do. Being damned, I am amused
to see the centre of love diffused
and the waves of love travel into vacancy.
How easy it is to make a ghost.

The weightless mosquito touches
her tiny shadow on the stone,
and with how like, how infinite
a lightness, man and shadow meet.
They fuse. A shadow is a man
when the mosquito death approaches.

ARISTOCRATS

'I think I am becoming a God'

The noble horse with courage in his eye
clean in the bone, looks up at a shellburst:
away fly the images of the shires
but he puts the pipe back in his mouth.

Peter was unfortunately killed by an 88:
it took his leg away, he died in the ambulance.
I saw him crawling on the sand; he said
It's most unfair, they've shot my foot off.

How can I live among this gentle
obsolescent breed of heroes, and not weep?
Unicorns, almost,
for they are falling into two legends
in which their stupidity and chivalry
are celebrated. Each, fool and hero, will be an immortal.

The plains were their cricket pitch
and in the mountains the tremendous drop fences
brought down some of the runners. Here then
under the stones and earth they dispose themselves,
I think with their famous unconcern.
It is not gunfire I hear but a hunting horn.

LANDSCAPE WITH FIGURES

I

Perched on a great fall of air
a pilot or angel looking down
on some eccentric chart, a plain
dotted with useless furniture,
discerns dying on the sand vehicles
squashed dead or still entire, stunned
like beetles: scattered wingcases and
legs, heads, appear when the dust settles.

But you who like Thomas come
to poke fingers in the wounds

find monuments and metal posies.
On each disordered tomb
the steel is torn into fronds
by the lunatic explosive.

II

On sand and scrub the dead men wriggle
in their dowdy clothes. They are mimes
who express silence and futile aims
enacting this prone and motionless struggle
at a queer angle to the scenery,
crawling on the boards of the stage like walls,
deaf to the one who opens his mouth and calls
silently. The décor is a horrible tracery
of iron. The eye and mouth of each figure
bear the cosmetic blood and the hectic
colours death has the only list of.

A yard more and my little finger
could trace the maquillage of these stony actors:
I am the figure writhing on the backcloth.

VERGISSMEINNICHT

Three weeks gone and the combatants gone,
returning over the nightmare ground
we found the place again, and found
the soldier sprawling in the sun.

The frowning barrel of his gun
overshadowing. As we came on
that day, he hit my tank with one
like the entry of a demon.

Look. Here in the gunpit spoil
the dishonoured picture of his girl
who has put: *Steffi. Vergissmeinnicht*
in a copybook gothic script.

We see him almost with content
abased, and seeming to have paid

and mocked at by his own equipment
that's hard and good when he's decayed.

But she would weep to see to-day
how on his skin the swart flies move;
the dust upon the paper eye
and the burst stomach like a cave.

For here the lover and killer are mingled
who had one body and one heart.
And death who had the soldier singled
has done the lover moral hurt.

Other warriors reflected on the luck of death in war.

AT SEA

After the attack
In the warm blue seas
We lazed and lolled
Floating at ease
As the long waves rolled
But men in the morning
Bomb blasted sea choked
Floundered and gasped
In these same blue seas
Some dead some drowned
Some rescued maybe
But we the killers
Lazed and lolled
Floating at ease
As the long waves rolled

Geoff Pearse

Faced with the death of friends, some had to seem almost callous to survive.

LA BELLE INDIFFERENCE

I hate that which is changing me
to treat all my past friends
with cold, impersonal disinterest.
Perhaps War makes inevitable
that false, local loyalty, only
to the immediate companions
of your own small circle.
One grows armoured like a lobster
against loss – can grow new limbs, claws.
Survival inhibits any feeling, save the joy
of survival. Your own miserable hide . . .
To hell with the Rest, England Home and Duty.

Take Terry, Company Clerk.
At Qassassin we shared spartan end of Coy. Office
shared Leave to Cairo, every darn thing
until I asked for a transfer to a fighting platoon.

A thousand miles later, up in the snows
of Florina Pass, just after the action
against the 'Adolf Hitler Leibstandarte' SS
the Coy. Commander comes over with, 'Your friend,
Lance Corporal Spears, has been wounded.
Took a Bren into the Railway Tunnel
so that you blighters could get out . . .
Caught it by blast. Both eyes.
Not likely to see again.'
                        I say nothing.
Betray no reaction. Cannot feel. Terry BLIND!
I cannot even breathe, 'Poor bastard.'
Now heading south in complete dark
only able to finger head bandages
in a stinking Red Crossed camion
on that bumping, rotten road.
Either I have a character defect
or else my loyalties froze hard up there.

We eye what's pitifully left of 'A' Coy.
Shrug. Crowd round the steaming brew.
Only the Section counts.

Victor West

MOTOR TRANSPORT OFFICER

Pyatt had something to do with horses.
No, that's not what I mean,
   wipe that smirk off your face.
I mean that in Civvy Street he had
   something to do with horses.
Not as a Trainer, you know, but in
   the buying and selling line.
A horse-chandler, or something.

We didn't have any horses in The Regiment,
   though we had some mules with us in Greece.
So we made him our Motor Transport Officer,
   as he was a Captain, and none of the other
   companies wanted him, not being a Gent.

He made a damn good transport officer, actually.
'Not afraid to get his head under the bonnet,'
   the Colonel always said.
And he could nurse a three-tonner back on the road,
   like a horse with an injured fetlock.

He didn't like the fighting much, and when shells
   fell, managed to be back with 'B' Echelon;
   and he drank too much.

But I wouldn't have wished his end, on man or beast.
Slewed a 15-hundredweight across the road, into a wall
   when he came upon a sudden roadblock.
Trapped in the cab, when the bastard truck caught fire.

Well, they shoot horses, don't they?

Colin McIntyre

INFANTRYMAN

When you have walked through a town, as an infantryman,
You'll never go through streets the same way again.

There is shoulder-ache from rifle-sling, and sore
butt-bruise, of bolt, on hip and thigh.

The walk comes somewhere between lope and slow hike,
a wary step, splay-footed, as drawers cellular,
catch in the crotch, twist centrifugally around.

Our lot moved at slow deliberate plod, eyes down, look out.
Ted walked on the left, looks right; I took the right,
looked left. Well spaced out, bloody tired all the time.

Ted and I had a reputation, in Four Section, for hitting
the deck, together, quick as a flash, at the first shell.
Ted had a nose for crossroads ranged by guns.

Infantrymen grow fat in later years, from never walking.
Ted would have become quite gross. But Ted's dead.
Stepped on an AP mine in champagne country.
Cheers, Ted, you old sod, you.

Colin McIntyre

Those who were gone left what they had to those who were still there.

'LET IT BE HUSHED'

Let it be hushed; let the deep ocean close
Upon these dead. Others may laud their parts,
Raise monuments of marble in their names.
But we who flew with them, and laughed with them –
We other crews who, living side by side,
In outward contacts slowly came to know
Their inmost parts, would rather leave untouched
The wound we healed, the love we buried there.
These men knew moments you have never known,
Nor ever will; we knew those moments too,
And talked of them in whispers late at night;

Such confidence was born of danger shared.
We shared their targets, too; but we came back.
Lightly we talked of it. We packed their kit;
Divided up such common useful things
As cigarettes and chocolate – rations stored
Against a rainy day that never came.
'And they cast lots among them!' someone said.
'It was a pity that he wore his watch;
It was a good one, twenty pounds he said
He paid for it in Egypt. Now let's see,
Who's on to-night? Ah, Taffy – you've a good one!
You'd better leave it with me.' And we laughed.
Cold, were we? Cold at heart. You get that way.
Sometimes we knew what happened; how they crashed.
It was not always on the other side.
One pranged upon the runway, dipped a wing.
The navigator bought it, and the gunner.
The other two got out – a little shaken.
Bob crashed when doing an air test; just low flying –
At least, they think it was, they couldn't say.
The plane was burning fiercely when they found it;
One man thrown clear, still living, but he died
On way to hospital. The loss was ours –
Because I shared an aeroplane with Bob.
We had to get another D for dog.
And some did not come back. We never knew
Whether they lived – at first, just overdue,
Till minutes changed to hours, and still no news.
One went to bed; but roused by later crews,
Asked: 'Were they back yet?' – and being answered 'No',
Went back to sleep.
One's waking eyes sought out the empty beds,
And – 'Damn', you said, 'another kit to pack.'
I never liked that part: you never knew
What privacies your sorting might lay bare.
I always tried to leave my kit arranged
In decent tidiness. You never know.
But that is past. The healing river flows,
And washes clean the wound with passing years.
We grieve not now. There was a time for tears,
When Death stood by us, and we dared not weep.
Let the seas close above them, and the dissolving deep.

David Raikes

THE MANTLE

Recruits are issued with dead soldiers' stock;
Field-muddied webbing, brasswork that must mock
Our novice hopes to get it clean.
No tragedy in that: what of the shock
At this first splash of blood I've seen –
This ground-sheet that has warmed some dying Jock?
'Royal Scots: Dunkirk'! so reads the rune.
– Blood and a name where heroism has been.

This hero's shroud must be my living hide
To shield and warm: Pity is in this pride:
My warmth will never quicken him.
And yet by this he shall be sanctified,
Through blood, and through a bullet's whim;
And the far, uncherished agony he died,
Kindling new life as life grew dim,
Shall lift a new vision above my vision's rim.

Stephen Haggard

THE DEATH OF THE BALL
TURRET GUNNER

From my mother's sleep I fell into the State,
And I hunched in its belly till my wet fur froze.
Six miles from earth, loosed from its dream of life,
I woke to black flak and the nightmare fighters.
When I died they washed me out of the turret with a hose.

Randall Jarrell

Hamish Henderson's Elegies *were among the best of the long poems written about the war.*

from ELEGIES FOR THE DEAD IN CYRENAICA
First Elegy: End of a Campaign

There are many dead in the brutish desert,
        who lie uneasy
among the scrub in this landscape of half-wit
stunted ill-will. For the dead land is insatiate
and necrophilous. The sand is blowing about still.
Many who for various reasons, or because
        of mere unanswerable compulsion, came here
and fought among the clutching gravestones,
        shivered and sweated,
cried out, suffered thirst, were stoically silent, cursed
the spittering machine-guns, were homesick for Europe
and fast embedded in quicksand of Africa
        agonized and died.
And sleep now. Sleep here the sleep of the dust.

There were our own, there were the others.
Their deaths were like their lives, human and animal.
There were no gods and precious few heroes.
What they regretted when they died had nothing to do with
        race and leader, realm indivisible,
laboured Augustan speeches or vague imperial heritage.
(They saw through that guff before the axe fell.)
        Their longing turned to
the lost world glimpsed in the memory of letters:
an evening at the pictures in the friendly dark,
two knowing conspirators smiling and whispering secrets;
        or else
a family gathering in the homely kitchen
with Mum so proud of her boys in uniform:
        their thoughts trembled
between moments of estrangement, and ecstatic moments
of reconciliation: and their desire
crucified itself against the unutterable shadow of someone
whose photo was in their wallets.
Then death made his incision.

There were our own, there were the others.
Therefore, minding the great word of Glencoe's
son, that we should not disfigure ourselves
with villainy of hatred; and seeing that all

have gone down like curs into anonymous silence,
I will bear witness for I knew the others.
Seeing that littoral and interior are alike indifferent
and the birds are drawn again to our welcoming north
why should I not sing *them*, the dead, the innocent?

Interlude: Opening of an Offensive

(*a*) the waiting

Armour has foregathered, snuffling
through tourbillons of fine dust.
The crews don't speak much. They've had
last brew-up before battle. The tawny
deadland lies in a silence
not yet smashed by salvoes.
No sound reaches us
from the African constellations.
The low ridge too is quiet.
But no fear we're sleeping,
no need to remind us
that the nervous fingers of the searchlights
are nearly meeting and time is flickering
and this I think in a few minutes
while the whole power crouches for the spring.
X – 20 in thirty seconds. Then begin

(*b*) the barrage

Let loose (rounds)
the exultant bounding hell-harrowing of sound.
Break the batteries. Confound
the damnable domination. Slake
the crashing breakers-húrled rúbble of the guns.

Dithering darkness, we'll wake you! Héll's bélls
blind you. Be broken, bleed
deathshead blackness!
       The thongs of the livid
firelights lick you
             jagg'd splinters rend you
                      underground
we'll bomb you, doom you, tomb you into grave's mound

(c) the Jocks

They move forward into no man's land, a vibrant sounding
board.
          As they advance
the guns push further murderous music.
In this all they will hear, this raucous apocalypse?
The spheres knocking in the night of Heaven?
The drummeling of overwhelming niagara?
No! For I can hear it! Or is it? . . . tell
me that I can hear it! Now – listen!

          Yes, hill and shieling
sea-loch and island, hear it, the yell
of your war-pipes, scaling sound's mountains
guns thunder drowning in their soaring swell!
– The barrage gulfs them: they're gulfed in the clumbering
          guns,
gulfed in gloom, gloom. Dumb in the blunderbuss black –
lost – gone in the anonymous cataract of noise.
Now again! The shrill war-song: it flaunts
aggression to the sullen desert. It mounts. Its scream
tops the valkyrie, tops the colossal
          artillery.

Meaning that many
German Fascists will not be going home
meaning that many
will die, doomed in their false dream

We'll mak siccar!
Against the bashing cudgel
against the contemptuous triumphs of the big battalions
mak siccar against the monkish adepts
of total war against the oppressed oppressors
mak siccar against the leaching lies
against the worked out systems of sick perversion
mak siccar
          against the executioner
against the tyrannous myth and real terror
mak siccar

Note to Interlude:

Scaling sound's mountains.

> Wi' nocht but the cry o' the pipes can Earth
> Or these – or silence – meet.

HUGH MACDIARMID. *Coronach*
for the End of the World.

Mak siccar (Make sure). One of the famous phrases of mediaeval Scottish history.

After Bruce had stabbed the Red Comyn in Dumfries Kirk he was found outside the building by Lindsay and Kirkpatrick. Lindsay asked if Comyn were dead. Bruce replied that he didn't know.

'Aweel,' said Kirkpatrick, 'I'll mak siccar.'

Stationed in Africa, Roy Fuller asked what would the fighting achieve or make of the troops.

THE LEGIONS

> When we have pissed away the marble walls,
> And turned a foreign vandyke in the suns,
> And lions wander in the ruined halls
> And come and lick the barrels of our guns,
> And the last letter has arrived and been
> Forgotten, and the nights are dreamless –
>
>   Then
> Shall we be free? And turn for home, as lean
> And baffled wolves turn for their starving den?
> Or shall we merely look upon our nails
> And see what kind of beast we have become;
> And weep at that: or, if our nature fails,
> Shrug, and descend to dancing and the drum?
>
> Exile has sores which battle cannot make,
> Changing the sick from sound, the truth from fake.

The Allied armies from North Africa crossed the Mediterranean to Italy. Harry Brown spoke of the nature of war when dealing with an American platoon landed on an invasion beachhead.

from *A WALK IN THE SUN*

It was strange to be so close to things and yet to be so far away. That was war. That was always war. It was confused and it was incoherent and it was unreasonable. Nothing ever happened quite on time, nothing ever happened exactly as was expected. War, itself a paradox, was full of paradoxes. A platoon of men, in on the first landing on an enemy coast, could be completely bypassed by events. They could sit in a hollow while all around them things went, or should be going, according to plan, and yet the platoon, itself an integral part of the whole operation, seemed to be entirely forgotten. Yet, had the platoon been unnecessary, it might very well have found itself caught underneath shells and planes, with machine guns and mortars and tanks battering away at it from all directions. The men of the Quartermaster Corps, who appear to lead quiet lives, unscarred by battle, could tell stories of just such occasions. They happen all the time. They probably always have happened.

War, without virtue in itself, breeds virtue. It breeds patience in the impatient and heroism in the cowardly, but mostly it breeds patience. For war is a dull business, the dullest business on earth. War is a period of waiting. Mainly it is a period of waiting for war to be over, but each day of it is crammed with the little hesitations of men uncertain of themselves and awed by the ghastly responsibilities, responsibilities of life and death, the responsibilities of gods, that have been thrust into their hands. The soldier waits for food, for clothing, for a letter, for a battle to begin. And often the food is never served, the clothing is never issued, the letter never arrives and the battle never begins. The soldier learns to wait meekly, hoping that something will happen. And, when the period of waiting is at an end, the something that does happen isn't what he expected. So in the end he learns to wait and expect nothing. That is patience. That is God's one great gift to the soldier.

But he refuses to confess his patience. He curses the fact that he has to wait. He howls at those who cause the waiting. He swears at himself for being such a fool as to wait. And that too is good, in a way. For the man who waits silently is not a good soldier. He is no more than a stone.

There was always more waiting than fighting, for action was rare. Tom Scott wrote of a canteen in West Africa.

CANTEEN

This boy dressed in dungarees draws my attention;
He stands alone in this smoke and haze
The air of a tropical A.F.N. and Army canteen
Among snappy white-khaki-clad soldiers
And over the counter the white-dressed white actresses;

He stands alone, his dungarees dirty
His old blue shirt stained with grease from some ship;
And I wonder why, browsing in the latest books
Seeking the Pimpernel unity on button-bright tunic
Suddenly this towsy-haired boy disturbs me;

Not that I want to be again in dungarees;
True to my time I am too proud (too afraid) for that;
Nor is it some fashionable flame; but still, coldly
Distantly I watch him alone among the bright uniforms;
I find his presence, like forgotten words,
         a bit puzzling.

The troops overseas had pin-ups on the walls of the barrack-rooms and went to the cinemas.

PIN-UP

On the walls
Above our beds
Are spreads
Of photogenic
Movie stars
In female
Attitudes.

Their heads
Are mostly
Teeth and smile
But they
Display
(Perhaps
Unwittingly)
That

Which spreads
Most fittingly
At heads
Of beds.

Ben Levy

TROOPS' CINEMA

Catcalls communicate
Unsatisfied desire,
But the hot cutie
Eludes the grasp;

Only those youths
Who feed on shadows
Shall hold her beauty
In their arms;

I feel frustrated –
And bored almost to tears –
Returning to duty
Beneath familiar stars.

R. N. Currey

*The front in India was so far away that death was nearer among the
people.*

UNCONSIDERED BODIES

Newspapers tabulate
Daily deaths;
But who cares a damn about
Passings of paupers?

Unconsidered bodies
Float down the tide
Of holy rivers;
Down the Ganges

With hunched shoulders
Past Benares' steps;
Godavery, Cauvery,
The River Kistna.

To-day I found
Under a dam,
Dedicate to Allah,
Blessed by Vishnu,

Serving provinces
With light and water,
A broken body
Stretched across a rock.

Coolies working near
Saw, but ignored it –
Nobody wanted it
Even for record.

R. N. Currey

POEM

Death is a matter of mathematics.

It screeches down at you from dirtywhite nothingness
And your life is a question of velocity and altitude,
With allowances for wind and the quick, relentless pull
Of gravity.

Or else it lies concealed
In that fleecy, peaceful puff of cloud ahead.
A streamlined, muttering vulture, waiting
To swoop upon you with a rush of steel.
And then your chances vary as the curves
Of your parabolas, your banks, your dives,
The scientific soundness of your choice
Of what to push or pull, and how, and when.

Or perhaps you walk oblivious in a wood,
Or crawl flat-bellied over pockmarked earth,
And Death awaits you in a field-gray tunic

205

Sights upright and aligned. Range estimated
And set in. A lightning, subconscious calculation
Of trajectory and deflection. With you the focal point,
The centre of the problem. The A and B
Or Smith and Jones of schoolboy textbooks.

Ten out of ten means you are dead.

Barry Conrad Amiel

Alun Lewis noted the journey towards the war front.

THE JOURNEY

We were the fore-runners of an army,
Going among strangers without sadness,
Danger being as natural as strangeness.

We had no other urge but to compel
Tomorrow in the image of today,
Which was motion and mileage and tinkering
When cylinders misfired and the gasket leaked.
Distance exhausted us each night;
I curled up in the darkness like a dog
And being a romantic stubbed my eyes
Upon the wheeling spokeshave of the stars.

Daylight had girls tawny as gazelles,
Beating their saris clean in pools and singing.
When we stopped they covered up their breasts;
Sometimes their gestures followed us for miles.
Then caravanserais of gipsies
With donkeys grey as mice and mincing camels
Laden with new-born lambs and trinkets,
Tentage and utensils and wicker baskets,
Following the ancient routes of the vast migrations
When history was the flight of a million birds
And poverty had splendid divagations.

Sometimes there were rivers that refused us,
Sweeping away the rafts, the oxen;
Some brown spates we breasted.

The jungle let us through with compass and machets.
And there were men like fauns, with drenched eyes,
Avoiding us, bearing arrows.

There was also the memory of Death
And the recurrent irritation of our selves.
But the wind so wound its ways about us,
Beyond this living and this loving,
This calculation and provision, this fearing,
That neither of us heard the quiet voice calling us,
Remorse like rain softening and rotting the ground,
We felt no sorrow in the singing bird,
Forgot the sadness we had left behind.
For how could we guess, oh Life, oh suffering and patient Life,
With distance spun for ever in the mind.
We among the camels, the donkeys and the waterfalls,
How could we ever guess,
Not knowing how you pined?

The fruits of war could be bitter.

THE BITTER MANGOES

I'll only tell the story once
it doesn't do to tell it twice;
the sergeant and the family man
will tell you that it isn't nice.
O the bitter mangoes O.

There were bamboos to the left of us
and bamboos to the right
bamboos all the morning
and thorns of course at night.
O the bitter mangoes O.

How shall we ever get there?
We shan't the captain said,
he fell among the cane trees
and broke his stupid head.
O the bitter mangoes O.

Stuck in the mud for lunchtime
stuck in the mud for tea
with centipedes and leeches
crawling round your knee.
O the bitter mangoes O.

Breaking your nails for supper
climbing up a cliff
trembling like a jelly
not daring once to sniff
O the bitter mangoes O

Crawling round for breakfast
under bamboo bush and tree
the ants are biting nicely
they're getting in your tea.
O the bitter mangoes O.

The rain is falling gently
the rain it's tumbling down
every single thing is wet
wouldn't you like to drown.
O the bitter mangoes O.

They're shooting in the pine trees
grenades are crashing down
the little man behind the tree
is going to get you soon.
O the bitter mangoes O.

George Scurfield

When the soldiers reached the front, there was hard fighting against the Japanese.

ARAKAN BOX

I thought,
Remembering the speech he made
Before they left us,
'The history of wars, when written down
'Has small reality,
'And no more semblance of life

'Than corpses in their graves, reduced by time to bones.
'In books it is a wearisome affair
'Of statesmen, wise or foolish,
'Of battles fought with men
'Who were not men, but figures
'Used to implement the plans
'Of sawdust generals.
'Flesh and blood are shown as oblongs
'Drawn on paper.'

But now,
There are only thirty of us left.
Five yards away my friend is lying dead,
Shot through the throat.
I dare not move to drive away the flies
But stare along the rough, hacked jungle lane
Peering through the dim leaf-filtered sunshine
For sign of any movement which will say
They come again,
A moving frond of fern, a trembling leaf;
My straining ears
Must catch the sound of snapping twig,
The rustle of some frightened forest beast
Through the close-pressing tangle of the undergrowth.

I must not wipe the sweat out of my eyes,
Nor let the jigging fraction of my mind
Stray to far hills, miraculously cool,
But think of killing.

He said,
'If you can hold them through the day,
'While we reorganise defences in your rear,
'You will make history.'
They have come twice already,
And many of the bastards lie
Heaps of old sacking, in the dying light.
The dark shadows on the path
Grow blacker every second.
We shall hold them.
It can't be long before they come again.

J. G. Millard

Death in war led to the same sort of burial.

MILITARY HONOURS

Across the path, deep with narrow tread,
the light is split by dim green angles
from the curious heads of palms
that cast a narrow eye along the dead

who passes in the breath defying heat,
between the rigid, gasping trees,
beneath a flag, and shaken by a lorry
slowed for the damp, uncaring feet

that march with stolid step beside.
Hard rifles glinting dully in the sun,
shirts dark with sweat, the lifting glare,
each head annoyed because he died

and trails them hot and cursing to the grave
to load and fire, repeat, repeat and wait
until the mumbled words are cold,
the bugle stilled. A mourner stoops to save

the flag, and carelessly the earth
descends from shovels slowly plied;
a quiet quick command, the ready cross
enfolds the hero buried into birth.

No grey, swift bullet burst his heart
or snuggled in his guts, or shell or bomb
from bitter foe, no sounding gesture
in retreat, or glory at the start

of the advance to stride the final crest;
unshaven, haggard on the bed,
he vomits, spatters sheets with bowel blood,
his blazing head against the venom breast

of dysentery, ironic germ within the pomp.

J. Alan Thompson

Alun Lewis finally died in the Burma campaign, leaving behind him as his memorial a fine body of stories and poems.

THE EARTH IS A SYLLABLE

'What I say is, if you're in trouble, take it easy,' the ambulance driver said. 'Always have done. Once I got a girl in trouble and I wasn't going to get grey hairs over that. And now I've bust the gasket and she won't budge and maybe the Jap is nearer than our own boys, but there you are, you're no better off if your nose bleeds, are you now?'

He'd often thought he'd die; it was a familiar idea; why shouldn't it be, if there's a war on and you're young and you try to be in it, somewhere? It had taken him a long time to succeed. He'd got into the army easy enough, but the war seemed to elude him all the time. If he was in England it would be in France in hot summer weather and he'd be eating Wall's ice-cream outside the barracks. If he was in India it would be in Egypt and he'd think of the Eighth Army glowing in the desert, attracting him like a moth to its fiery circle. He used to fancy himself flying there like a queen ant on her nuptial flight, and shedding his wings when he lighted, and going to ground there. And now that he had caught up with it, here in Burma, well, it hadn't been much of a show. But he'd never liked the idea of Burma. He'd always known he'd die if he caught up with it in Burma. 'Can't you stop tossing and kicking them blankets?' the ambulance driver said. 'Wear yourself out quicker like that. Take it easy, I say. I been in some bad spots off and on. Narvik for a kick-off, and Crete for a birthday, and a bloody narrow escape from going into Libya with Ritchie; thought I was lucky once being sent out here instead. But I reckon it's all the same where I go. There's sure to be a war there.' He spoke very mournfully, a sort of thoughtful incantation. 'I've had more crump than crumpet this war. That's why I take it easy, mate. You got to last a long time, you know. A long time.'

The driver had given up trying to repair the damage to the cylinder head of his 15-cwt. Bedford; the tropical heat and the dust of the bumpy track that cavorted through the misleading jungle had dried up his water and blown the gasket. It was useless. They were on their way to the rendezvous where the wounded from the advanced dressing stations were handed over to the main dressing station ambulances. To-morrow they'd have to find out where the new rendezvous was; it changed daily, same as everything else changed daily; the situation was very confused, the Japs were said to have worked right round their left flank somewhere up the Sittang, and to have landed above Rangoon.

To-morrow they'd have to find out where the new rendezvous was, if it still mattered.

He was lying on a stretcher in the back of the truck and it was a bit awkward because the truck was tilted steeply, one side in the ditch so as to let the traffic pass up the track to the front, what front there was. The rear flaps were strapped up to give him some air and he could see the darkness of the jungle encircling them. It was dark and soft like a mass of congealed blood. If the Japs were there they'd be sleeping. They had to sleep. Or a snake or a tiger would get them, they weren't all that clever. Any case you could hear them if they were there, calling each other like owls, because they were lonely, maybe. And the jungle was utterly silent, dark and shimmering with darkness like ebony, and malevolent. And he was quite at peace. He'd been more nervous in India than he was here. It was lonely in India, no friendship there, nor any active hostility to brace you. Just loneliness and strangeness. It wasn't dangerous there; just nerves, that's all. You couldn't walk into a native village and have a good time like you wanted to. QUIT INDIA they painted on the walls, Quit India. The silly fools. How can we? India is part of the world. It's the world we can't quit. No, it was just nerves in India. Riding back to camp after the pictures in a trotting tonga with the bells tinkling on the skinny mare's back, it was so dark it was like riding to your death. Just nerves. Here he was quite peaceful.

There was a sudden murmur in the jungle, a sigh, a growing perturbance. Dust. The wind puffed up with a hot dry sigh and the dust came riding in on them in a thick irritating column, into their eyes and mouths, making them swear and spit and blink, and extinguishing the petrol cooker on which the driver was brewing some char. His own lamp spat a high flame and cracked the glass and then subsided. He didn't move. He liked the dust storms by day, the whirling cylinder of tall red dust moving across the plain, the moving red towers that touched the blue sky. He didn't like it at night so much; now when he put his hand over his face his skin was dry and dusty like a statue in a dilapidated museum, like an embalming. The blanket was filthy, it set the skin of his fingers on edge, and he saw with sudden distaste that it was covered with hairs and dandruff under his cheek. It made him think of his wife, she'd written to say he'd left some hairs on his pillow the time he was on embarkation leave, and she'd felt terribly cruel to shake them off, she said. But she was so beautiful and fresh always, and the house always so clean and simple, with the sun or the snow always lighting it. She wouldn't like this dust.

'Well, we'll have to go without a cup of you an' me,' the driver said, grinning and sweating as he leaned over the tailboard to stow the cooker away. ''Tisn't the first thing I've gone without by a long chalk. Christ, I've been without work before now. That's a real nasty thing, being without work. I don't suppose you've been without work, chum, being an officer?'

His mouth was bitter and dry and it hurt him when he smiled. It was the lump the shrapnel had taken out of his throat was hurting now when he smiled. Life had been pretty heartless off and on, but you usually got a laugh out of it. When he'd written three novels one after the other and failed to sell any of them, and gone round to an agency for a job and the old clerk asked him if he could type and he said two fingers only and the clerk said No Good, and he went to sea then as a trimmer. He'd never thought of dying in those days, though, it didn't seem a physical fact at all. Just something you wrote and theorised about. Not like *this*.

'Speaking for myself,' said the driver, 'I've found it a bloody sight easier with a war on. You don't have to bother now. It's all buttoned up. Food and clothes and dentists, trucks to drive, loads to carry, allowances for the missus. It's all laid on for you now. You don't have to bother.'

Yes, he thought, it's been pretty easy. You sink your scruples in conscription, and then there's always something interesting if you take the trouble of finding it. Infantry schemes, sleeping under hedges, swimming a river in full kit, being hungry, talking to a stranger. And since his regiment had been mechanised the tanks had him by the hair – the iron maidens – he'd never tire of pulling on the Tiller bars and stamping on the clutch and pulling like hell on the gear lever and the thrill as she surged softly forward, grunting peacefully and bellying over a slope so sweet and easy. And the big 75 mm. gun and the voices of your friends in your headsets coming over the air. And the queer consolation of the other things he'd tried and written off as failures and now recalled – the little meetings he'd tried to run, debates round a hurricane lamp on the FUTURE, talks he'd carefully put together on RECONSTRUCTION, gramophone records he'd borrowed and played for the lads, the choir he'd tried to make something good of; naturally it was no good for a few odd men to sit round and discuss how to prevent another war, naturally they couldn't 'succeed'. Still, it was all right to remember it.

No. The terrible struggles had been quieter and less obvious than voyages and armoured regiments. They were just something inside you – simply whether to say Yes or No to a thing – to chastity or pity or love or a drink with another man's wife. Maybe if you could avoid saying Yes or No to life, and yet be free, you'd be stronger, better? Would you? How did the dust columns form? What did the Upanishads say? The earth is a syllable. 'I'm turning in, mate,' said the driver. 'There ain't nothing I can do till a truck comes along. Get you back then, if a truck comes along. It's so bleeding quiet in these parts, that's what I don't like. Makes you think we missed the road back somewhere, or missed the war or sommat. I never did like the quiet. Give me a pub that can sell its liquor, not keep it. Give me a call if your pains come back, chum, though there ain't nothing I can do. Jesus, I'm tired. Good-night, cocky.'

He stumped up the road a few yards to where he'd slung his mosquito net among the bushes. He sighed aloud as he pulled each boot off.

Now he was left alone and whatever he had he was alone with it. It was all right as long as he was alone. Whatever he had he could manage it now. His lamp still burned calmly and it might last an hour yet. He didn't want the dark to come any nearer. He could see exactly where it started, just this side of his feet. And then it went on and on. The dawn is the head of a horse. He lay quietly among the crickets and the darkness and the moths came suddenly tilting head-on against this lamp and righted themselves on his face and flew on again. It was very still, except for the pain. There was a translucent golden influence at the core of his being. He could see his wife. She'd wanted a child before he left England but it hadn't turned out that way. And now in a way he was glad. There was only her left, besides himself. She would understand. He'd tried bloody hard; he'd roughed it now and he was cut up a lot and he could smell the poison where the left shoulder and arm had been. But he was still her little house. That was all. He didn't want to go to Burma; he knew it would be a bad place for him. But all striving is a blind guess, and he wasn't in Burma now, he was in the night in the common ground of humanity, and he wasn't alone now.

He wanted to get up and enter the darkness and enter the silent village under the hill and enter it with his wife alone. Not in a tank, for that was a schoolboy's thrill, nor in Burma, because it was a bad place for him. So he pushed himself up on his spare arm and sweated all over; Judas! it hurt. But he hated the dirt and hair of his blanket, and being hot in bed, and he wanted to have his little walk. So he went across the plain in the night and the darkness was hot and tepid and after a while he didn't know where the hell he was, but he knew he was all right, and he loved her so much that he knew he could throw the darkness over the hill.

The driver found him five yards away from the truck.

7
Carrying On

STRENGTHEN THE HOME FRONT

YOU can't depend on them getting home to meals on time these days ; and when they're tired after hard work, their appetites need tempting. That's when OXO comes in so well for family cooking—it gives that extra flavour and richness.

OXO CUBE

OXO

MAKES MEATIER MEALS

We had settled down to war, accepting it almost like a game of chess. 1941, 1942; they were years in which the political strands of earlier eras – frustrated hopes, careless peace-treaties, wilful blindness – now stood out like boulders in a river. Men were moved about like counters; armies slid out from northern ports in long, grey convoys; trains pulled up in country-sidings, their blinds drawn and their corridors filled with sprawling, sleep-swollen men separated by kit-bags. Signposts lost their markings, the black painted names of villages rubbed out like casualties. Rubbish dumps increased; awkward piles of scrap-iron sprouted in a countryside increasingly barbed-wired. Strange white cones, like stone flowers, were planted in fields to stop enemy tanks from passing. Aerodromes like beehives hummed at night and were almost unfindable by day. On clear days, during 'office-hours', war was as unreal as faded photographs. It was fictional; a mass-fantasy shared through news bulletins and over cups of tea; through almost mythical fire-watching and bomb stories; through the faceless, uniformed figures seen unhappily in towns, searching for Y.M.C.A's and some violent but human contact for their raw bodies. Then at dusk, with the lines of bombers throbbing overhead, the occasional heart-stabbing sirens, the nerves of reality, like nerves in teeth, re-asserted the ache of their existence.

Daily the newspapers flung out their headlines – frantic arms, like those of wounded men, clamouring for recognition. Yet, despite moments of heroic indulgence, the patterns of life were strangely unemotional, strangely unresponsive to drama. Or so it seems now. The whole sequence of events, like a convoy moving in echelon, seemed pre-ordained to an inevitable destination. No one knew how long it might take, nor where the port of arrival might be. But everything seemed of a piece, society, the war, ourselves, confined within mutual limits on which we were all dependent.

Certain events, nonetheless, acted as arbitrary time-divisions – work-men's lanterns in the long tunnel through which we raced at moments, dragged interminably at others. Pearl Harbor; The Battle of the Atlantic; El Alamein; the sinking of the *Graf Spee* and the *Bismarck*. Now in strict chronology their dates no longer matter. They have come to be human symbols on which we rely, by which to a greater or less degree we were affected.

The Americans arrived in London, bringing with them much of a crude vitality that was generously if unsubtly expended on all manner of things. They brought with them Times Square and Broadway; West Point attributes and Hollywood habits; money and accents and chewing-gum and hats like up-turned chambers. They left the discarded safeguards of sex like pricked children's balloons in piles round Shaftesbury Avenue and Green Park; they failed to hold their liquor and London became fertile with oases of sad-faced enlisted negroes wandering up Piccadilly and the Charing Cross Road. But, all in all, the Americans brought a feeling of solidity, a coarse, numerical conceit, which expressive as it was of military power, was almost wholly agreeable. We reached, with their arrival and appropriation of artificial London life, what came to be called 'the end of the beginning'.

Alan Ross

The blackout still created a different world at night.

BLACKOUT

Walking the dark this night might be anywhere,
Anywhere, that is, where the war is here:
The searchlights prying on the loves of clouds
Like constables, the guns waiting to hiccough,
The tea-drinking basements waiting for the All-Clear.

Some waiting but not hating,
Some hating and anticipating,
Fearing and perhaps jeering,
Or drinking without thinking,
Or in blankets shrinking,
Or with crisp confident walking
And subdued talking;
In dressing-gown complaining
On flags in farmyard kitchen
Under flitch of bacon;
Firewatching with eyes straining
On the inflammable, oh so wooden wharf,
Or under trees three-quarters stripped of leaf
By gun-site, or at warden's post,
Or glued to earphones on the humming coast.

Starlight, lovers under ivy wall, I saw,
Whispering, it might be so, *Io t'amo*,
Ich liebe dich, as well as I love you.

The mind rocks softly on its pedestal
Like dusty chalk-eyed Roman emperor.

What time is it, please, and what are we doing where?

I might be myself or, if I am not here,
That man's or my own fair murderer.

Kenneth Allott

Although the blitz was over, there was still no light at the end of the tunnel.

from THE HEAT OF THE DAY

That autumn of 1940 was to appear, by two autumns later, apocryphal, more far away than peace. No planetary round was to bring again that particular conjunction of life and death; that particular psychic London was to be gone for ever; more bombs would fall, but not on the same city. War moved from the horizon to the map. And it was now, when you no longer saw, heard, smelled war, that a deadening acclimatization to it began to set in. The first generation of ruins, cleaned up, shored up, began to weather – in daylight they took their places as a norm of the scene; the dangerless nights of September two years later blotted them out. It was from this new insidious echoless propriety of ruins that you breathed in all that was most malarial. Reverses, losses, deadlocks now almost unnoticed bred one another; every day the news hammered one more nail into a consciousness which no longer re-sounded. Everywhere hung the heaviness of the even worse you could not be told and could not desire to hear. This was the lightless middle of the tunnel. Faith came down to a slogan, desperately re-worded to catch the eye, requiring to be pasted each time more strikingly on to hoardings and bases of monuments . . . No, no virtue was to be found in the outward order of things: happy those who could draw from some inner source.

Elizabeth Bowen

Unfortunately, there was a black market and war profiteering displayed at the big hotels and restaurants.

THE PASSIONATE PROFITEER TO HIS LOVE
[*After Christopher Marlowe*]

Come feed with me and be my love,
And pleasures of the table prove,
Where *Prunier* and *The Ivy* yield
Choice dainties of the stream and field.

At *Claridge* thou shalt duckling eat,
Sip vintages both dry and sweet,
And thou shalt squeeze between thy lips
Asparagus with buttered tips.

On caviare my love shall graze,
And plump on salmon mayonnaise,
And browse at *Scott's* beside thy swain
On lobster Newburg with champagne.

Between hors d'œuvres and canapés
I'll feast thee on *poularde soufflé*
And every day within thy reach
Pile melon, nectarine and peach.

Come share at the *Savoy* with me
The menu of austerity;
If in these pastures thou wouldst rove
Then feed with me and be my love.

Sagittarius

THE MILLLIONAIRE
A man went out
With a million pounds
Bought a virginity,
Ten reputations,
Truth (by the column),
And the O.B.E.
God's indulgence,
Poet's immortality,
His best friend's wife.
Glimpses round a table of
The after-life.

Virility,
Big cigars,
Motor-cars,
A chinese vase
And every other thing
That money buys –
A pain in the belly,
Hammers in the head.
Fear of getting hurt,
Fear of being dead.
Fear of going bust,
Fear of going crazy,
Fear of being dead
And
Fear of being dead.

Jack Beeching

Taking the train was no picnic for civilians nor for soldiers on their necessary journeys.

THE TRAIN

There is no joy upon this train.
The lavatory is out of order.
Do not spit. The corridor is guarded
By a warder.
Why? It's requisite.
Anything desired is strictly guarded
And forbidden.
Love is hidden
In the luggage-van.
No man
Must sit too long, nor stand too long,
Nor lose his ticket.
(If his ticket is not seen
By every one of ten collectors
Once an hour, the man is shot.
There are a lot
Of bodies in the furnace –
They dispose them there.)
You may not sleep –

221

It indicates desire to dream;
Nor may you weep –
It shows desire for better things.
There must be no wings
Desired nor thought upon.
This train will take their place. Get on.

J. B. Pick

STEEL CATHEDRALS

It seems to me, I spend my life in stations.
Going, coming, standing, waiting.
Paddington, Darlington, Shrewsbury, York.
I know them all most bitterly.
Dawn stations, with a steel light, and waxen figures.
Dust, stone, and clanking sounds, hiss of weary steam.
Night stations, shaded light, fading pools of colour.
Shadows and the shuffling of a million feet.
Khaki, blue, and bulky kitbags, rifles gleaming dull.
Metal sound of army boots, and smoker's coughs.
Titter of harlots in their silver foxes.
Cases, casks, and coffins, clanging of the trolleys.
Tea urns tarnished, and the greasy white of cups.
Dry buns, Woodbines, Picture Post and Penguins:
and the blaze of magazines.
Grinding sound of trains, and rattle of the platform gates.
Running feet and sudden shouts, clink of glasses from the buffet.
Smell of drains, tar, fish and chips and sweaty scent, honk of taxis;
and the gleam of cigarettes.
Iron pillars, cupolas of glass, girders messed by pigeons;
the lazy singing of a drunk.
Sailors going to Chatham, soldiers going to Crewe.
Arching bulk of kit and packs, tin hats swinging.
The station clock with staggering hands and callous face,
says twenty-five-to-nine.
A cigarette, a cup of tea, a bun,
and my train goes at ten.

D. Van Den Bogaerde (*Dirk Bogarde*)

Even those wearing a uniform found the middle of the war a wearing time.

THE MIDDLE OF A WAR

My photograph already looks historic.
The promising youthful face, the matelot's collar,
Say 'This one is remembered for a lyric.
His place and period – nothing could be duller.'

Its position is already indicated –
The son or brother in the album; pained
The expression and the garments dated,
His fate so obviously preordained.

The original turns away: as horrible thoughts,
Loud fluttering aircraft slope above his head
At dusk. The ridiculous empires break like biscuits.
Ah, life has been abandoned by the boats –
Only the trodden island and the dead
Remain, and the once inestimable caskets.

Roy Fuller

Leaves were always short; death remote, but always present.

A BALLAD OF 1941

Two lovers walked down a Tooting street
To the three-roomed flat at the Radio Store,
'Have you got the key to the door, my sweet?'
Then up the stairs to the Second Floor.
Put up the black-out, switch on the light,
Pop goes the gas-fire's cosy glow.
Shut out the hum and the noise of the night,
The chatter of life in the streets below.

The wail of a bus as it changes gear,
The smell and the cries of the fading light,
The raucous song of men on the beer
All, all are gone, and we have tonight.

And the man who is weary of marching days
Lists to the music the great bed makes,
'Forget your dull drab khaki ways,
Sleep the sweet sleep from which no man wakes.'

The faint aroma of coffee flows
Like tropical musk from the kitchen door
A match is struck – a cigarette glows –
The shadows dart across the floor.

Outside the wind and the raindrops beat
And the pitter-patter of hurrying feet.

'Press your lips close to mine, my love,
Hold my fair form till I cannot breathe
Take my body and soul, O God, above,
This passionate fire, all, all I give.'

'Your soft nude life beside me lies –
You flame of desire, you draw me on.
O sweet, your eyes are like starlit skies,
Your breasts are the hills of Avilion.

'Tonight is ours, all ours to take.
These are the days of eternity,
Tomorrow we kiss and our hearts will break
In the first grey light when the shadows flee.'

The tired man slept and the night grew old,
But the dark-eyed girl saw the break of dawn –
Saw endless days that were wan and cold,
And the dull ache grew in the coming morn.

Thoughts of the devils who make the wars,
Who strum the music of flaming steel.
And force their slaves to their bloody cause
Till the dead and dying the cities seal –

– Till the daylight fades in the lurid sky
And the night dew bathes the rotting dead.
'What does it matter, we all must die,
In a blood-stained field or a quiet bed.'

No, no, dear God, that cannot be,
Surely you cannot stand aside
And see the world in agony;
Or do the stars your laughter hide?'

The great sun rose like a ball of gold
And the sleeper moaned, 'My love has gone.
The endless days are wan and cold.
Dear one, did I dream of Avilion?'

The milkman's cry in the drowsy street,
The postman's knock, the *Daily Mail*,
The last few hours of bittersweet,
Tomorrow the draft – and the troopships sail.

You fools of men – how fair the earth,
– Of gods I have dreamed, and Paradise –
Surely the devil gave you birth,
The spawn of all evil, creator of lies.

Francis Gelder

THINKING OF WAR

If I must die, forget these hands of mine
That touched your body into tiny flames:
Forget our faith, our strength, and each least sign
– The whispered wonder of our own two names
And all great words we said: how love was true
And seemed immortal. O, forget, my love,
That there was one on earth who worshipped you
And only for your sake desired to live.
I shall forget. As if I never lived
Will be the hours we had, the years we missed,
And your grief too. These hands that have so loved
Will be dumb then as hands you never kissed,
And all my body will not know your name.
I shall have broken our faith: do you the same.

John Jarmain

Appreciation of the arts flourished during the war, as Stephen Spender noticed.

from WORLD WITHIN WORLD

. . . There was a revival of interest in the arts. This arose spontaneously and simply, because people felt that music, the ballet, poetry and painting were concerned with a seriousness of living and dying with which they themselves had suddenly been confronted. The audiences at the midday concerts of the National Gallery, or at the recitals of music and ballet in provincial towns and at factories, sat with a rapt attention as though they were listening for some message from the artist, who, though perhaps he had lived in other times, was close to the same realities as themselves – and to the pressing need to affirm faith and joy within them. There was something deeply touching about this interest in the arts; it was one of the few things which can still make me regret the war.

The affirmation of these timeless qualities was the only answer of human personality to war. In a word, it was – survival. It answered that side of humanity which had produced the war with the in-destructibility of this other side – human love.

The cinema and the newsreel brought close the pictures of the war.

THE NEWS-REEL

Since Munich, what? A tangle of black film
Squirming like bait upon the floor of my mind.
And scissors clicking daily. I am inclined
To pick these pictures now but will hold back
Till memory has elicited from this blind
Drama its threads of vision, the intrusions
Of value upon fact, that sudden unconfined
Wind of understanding that blew out
From people's hands and faces, undesigned
Evidence of design, that change of climate
Which did not last but happens often enough
To give us hope that fact is a façade
And that there is an organism behind
Its brittle littleness, a rhythm and a meaning,
Something half-conjectured and half-divined,
Something to give way to and so find.

Louis MacNeice

NEWS-REEL OF EMBARKATION

Where are you going to, laughing men?
    For a holiday on the sea?
Laughing, smiling, wonderful men,
    Why won't you wait for me?

God, how I love you, men of my race,
    As you smile on your way to a war.
How can you do it, wonderful face,
    Do you not know what's before?

Laugh, laugh, you soldier sons,
    Joke on your way to the war,
For your mothers won't laugh at the sound of
        the guns
    And the tales of the filth and the gore.

Smile and joke, young sailor Jack,
    For it's the same old story.
There'll be no jokes when you come back,
    And bloody little glory.

                                Timothy Corsellis

THIS IS MERELY PART OF THE STUDIO TOUR

On Stage Seven we are shooting an historical epic,
And today we are taking angle shots of the Four Horsemen,
Who are somewhere in the background of every scene,
Four fine old actors hired through Central Casting,
Only one has grown fat, the others are very lean.

The stars of the picture are scattered about the set:
That one with the pout is the villain, this one dies in Reel Four,
That girl is fine in portrayals of outraged honour.
No one is ever sure whom she plays, and yet at her appearance
The audience cheers, and critics heap praise upon her.

The Assistant Directors have finished their shouts of 'Quiet!'
The stand-ins have ended their work beneath the Kliegs,
Now all is ready, and this is the actual take.

Microphones hang from their booms in the best positions
To pick up the thunderous noises the horsemen make.

They are riding a treadmill through manufactured smoke.
It will, on the screen, be a terrifying prospect,
Not recommended for children. Their mothers will protest,
Saying it makes them sweat or scream from their pillows,
Or somehow disturbs their innocent, silly rest.

O, watch those four old character actors, hired
Through Central Casting, one of them fat, three lean.
They perform as though they all were quite inspired,
And yet they all have moved across the screen
For longer than I can remember. They must be very tired.

Harry Brown

PRISONERS' RETURN

Tonight I saw the wounded come ashore . . .
In Liverpool? No, man, the local flicks,
and, sure, saw more
than any at the quay.
The most they'd get was a peep, with shoves and kicks
from other hollering patriots; for me
a ringside seat, red plush, price half a crown –
but, there, never mind me. I was in the last.
I saw some good ones go. I saw some drown
later in peace's smooth, oblivious tide.
And maybe I muddle your future with my past.
Maybe I'm sour and grey . . .
Sure, this, tonight, this got my dull eyes stinging –
those docks like Whitehall, Coronation day,
all jumbled with handkerchiefs, but full of singing
and words without meaning that meant welcome home,
and every tug was hooting welcome home,
and through it all that ship, those curious faces
of shattered, smiling boys.
                              A camera,
we say, is heartless – and this one lent no graces
to a peasant grin or an uncouth, graceless hand,
or some it startled as from a reverie

in the pit where agonies are.
Heartless – but there was one marvel it did not hide;
the involuntary eyes towards their land
like dreamers to an unequivocal star.

On shore, a general and a microphone.
They listened from the ship. They lined her side.
He read his speech. 'The motherland,' he read,
'will care for you.'
Then there they came, the limbless and the blind,
the helped and the helpful, and the crutches clumsily new.
Ay, there they came, the undemonstrative few,
the stretcher cases with bandaged, rigid head
(or Dunkirk relics or left by a Libyan car-track
and left for dying or dead).
Then bland reporters came
with 'who's from old Scotland?' and 'well, lad, let's have your
          name'
and 'you were in France – just where?' They answered 'Arras'
or 'Cambrai' or 'Saint Omer'.
                              Not much to follow –
more waving – an infant kissed – a train receding
to a song of their own and (how these things are changeless)
the song was triumphant German, anglicised,
just as we used to do. And that was the end . . .
But not quite the end for me . . . Through the last notes, fading,
I heard gaunt voices singing in the Strand
and I saw a dishonoured uniform, that cloth
of the glazed, ex-Service blue, their medals too
and the flag of the cap-in-hand.
And there, beyond,
was a pavement-piano in Trafalgar Square
with 'Arras' chalked up and 'Cambrai', each with the date
when those dots on a foreign map grew suddenly great
with our wooden crosses, and when I was there.

So you call this retrogressive? old? not fair
to plans, unsentimentally profound?
Well, you may be right; that audience tonight
assuredly said so; for their money talked.
(Oh – after the film a Red Cross box went round
to a jingling profusion of uncounted coins
and each coin seemed a shining resolution

to do the thing well this time.)
                                    But I was thinking:
ten years from now were the better time to see
this fragment from the desolate heaps of war.
Ah! then it would be a probe – how deeply sinking
through how much obliterating moss, before
it struck the embedded stone, that brave, first stone
on which a templed peace was planned to be . . .?

So at the last I am frank and will not own
I am blinded by bitterness. Come ten years later –
my friend, come then and say: this bitterness
was blind. And say your plans were greater
than all the powers of forgetfulness.
Come ten years later. Say you have found redress
for the wreck of the world and for wrecks of wounded men;
and humbly I shall listen to you then.

James Monahan

*Writers such as H. E. Bates under the pseudonym of Flying Officer X
and artists such as Paul Nash were engaged by the Air Ministry in order
to create stories and pictures. Nash had always dreamed of flying as a
child and painted the ultimate picture of the Battle of Britain, the dead
sea of wrecked German aeroplanes,* Totes Meer.

from *AERIAL FLOWERS*

When the War came, suddenly the sky was upon us all like a huge
hawk hovering, threatening. Everyone was searching the sky expecting
some terror to fall; I among them scanned the low clouds or tried to
penetrate the depth of the blue. I was hunting the sky for what I most
dreaded in my own imagining. It was a white flower. Ever since the
Spanish war the idea of the *rose of death*, the name the Spaniards gave
to the parachute, had haunted my mind so that when war overtook us
I strained my eyes always to see that dreadful miracle of the sky
blossoming with these floating flowers. The first picture I made of the
War was a collage of the Rose of Death. But it was not on the score of
this prophetic fantasia that I was later, considerably to my surprise,
appointed official artist to the Air Ministry . . . I was quickly involved
in the Battle of Britain. What fascinated me particularly were the
incongruous disasters befalling the Luftwaffe aircraft day by day;

crashing into the cornfield or tearing up the seashore, burning themselves away in the summer coverts, disturbing the pheasants, and so
on. Most of my first pictures recorded these happy disasters. I selected
them first because they interested me acutely, and also for their
propaganda value as images encouraging for our people and depressing
for the enemy. But my employers did not look at it that way. I was
made to feel that to make a picture of the wreck of an enemy machine
on the ground was rather like shooting at a sitting bird. In the slang of
the moment, they took a poor view of it. But they were better pleased
when I began to depict aeroplanes in flight, but again there was
something not right. The fact was I had again approached the machine
from the wrong standpoint. Without a number of illustrations at hand
it is useless to dilate; my record of *Aerial Creatures* will, I hope, some
day speak for itself. It is enough to say that what appealed to me were
the diverse, distinct personalities of these enchanting monsters, a point
of view I soon found support and sympathy for among the airmen
themselves. It was from this aspect I explored them and set down my
impressions, but by the time I left the service of the Air Ministry I
had already encountered the fantastic phenomenon of Totes Meer . . .
Death, about which we are all thinking, death, I believe, is the only
solution to this problem of how to be able to fly. Personally I feel that
if death can give us that, death will be good.

Paul Nash

*Many of the artists went into camouflage and tried to deceive the enemy
about the position of weapons.*

REPRISAL

They worked all night with cardboard and with wood
to make those dummy planes to hoodwink the foe,
and in the chilly morning solitude
wheeled out the dummies to places they should go
on the dispersal fields, and went away;
the hours passed uneventfully, and even
no reconnaissance planes were overhead that day.
They evacuated in the twilight, just after seven,
and when they'd gone the Germans flew above the drome
and by each plane they dropped a wooden bomb.

Herbert Corby

The war made the task of the writer difficult. Its horrors were beyond description, and serving it took away inspiration.

THE NOVELIST

Encased in talent like a uniform
The rank of every poet is well known;
They can amaze us like a thunderstorm,
Or die so young, or live for years alone.

They can dash forward like hussars: but he
Must struggle out of his boyish gift and learn
How to be plain and awkward, how to be
One after whom none think it worth to turn.

For, to achieve his lightest wish, he must
Become the whole of boredom, subject to
Vulgar complaints like love, among the Just

Be just, among the Filthy filthy too,
And in his own weak person, if he can,
Must suffer dully all the wrongs of Man.

W. H. Auden

THE WRITER

The bitter wind that blows against
The windows of my squalid cell
Re-assures me, if need were,
In all this world nothing is well.

The liar with the microphone
The liar with the printer's ink
The vain with their stupid fantasies
Are shouting what they hope they think.

A rustling pendulum of bones
Parades as the traditional spook
But, hung from an observant skull,
It writes its thoughts down in a book.

C. H. Sisson

THE SOLDIER POET

The soldier poet through the mud
Repeats along his curious road
The bygone rhythms of his blood,
Forgets his shoulder's triggered load.

In nice suspension he obeys
Commands with a poetic ring.
(His lighter verse, of late, displays
A somewhat military swing.)

His eyes are crossed, his glance is split;
The metric shell explodes in rhyme.
O ask not where his talents fit,
Or if he's out of step with time,

For he must choose like any man
Who faces flames in a burning Rome:
Train that gunsight if he can,
Or fiddle, if he can, a poem.

Wilfred Gibson

WAR POET

I am the man who looked for peace and found
My own eyes barbed.
I am the man who groped for words and found
An arrow in my hand.
I am the builder whose firm walls surround
A slipping land.
When I grow sick or mad
Mock me not nor chain me:
When I reach for the wind
Cast me not down:
Though my face is a burnt book
And a wasted town.

Sidney Keyes

TO A FIREMAN-POET

You burn with zeal to fight a fire
Who never had a fire to fight
Save that within, which you aspire
(In vain?) to set and keep alight.

Patric Dickinson

A WRY SMILE

The mess is all asleep, my candle burns.
I hear the rain sharp on the iron roof
And dully on the broad leaves by the window.
Already someone moans, another turns
And, clear and startling, cries 'Tell me the truth.'

The candle throws my shadow on the wall
And gilds my books: tonight I'd like to bring
The poets from their safe and paper beds,
Show them my comrades and the silver pall
Over the airfield, ask them what they'd sing.

Not one of them has had to bear such shame,
Been tortured so constantly by government,
Has had to draw his life out when the age
Made happiness a revolution, fame
Exile, and death the whimsy of a sergeant.

But without envy I remember them,
And without pity look at my condition:
I give myself a wry smile in the mirror
– The poets get a quizzical ahem.
They reflect time, I am the very ticking:

No longer divided – the unhappy echo
Of a great fault in civilization; inadequate,
Perhaps, and sad, but strictly conscious no one
Anywhere can move, nothing occur,
Outside my perfect knowledge or my fate.

Roy Fuller

234

POEM IN 1944

No, I cannot write the poem of war,
Neither the colossal dying nor the local scene,
A platoon asleep and dreaming of girls' warmth
Or by the petrol-cooker scraping out a laughter.
– Only the images that are not even nightmare:
A globe encrusted with a skin of seaweed,
Or razors at the roots. The heart is no man's prism
To cast a frozen shadow down the streaming future:
At most a cold slipstream of empty sorrow,
The grapes and melody of a dreamed love
Or a vague roar of courage.
                                No, I am not
The meeting point of event and vision, where the poem
Bursts into flame, and the heart's engine
Takes on the load of these broken years and lifts it.
I am not even the tongue and the hand that write
The dissolving sweetness of a personal view
Like those who now in greater luck and liberty
Are professionally pitiful or heroic . . .

Into what eye to imagine the vista pouring
Its violent treasures? For I must believe
That somewhere the poet is working who can handle
The flung world and his own heart. To him I say
The little I can. I offer him the debris
Of five years' undirected storm in self and Europe,
And my love. Let him take it for what it's worth
In this poem scarcely made and already forgotten.

Robert Conquest

WAR POET

We in our haste can only see the small components of the scene
We cannot tell what incidents will focus on the final screen.
A barrage of disruptive sound, a petal on a sleeping face,
Both must be noted, both must have their place;
It may be that our later selves or else our unborn sons
Will search for meaning in the dust of long deserted guns,

We only watch, and indicate and make our scribbled pencil
    notes.
We do not wish to moralize, only to ease our dusty throats.

Donald Bain

*Many witnesses feared the effect of propaganda and censorship on the
truth which they were allowed to read in wartime.*

NOVEMBER NEWS: 1941

Now presses print the Winter lies,
Eyes for the blind, for hate must surely bind;
And on the breasts of those who groan
    The medals gleam.

    Lies printed on the Winter leaves
Let fall the germ, hatch where the muscles join,
And by the waters of the lonely weir
    Hang entrails on the wire.

    Love's engine on the bridge of life
Lets fall its spark, implores my heart to speak.
But death is usual, and the smoke of war
    Clings to the cloud.

Peter Yates

PROPAGANDA

Nor shot, nor shell, but the fused word,
That rocks the world to its white root,
Has wrought a chaos in the mind,
And drained the love from the split heart;

Nor shock, nor shower of the sharp blows,
That fall alike from life and death,
But some slow subsidence within,
That sinks a grave for the sapped faith.

R. S. Thomas

'FROM MANY A MANGLED TRUTH A WAR IS WON'

From many a mangled truth a war is won
    And who am I to oppose
    War and the lie and the pose
Asserting a lie is good if a war be won?

From many a mangled truth a war is won
    And many a truth has died
    That has lived undenied
For always there must be loss that a war be won.

From many a mangled truth a war is won
    And when no thought is pure
    Who of us can be sure
Of lie and truth and war when the war is won?

Clifford Dyment

HOMAGE TO OUR LEADERS

These larger-than-life comic characters,
Churchill the moonface moocow chewing
A permanent cigar, Roosevelt the gigantic
False Liberal mask with syrup smile,
Medicine-man Stalin like Aunt Sally at a fair,
All snapping like canvas in the wind . . .

Our world, our time, our murder
Evolved these monsters: who like the allosaurus
Should be remembered as a stupidity
We have outgrown. Now they sprawl across
Hoardings, papers, radios, these simple shapeless demons.
Friend, lock your door at night: watch neighbour and wife,
See that your eyes are hidden behind dark glasses,
Remember that you live by permission of the police.

Julian Symons

Virginia Graham could mock at the necessities of waging war.

MY BONNY

(To be sung to the old tune)

My Bonny is stationed at ▆▆▆
But nobody knows it, you see,
Except all the people of ▆▆▆
And all his relations and me.

The ▆▆▆ he is manning at ▆▆▆
Sticks seventy feet in the air,
But don't tell a soul it's at ▆▆▆
For *nobody* knows it is there.

SWITCH IT OFF!

Any news on the wireless today? . . .

Nothing to speak of, Madam.
Only a few bombs here and there
(they didn't, of course, say exactly where) –
Oh, we've lost some planes in a raid off Crete,
and ten small ships of the Merchant Fleet.
They say there's a billion men in Russia
fighting a billion men from Prussia,
and hundreds are dying like flies in the sand
in Libya and the Holy Land . . .
Thank you, May, so there isn't much news?

Nothing to speak of, Madam.

The headlines were not all in the news.

BEYOND THE HEADLINES

Then I saw the wild geese flying
In fair formation to their bases in Inchicore
And I knew that these wings would outwear the wings of war
And a man's simple thoughts outlive the day's loud lying.
Don't fear, don't fear, I said to my soul.

The Bedlam of Time is an empty bucket rattled,
'Tis you who will say in the end who best battles.
Only they who fly home to God have flown at all.

P. J. Kavanagh

HOMO SAPIENS 1941

Murmuration of engines in the cold caves of air,
And, daring the starlight above the stiff sea of cloud,
Deadly as a falcon brooding over its prey
In a tower of spirit-dazzling and splendid light,
Pedestrian man holds grimly on his way.
Legions of winds, ambushed in crystal corries,
Conspiring to destroy him, and hosts of ice,
Thronging him close, weigh down his delicate wings;
But loud as a drum in his ear the hot blood sings,
And a frenzy of solitude mantles him like a god.

R. S. Thomas

There had to be a new education for those who fought.

THE NEW LEARNING

With hatred now all lips and wings
the human mind does silly things.
Common sense has fled, and reason
is definitely out of season.

In nature class the schoolboy's head
is taught to contemplate, instead
of flower pot and cactus stump,
a budding aluminium dump.

Can God that made the cactus grow
do miracles, he wants to know?
Can He that made the water wine
make Spitfires of a pot and pan?

He knows that, loving human life,
God strongly disapproves of strife

and doesn't care a damn for guns
except if they are British ones.

'The British blockade will bring salvation'
(he's told) 'to every neutral nation.'
So starve them! then, their lands restored,
they'll all be free to praise the Lord.

'You think the Bible's right – it ain't
now that a murderer's a saint.'
The new commandment's "Thou shalt kill
in order to effect God's will".'

And so with tanks for people's toes
the Christian soldier onward goes.

                                    Ian Serraillier

*The experience of the Second World War changed the remembrance of the
First.*

ARMISTICE DAY

I stood with three comrades in Parliament Square
November her freights of grey fire unloading,
No sound from the city upon the pale air
Above us the sea-bell eleven exploding.

Down by the bands and the burning memorial
Beats all the brass in a royal array,
But at our end we are not so sartorial:
Out of (as usual) the rig of the day.

Starry is wearing a split pusser's flannel
Rubbed, as he is, by the regular tide;
Oxo the ducks that he ditched in the Channel
In June, 1940 (when he was inside).

Kitty recalls his abandon-ship station,
Running below at the Old Man's salute
And (with a deck-watch) going down for duration
Wearing his oppoe's pneumonia-suit.

Comrades, for you the black captain of carracks
Writes in Whitehall his appalling decisions,
But as was often the case in the Barracks
Several ratings are not at Divisions.

Into my eyes the stiff sea-horses stare,
Over my head sweeps the sun like a swan.
As I stand alone in Parliament Square
A cold bugle calls, and the city moves on.

Charles Causley

For Kathleen Raine, it was no war for heroes, but for survivors.

HEROES

This war's dead heroes, who has seen them?
They rise, in smoke above the burning city,
Faint clouds, dissolving into sky.

And who, sifting the Libyan sand, can find
The tracery of a human hand,
The faint impression of an absent mind,
The fade-out of a soldier's day dream?

You'll know your love no more, nor his sweet kisses –
He's forgotten you, girl, and in the idle sun
In long green grass that the east wind caresses
The seed of man is ravished by the corn.

GRANTCHESTER – AGAIN

I think that if there is a God
One would realize it at Grantchester;
Old men may talk of youth as pawns
Under the name of man power;
Young men, some with imagination,
May talk of killing and being killed,
And of how much more effective
This method of destruction
May be than that; and all the shame

Of war may be apparent
To violate the peace of summer,
Even in the calm of Grantchester.

The path of man is difficult,
Much water will flow through Grantchester
Before God's way is understood,
For man has very far to go.

C. R. Sanderson

William Soutar described in two poems a war without winners or losers.

THE PERMANENCE OF THE YOUNG MEN

No man outlives the grief of war
Though he outlive its wreck:
Upon the memory a scar
Through all his years will ache.

Hopes will revive when horrors cease;
And dreaming dread be stilled;
But there shall dwell within his peace
A sadness unannulled.

Upon his world shall hang a sign
Which summer cannot hide:
The permanence of the young men
Who are not by his side.

REVELATION

Machines of death from east to west
Drone through the darkened sky:
Machines of death from west to east
Through the same darkness fly.

They pass; and on the foredoomed towns
Loosen their slaughtering load:
They see no faces in the stones:
They hear no cries of blood.

They leave a ruin; and they meet
A ruin on return:
The mourners in the alien street
At their own doorways mourn.

In wartime, there was still the refuge of reading and writing letters.

READING IN WARTIME

Boswell by my bed,
Tolstoy on my table:
Though the world has bled
For four and a half years,
And wives' and mothers' tears
Collected would be able
To water a little field
Untouched by anger and blood,
A penitential yield
Somewhere in the world;
Though in each latitude
Armies like forests fall,
The iniquitous and the good
Head over heels hurled,
And confusion over all:
Boswell's turbulent friend
And his deafening verbal strife,
Ivan Ilych's death
Tell me more about life,
The meaning and the end
Of our familiar breath,
Both being personal,
Than all the carnage can,
Retrieve the shape of man,
Lost and anonymous,
Tell me wherever I look
That not one soul can die
Of this or any clan
Who is not one of us
And has a personal tie
Perhaps to someone now
Searching an ancient book,
 Folk-tale or country song

In many and many a tongue,
To find the original face,
The individual soul,
The eye, the lip, the brow
For ever gone from their place,
And gather an image whole.

Edwin Muir

WAR LETTERS

The letters are shockingly real,
Like the personal belongings
Of someone recently dead.

The letters are permanent,
And written with our hands,
Which crease into their lines

And breathe, but are not so
Living as these letters.
Our hands are seas apart;

A pair might cease to live
While the indestructible letter,
Turned lies, flew to the other.

The letters express a love
We cannot realize:
Like a poignant glove

Surviving a well-known hand,
They can outlast our bodies
And our love transcend.

Roy Fuller

Britain was beginning its counter-attack in Europe, testing the German defences across the Channel.

DIEPPE

19 August, 1942

It started early, the attacking trek
by sea and sky. Early
and quietly, like a well-told lie.

His hair was very crisp and curly.
I ran my fingers through his hair while he expressed his views
on this and that and my new hat and the length of the movie
queues.
Nothing dramatic. And now he's – there. And I tune-in to the
News.

The barge-like boats, packed panting tight,
eat up the narrow strip of water,
and in the sky the grey wings wait
poised on the edge of a well-planned slaughter.

I wait as well and see it right
in my mind's eye.
Then suddenly a white
smoky curtain covers the beach where the forsaken promenade
winds its course,
and men charge up from the sea, hoarse
with excitement, afraid to swallow lest they miss a sound.
Then everywhere
the carefully planned attacks mass in their place
and hundreds, hundreds falling in the race
for shelter from the stuttering guns; falling face-
downwards, just a mile or two of sea between
them and us and all that might have been,
the trampled sand blinding already sightless eyes.

Yet, when all's said and done, who'd have it otherwise?
Not they.
Women wait long enough for paradise
and if it's now – or in a million years –
it makes no odds. Their blood flows, and my tears
If I could shed them.

There's the pips
and the news again of men and planes and ships.
But I already know, and feel my lips
grow cold and my heart a hot, hard ball
wedged in my throat. I knew they could not all
come back.

Joyce Rowe

The war progressed towards a victory in Europe.

from THE HEAT OF THE DAY

1942, still with no Second Front, ran out: nothing more than a sort of grinding change of gear for the up-grade was to be felt till the next war year steadied into its course. Cryptic were new 1943 block calendars. February, the Germans capitulated at Stalingrad; March, the 8th Army broke through the Mareth Line. North African spring teemed with pursuits and astronomic surrenders, with a victoriousness hard, still, not to associate with the enemy. July, the Sicilian landings; the Russian opening of their great leafy Orel summer drive. Mussolini out. September, Italians out, but leaving Italy to it. Landings, beach-heads, Russian tanks lurching across the screens in London; November, Italian rivers, however, being crossed by us in strength. Winter known to have come by the Germans having their winter line shattered. Mussolini back. Pictures, less to be relished than had been hoped, of Berlin learning how it had been for London. The Big Three photo-graphed smiling at Teheran. The idea of the European Fortress. The day after Christmas we sank the *Scharnhorst*, and upon the Russians having advanced up to sixty miles in five days in the Kiev salient, at the same time widening a breach to a front of a hundred and eighty miles, 1943 expired.

War's being global meant it ran off the edges of maps; it was uncontainable. What was being done, for instance, against the Japanese was heard of but never grasped in London. There were too many theatres of war.

1944 was the year in which there could not but be the Second Front. General Smuts called it the Year of Destiny; the bombers continued to carry on preparatory work. As early as January we broke the Gustav line; the Russians announced the lifting of the blockade of Leningrad. February, in Italy we encircled ten enemy divisions, but the Germans opened up against Anzio beach-head, which held. The

246

wiping-out of Monte Cassino caused an uncertain breath to be drawn in cinemas: all this was going to be necessary, and more. Reflections were cut short by the renewal of air attacks on London – a five-night February season to be known as the Little Blitz.

Elizabeth Bowen

When D-Day came and the Allies crossed to France, the long seasons of waiting were over.

CALENDAR SONG

The apples I ate in Bedfordshire
   mocked me with red from Alamein
and yellow from sand and the sun that's there
   and green from the wounds in Englishmen.

The leaves that tumbled on Somerset
   like parachutists from a war
brushed down my khaki battle-suit
   shaming my millions everywhere.

The big bare trees in St. James's Park
   stretched out their arms like camouflage
and ducks came down like Sunderlands
   and kids pushed off in a landing barge.

I lay by daffodils in Kent
   while men in steel drove up the sky
to toss the earth at an enemy point
   and my colonel said leisurely, by and by.

But O, when they woke me up in June
   and told all thumbs to touch the news
I heard my boats grind into France
   and the prisoning seasons let me loose.

Arnold Rattenbury

The women on the home front had to adapt to survive the war.

IN THESE FIVE YEARS

In these five years
we grew,
out of the mire of ease,
into the rhythm of reality;
we came alive,
and part of this new world,
in which the fact of life and death
discarded frill and fantasy.
We saw our lovers,
and our brothers go to war,
heard their defeats with fear,
their gains with adulation,
but outside the circle of their lives,
the whole was lost
to the small infinities of our minds.

So the years have wandered,
winding us into the pattern,
until we learnt the meaning
of our life and theirs.
The anchor of our homes
lie far behind,
we are, as we can make ourselves,
without surrounding prejudice.

To be a woman now
it is expected that you live
like men,
and work like men,
yet struggle always to remain
fundamentally feminine.
But in our new born hearts,
has grown the urge to act
in equal part of fight and fear,
we want no time to weep,
only the wasted hours bring despair.

And we have learnt
submission,

to have our lives laid out
not by personality,
but by position,
with undefeated soul
we have our minds,
and they are still ours
to control.

Out of the chrysalis we came,
young and foolish,
eager undecided,
if we have hardened,
fought to brush aside
the heartache and the fear,
should we be blamed?
learning endurance even men have changed,
and these five years have been strong stuff
to give these women.

Daphne Nixon

Already people began to plan for the peace, for a new society based on the comradeship of war.

THE TWO PULLS

I

They were reared to adore the snug limit –
door closed on the world, and family-awe,
kitchenglow, bedroom's tepid climate,
Father's word as law.

Through years of school or work they've striven
to keep the burrowing fear entire.
The world by the money-storm is driven;
shelter of home is their deepest desire.

And now the facade has fallen away
maimed in a blitz; and the draggled fragments
of that doomed life obtrude on the day
pathetic shards of a privacy shamed.

But they want to get back to that street, the same one,
rebuilt perhaps with a few more conveniences;
Civvy Street lights in their hearts that flame,
moated parlour, no-trespassing fences.

That is the dream which slumbers unstirred
by ABCA post-war reconstructions,
or the Platoon Red's goading words:
One letter from home explodes all abstractions.

Yes, admit it. They are certainly shy-birds.
It's not that they're obstinate – not that only.
Not that they're stupid, cynical, tamed,
fed far too long on the fake and the phoney.

II

Great changes do not come as blueprints, though
blueprints are born of them; but first as fissures
they come, as turmoil, dreamtangle, and slow
evacuation of untenable positions.

The basic conflict wrestles out of sight,
in terms long hid from workaday consciousness.
'Bill's papership's gone broke, it isn't right.'
Small angers accumulate, and large distress.

So here. New ways of life beget new habits.
Not only resistance springs from army-ways.
In this communal life new potences
are veining out, to bridge the abrupt gap.

Jokes weld it, jokes against it. In the laughter
new bonds are warmly struck. It first appears
in mess-room, sleeping-hut, in common fears
and hopes. It is completed some time after.

The sense of a different union at last coheres
in anger that can kill. Terror shakes it,
fails and finally forms it. Life is good
in that murderous circle of brotherhood.

Jack Lindsay

WAR AIMS: PLANNING

Plan me a merry-go-round in a great big roaring
    Blackpool;
plan me a seat between a harlot's breasts;
plan me a million pounds or a dinner at the Ivy,
plan me a Chilprufe for my vests.

Plan me everything I saw to-day in Selfridge's;
plan me that politician's ninety horse-power car;
plan me a shooting box in Argyllshire or Banff;
plan me a six-foot cigar.

Plan me six nights with the girl in the kiosk,
plan me a blind with a row of smutty jokes;
plan me some lime water ready for the morning;
but not, please, not another international hoax!

John Atkins

MY WORK

To break new ground
To take small weak dark seeds
Out from unfertile sand
Then to throw them
Proudly at the sun.

To put dignity into a question
And simplicity into a song;
To take plain, common, ordinary men
And give them the power,
To see themselves Kings.

To sing on –
Until the world is Blackpool
In August
In the afternoon.

Paul Potts

*The Beveridge Report, which sold more than half a million copies,
promised a welfare state in post-war Britain.*

from a SPEECH BY SIR WILLIAM BEVERIDGE

'Social Insurance and the Allied Services'

The first principle is that any proposals for the future, while they
should use to the full the experience gathered in the past, should not
be restricted by consideration of sectional interests established in the
obtaining of that experience ... A revolutionary moment in the
world's history is time for revolutions, not for patching.

The second principle is that organization of social insurance should
be treated as one part only of a comprehensive policy of social
progress. Social insurance fully developed may provide income security; it is an attack upon Want. But Want is one only of five giants on
the road of reconstruction and in some ways the easiest to attack. The
others are Disease, Ignorance, Squalor and Idleness.

The third principle is that social security must be achieved by co-
operation between the state and the individual. The state should offer
security for service and contribution. The state in organizing security
should not stifle incentive, opportunity, responsibility; in establishing
a national minimum, it should leave room and encouragement for
voluntary action by each individual to provide more than that minimum
for himself and his family.

*Nobody wanted a repetition of the failure of reconstruction after the First
World War.*

WILL IT BE SO AGAIN?

Will it be so again
That the brave, the gifted are lost from view,
And empty, scheming men
Are left in peace their lunatic age to renew?
Will it be so again?

Must it be always so
That the best are chosen to fall and sleep
Like seeds, and we too slow
In claiming the earth they quicken, and the old usurpers reap
What they could not sow?

Will it be so again –
The jungle code and the hypocrite gesture?
A poppy wreath for the slain
And a cut-throat world for the living? that stale imposture
Played on us once again?

Will it be as before –
Peace, with no heart or mind to ensue it,
Guttering down to war
Like a libertine to his grave? We should not be surprised: we
    knew it
Happen before.

Shall it be so again?
Call not upon the glorious dead
To be your witnesses then.
The living alone can nail to their promise the ones who said
It shall not be so again.

Cecil Day Lewis

8

A Terrible Victory

THE SIGN

The flying bombs, the V.1.s and the V.2.s, were Hitler's retribution for the invasion of France.

from WESTMINSTER IN WAR

Flying-bombs were particularly disliked for their automatic nature, their unpleasant unreality. It was difficult to imagine a machine flying by itself, it was easier to picture a kind of grim steel automatic pilot cast in the shape of a man, flying straight, freeing the last control with a sightless jerk of his arm. Such nightmares came easily to a people removed from centuries of superstition by only a few years. The new things were supernatural. The idea of a grey-clad pilot with Nazi-blond hair seemed almost affectionate in comparison. But in addition to such a concrete vision, a curious psychological situation evolved – for this was the first time in their lives that people had been faced with a *purely arbitrary fate*. Hitherto, every bombardment might at least be thought to have had a target, a direction: and there had always been contrary devices to deflect the attack. But here in these first days (and this feeling was to develop further with the Long-Range Rocket) the sound of a flying-bomb approached like a straight line, so that every-body in the half-circle of its fanning-forward sound attached the bomb to themselves and knew that without any particular reason it could drop at any time and any place. It could drop anywhere. It was absolutely reasonless, the first purely fatal agent that had come to man for centuries, tempting him to cross his fingers again, bringing a rebirth of superstition.

Lastly, in more material mind, the people saw this as destruction at its most wanton. Now they could see no possible excuse of military targets. Homes, women, children and old people were openly the slaughter-toys of the German. So a grim fury was generated that to an extent must have recuperated the shocked spirits of a people who now, after all they had suffered, were faced with renewed and fiercer attack, with a Secret Weapon (the war of nerves was not altogether unsuccess-ful) and an unpredictable future. There was always, too, the thought to sustain the spirit of the land battles in France. People thought that even though this was bad, there was worse being endured over the other side.

William Sansom

DURING A BOMBARDMENT BY V-WEAPONS

The little noises of the house:
Drippings between the slates and ceiling;
From the electric fire's cooling,
Tickings; the dry feet of a mouse:

These at the ending of a war
Have power to alarm me more
Than the ridiculous detonations
Outside the gently coughing curtains.

And, love, I see your pallor bears
A far more pointed threat than steel.
Now all the permanent and real
Furies are settling in upstairs.

Roy Fuller

When his friend the poet Julian Orde died, David Wright remembered the London summer of the flying bombs.

ON A FRIEND DYING

I should speak in the past tense
But do not, for it seems
What was has an existence,
If only of images.

Remains a scene as still
As water, as fragile,
Floating a ghostly
Reflection. Immobile

Summer of long late-lit
Evenings in a dingy street.
A swung glow of the Marquis
Door seen from Rathbone Place.

And there remains a large room full of flowers
    Imaged on canvases, the real ones still in the garden,
And books and objects I've known for thirty years.
    Unknown to me I am taking a final leave of them.

And the woman no longer young but more beautiful
    Than the young girl had been, who held all these
            together.
Yet that web woven over so long shall not unravel,
    Though the lives and bonds disperse like the furniture

To dissociation. Eternity, when one thinks of it,
    Exists in what has been, there residing.
In what's done and can't be changed is immortality,
    Though I may not be long remembering.

The summer of pilotless planes,
Of searchlit nights and soft,
When once upon a scare
Together we ran out

Into the naked garden
High over Archway, and
The warm leaves of laurel
Trembled in no wind.

Larger in death, mythical, those figures,
Yankel Adler, David Archer, Colquhoun and MacBryde;
Not failed gods, because our gods were failures
Standing in broken shoes with half-pints of Scotch ale.
Now would I say that it is nine o'clock at the Wheatsheaf,
That it will not be long before the place is full.

Who was it who said
Friends are born, not made?

I remember, as now
You no longer do,

The recognition
Across a long room;

After the eyes met
Was articulate

Before we had spoken
What had always been.

William Plomer treated the German attack with his usual witty elegance.

THE FLYING BUM: 1944

In the vegetarian guest-house
All was frolic, feast and fun,
Eager voices were enquiring
'Are the nettle cutlets done?'
Peals of vegetarian laughter,
Husky wholesome wholemeal bread,
Will the evening finish with a
Rush of cocoa to the head?

Yes, you've guessed; it's Minnie's birthday,
Hence the frolic, hence the feast.
Are there calories in custard?
There are vitamins in yeast.
Kate is here and Tom her hubby,
Ex-commissioner for oaths,
She is mad on Christian Science,
Parsnip flan he simply loathes.

And Mr Croaker, call him Arthur,
Such a keen philatelist,
Making sheep's-eyes at Louisa
(After dinner there'll be whist) –
Come, sit down, the soup is coming,
All of docks and darnels made,
Drinks a health to dear old Minnie
In synthetic lemonade.

Dentures champing juicy lettuce,
Champing macerated bran,
Oh the imitation rissoles!
Oh the food untouched by man!
Look, an imitation sausage
Made of monkey-nuts and spice,
Prunes tonight and semolina,
Wrinkled prunes, unpolished rice.

Yards of guts absorbing jellies,
Bellies filling up with nuts,
Carbohydrates jostling proteins

Out of intestinal ruts;
Peristalsis calls for roughage,
Haulms and fibres, husks and grit,
Nature's way to open bowels,
Maybe – let them practise it.

'Hark, I hear an air-raid warning!'
'Take no notice, let 'em come.'
'Who'll say grace?' 'Another walnut?'
'Listen, what's that distant hum?'
'Bomb or no bomb,' stated Minnie,
'Lips unsoiled by beef or beer
We shall use to greet our Maker
When he sounds the Great All-Clear.'

When the flying bomb exploded
Minnie's wig flew off her pate,
Half a curtain, like a tippet,
Wrapped itself round bony Kate,
Plaster landed on Louisa,
Tom fell headlong on the floor,
And a spurt of lukewarm custard
Lathered Mr Croaker's jaw.

All were spared by glass and splinters
But, the loud explosion past,
Greater was the shock impending
Even than the shock of blast –
Blast we veterans know as freakish
Gave this feast its final course,
Planted bang upon the table
A lightly roasted rump of horse.

Elizabeth Bowen found that the extensive blast had led to a new form of house decorating.

CALICO WINDOWS

Calico windows are something new – in a summer bare of fashions, 'crazes' or toys. They pitch home life in a hitherto unknown mood. In the theatrical sense, they rank as 'effects' of the first order. They cast on your ceiling, if you have a ceiling left, a blind white light, at once dull and dazzling, so that your waking thought every morning continues to be, 'Why, it must have snowed!' They lighten and darken slowly: inside calico windows it might be any time of year, any time of day. Through their panes you hear, with unexpected distinctness, steps, voices and the orchestration of traffic from the unseen outside world. (Talkers outside a calico window should be discreet.) Glass lets in light and keeps out sound; calico keeps out (most) light and lets sound in. The inside of your house, stripped of rugs, cushions and curtains, reverberates.

Few of these new-fashion windows are made to open: you cannot have everything. However, the sashes of those that do fly up with ghostly lightness, almost before you touch, showing you summer still outside.

This cotton and cardboard 1944 summer home, inside the shell of the old home, is fascinating. With what magic rapidity was it improvised and tacked together by the kind workman. The blast of the buzz bomb marked the end of the former phase. The dreamlike next phase began with the arrival of workmen. As though just hatched, or dropped from the skies, these swarmed in their dozens in your street. Soon they had disappeared, without trouble, inside the blasted-open front doors – yours having its share. So many and so alike were the workmen that, still dazed, you failed to distinguish one from the other, and only attempted to guess their number when it came to finding cups for their tea. They were at it almost before you knew they were there – smashing out what was left of glass, smashing down what was left of plaster, wrenching out sagging frames and disjointed doors. The noise they made at their beginning, if just less, was more protracted than that of the explosion. But nothing makes you feel calmer than being taken in hand.

Coughing in the fog of dust they had raised, scrunching over chips of glass on the floors, the workmen, godlike, proceeded towards their next stage, that of sweeping, hauling, measuring, hammering. Only just pausing, they listened patronizingly to other buzz bombs passing across the sky: you knew nothing more could happen while they were with you. To watch them filled your post-blast blankness; to watch them made you feel you were doing something yourself; and to know that *you* were not paying them was most heartening.

The calico for the windows arrived in bales, along with the felt and boarding. Workmen carrying these in wove their way between workmen carrying rubble out. The rubble was tipped from baskets on to a mounting mountain outside your doors; and the mountain was by-passed by still more workmen with tarpaulins with which to drape your roof – these last disappeared upstairs and, for all you knew, never came down again.

The whole scene was one of rhythm and, soon, of order. Watching the bold creation shape itself, you exclaimed, 'Of course, of course!' The light new window-frames, primitive as a child's drawing, which have been constructed out on the pavement, are now fitted into the old windows. The outside world disappears. The workmen's are the first faces you see in this to-be-familiar calico light. You have now been tied up, sealed up, inside a tense white parcel. The workmen see it is good. They go.

You are left alone with your new sensations. The extraordinary is only at the beginning of its long reign. So many footprints are in the dust that you lose track of your own; you lose track of yourself, and you do not care. The peace of absolute dislocation from everything you have been and done settles down. The old plan for living has been erased, and you do not miss it. Solicitous for the safety of your belongings, the considerate workmen have hidden everything: the lamps are in the hat-cupboard; the telephone has been rolled up inside a mattress; your place in the book you were reading when the bomb went off has been religiously marked with a leg that blew off the sofa; more books are in the bath. And everything seems very well where it is. Especially does it seem good that the position of the telephone makes it impossible for you to tell anyone what has happened, or to reply if anyone asks you. Already you feel secretive about your pleasure at the dawn of this new, timeless era of calico.

And next door? For you are not the only one. You run in to ask how the next-doors sustained the blast, but how they feel inside their white box is a more intimate question. Next door – now that you come to listen – sounds remarkably silent: can they have gone to the country? If so, have they any notion how much they miss? Next-door-but-one, and next door to that, add their quota to the deserted silence.

No doubt, however, everyone else, like you, is standing still, taking stock, looking round. Now you think, you find you are making no noise yourself – they probably think you have gone away.

But perhaps as that first dusk falls your curiosity heightens, till you go out to make a reconnaissance. Your street, chequered over with black and white, looks somehow coquettish and self-conscious. Going farther, you are perhaps diminished by finding your entire neighbour-hood endowed with this striking new thing in panes. Seen from the outside, all the way down a street, calico windows lose tone. You begin to wonder, inimically, how long these good people's windows will stay clean, and what they will look like when they no longer are. Now, in this hour before black-out, lights flower behind the criss-crossed frames. Do that young couple realize, or should you tell them, that they perform a shadow-play on a screen? No polite person stares in at a lighted window, but what is to stop you staring at calico?

Back home, you remember you have no black-out. You grope to bed in the calico-muffled dark.

Those first twenty-four hours are only the sharp-edged beginning of the mood. You must live, of course; you must pick up at least some of the pattern; you must at least play house. You discover that what turned on, turns on still – hot water, wireless, electric light. Whether willing or not, you disinter the telephone from the mattress, to explain you are quite safe, perfectly all right, happy; and to learn, from the pause on the wire, that you are disbelieved.

But everything comes from a distance; nothing disturbs you. Each time you return home, shutting the door behind you, you re-enter the mood. The hush of light, the transit of outdoor sounds, the bareness in here become familiar without losing their spell. Life here – life in a blasted, patched-up house – is *not* life, you have been indignantly told. What is it, then – a dream? We are, whatever else we may be, creatures of our senses, varying with their food. Is this different food for our senses making us different creatures?

This tense, mild, soporific indoor whiteness, with, outside, the thunder of world events, sets the note of the summer for Southern England. I say to myself, all my life when I see a calico window, I shall be back in summer 1944. Then I remember – when war is over, there will be no more of this nonsense; we shall look out through glass. May the world be fair!

Cyril Connolly described new vistas in London.

from *THE CONDEMNED PLAYGROUND*

It is sad on a spring evening to walk through the bombed streets of Chelsea. There are vast districts of London – Bayswater, for example, or Kensington – which seem to have been created for destruction, where squares and terraces for half a century have invited dilapidation, where fear and hypocrisy have accumulated through interminable Sunday afternoons until one feels, so evil is the atmosphere of unreality and suspense, that had it not been for the bombers, the houses would have been ignited one day of their own accord by spontaneous combustion. Behind the stucco porches and the lace curtains the half-life of decaying Victorian families guttered like marsh-gas. One has no pity for the fate of such houses, and no pity for the spectacular cinemas and fun-places of Leicester Square, whose architecture was a standing appeal to heaven to rain down vengeance on them. But Chelsea in the milky green evening light, where the church where Henry James lies buried is a pile of red rubble, where tall eighteenth-century houses with their insides blown out gape like ruined triumphal arches, is a more tragic spectacle. For here the life that has vanished with the buildings that once housed it was of some consequence: here there existed a fine appreciation of books and pictures, and many quiet work-rooms for the people who made them. Here was one of the last strongholds of the cultivated *haute bourgeoisie* in which leisure, however ill-earned, has seldom been more agreeably and intelligently made use of. Now when the sun shines on these sandy ruins and on the brown and blue men working there one expects to see goats, and a goatherd in a burnous – 'sirenes in delubris voluptatis' – pattering among them.

The war in Europe progressed towards its conclusion. The Americans were fighting with the British forces.

MEMORIES OF A LOST WAR

The guns know what is what, but underneath
In fearful file
We go around burst boots and packs and teeth
That seem to smile.

The scene jags like a strip of celluloid,
A mortar fires,
Cinzano falls, Michelin is destroyed,
The man of tires.

As darkness drifts like fog in from the sea
Somebody says
'We're digging in.' Look well, for this may be
The last of days.

Hot lightnings stitch the blind eye of the moon,
The thunder's blunt.
We sleep. Our dreams pass in a faint platoon
Towards the front.

Sleep well, for you are young. Each tree a bush
Drips with sweet dew,
And earlier than morning June's cool hush
Will waken you.

The riflemen will wake and hold their breath.
Though they may bleed
They will be proud a while of something death
Still seems to need.

Louis Simpson

FORESIGHT

Previsioning death in advance, our doom is delayed.
I guess mine:
I'm driving for some dumb officer on this raid:

I can't doubt his sense of direction, his perfect right.
Still, he's wrong.
I hint we're too far front. Been warned plenty about this before.

Base far off. No lights may be shown. He starts to get sore.
Lost, our road.
He feels he's failed. Abruptly down drops night.

Anticipate panic: his, mine, contagions fear takes.
THIS IS IT.
Not good. I invoke calm plus prayer for both our sakes.

Calm makes sense. Prayer is less useful than gin or a smoke.
Where are we?
If this ass hadn't tried to crack his great big joke,

Pushing beyond where he knew well we were told to go,
We'd be safe.
Checking my estimate, my unvoiced I Told You So,

Granite bang-bangs blossom all over hell and gone.
Let me Out!
My foreseen fright swells, a warm swarm and we're sure done

In by Mistake, including his fright, faking him brave;
Me the same,
Making me clam tight when I oughta had the brains to save

Our skins, sparing official pride by baring my fear:
(Please, sir. *Turn*.)
Sharing his shame with me, who, also, deserve some. Oh dear,

It's too late. The end of two nervous careers,
Oh dear me,
And him, dear doubtless to someone, worth her dear tears.

Lincoln Kirstein

Poets and artists came to the death-camps.

A CAMP IN THE PRUSSIAN FOREST

I walk beside the prisoners to the road.
Load on puffed load,
Their corpses, stacked like sodden wood,
Lie barred or galled with blood

By the charred warehouse. No one comes today
In the old way
To knock the fillings from their teeth;
The dark, coned, common wreath

Is planted for their grave – a kind of grief.
The living leaf
Clings to the planted profitable
Pine if it is able;

The boughs sigh, mile on green, calm, breathing mile,
From this dead file
The planners ruled for them . . . One year
They sent a million here:

Here men were drunk like water, burnt like wood.
The fat of good
And evil, the breast's star of hope
Were rendered into soap.

I paint the star I sawed from yellow pine –
And plant the sign
In soil that does not yet refuse
Its usual Jews

267

Their first asylum. But the white, dwarfed star –
This dead white star –
Hides nothing, pays for nothing; smoke
Fouls it, a yellow joke,

The needles of the wreath are chalked with ash,
A filmy trash
Litters the black woods with the death
Of men; and one last breath

Curls from the monstrous chimney . . . I laugh aloud
Again and again;
The star laughs from its rotting shroud
Of flesh. O star of men!

Randall Jarrell

AUGUST, 1945

Feeble Caligula! to say
You wished mankind one only neck.
The dying guards might dance that day
At Auschwitz and at Maidanek,
Seeing their bloody seed begin to swell
Where the two cities fell.

That was our deed, without us done.
Great murder in the earth was set
That day to grow, and for us won
A present freedom to regret
Necessity, that once had made us, blind,
The saviours of mankind.

The pluming shadow of that plant,
A tragic actor now grown tall
To toppling, sounds the haughty cant
And birdlike flutes of sorrow, all
That power cracked at the root and manifest
In the burnt Phoenix' nest.

Howard Nemerov

THE CONSUMPTIVE. BELSEN 1945

I

If seeing her an hour before her last
Weak cough into all blackness I could yet
Be held by chalk-white walls, and by the great
Ash-coloured bed,
And the pillows hardly creased
By the tapping of her little cough-jerked head –
If such can be a painter's ecstasy,
(Her limbs like pipes, her head a china skull)
Then where is mercy?
And what
Is this my traffic? for my schooled eyes see
The ghost of a great painting, line and hue,
In this doomed girl of tallow?
O Jesus! has this world so white a yellow
As lifts her head by but a breath from linen
In the congested yet empty world
Of plaster, cotton, and a little marl?
Than pallor what is there more terrible?

There lay the gall
Of that dead mouth of the world.
And at death's centre a torn garden trembled
In which her eyes like great hearts of black water
Shone in their wells of bone,
Brimmed to the well-heads of the coughing girl,
Pleading through history in that white garden;
And very wild, upon the small head's cheekbones,
As on high ridges in an icy dew,
Burned the sharp roses.

II

Her agony slides through me: am I glass
That grief can find no grip
Save for a moment when the quivering lip
And the coughing weaker than the broken wing
That, fluttering, shakes the life from a small bird
Caught me as in a nightmare? Nightmares pass;
The image blurs and the quick razor-edge

Of anger dulls, and pity dulls. O God,
That grief so glibly slides! The little badge
On either cheek was gathered from her blood:
Those coughs were her last words. They had no weight
Save that through them was made articulate
Earth's desolation on the alien bed.
Though I be glass, it shall not be betrayed,
That last weak cough of her small, trembling head.

Mervyn Peake

Many of the prisoners of war had served a long time before their release.

THE PRISONERS

Far far the least of all, in want,
Are these,
The prisoners
Turned massive with their vaults and dark with dark.

They raise no hands, which rest upon their knees,
But lean their solid eyes against the night,
Dimly they feel
Only the furniture they use in cells.

Their Time is almost Death. The silted flow
Of years on years
Is marked by dawns
As faint as cracks on mud-flats of despair.

My pity moves amongst them like a breeze
On walls of stone
Fretting for summer leaves, or like a tune
On ears of stone.

Then, when I raise my hands to strike,
It is too late,
There are no chains that fall
Nor visionary liquid door
Melted with anger.

When have their lives been free from walls and dark

And airs that choke?
And where less prisoner to let my anger
Like a sun strike?

If I could follow them from room to womb
To plant some hope
Through the black silk of the big-bellied gown
There would I win.
No, no, no,
It is too late for anger,
Nothing prevails
But pity for the grief they cannot feel.

Stephen Spender

THE PRISONER

Today, Cheng, I touched your face
with two fingers, as a gesture of love;
for I can never prove enough
by sight or sense your strange grace,

but mothwise my hands return
to your fair cheek, as luminous
as a lamp in a paper house,
and touch, to teach love and learn.

I think a hundred hours are gone
that so, like gods, we'd occupy.
But alas, Cheng, I cannot tell why,
today I touched a mask stretched on the stone

person of death. There was the urge
to break the bright flesh and emerge
of the ambitious cruel bone.

Keith Douglas

PRISONERS OF WAR

Like shabby ghosts down dried-up river beds
The tired procession slowly leaves the field;
Dazed and abandoned, just a count of heads,
They file away, these who have done their last,
To that grey safety where the days are sealed,
Where no word enters, and the urgent past
Is relieved day by day against the clock
Whose hours are meaningless, whose measured rate
Brings nearer nothing, only serves to mock.

It is ended now. There's no more need to choose,
To fend and think and act: no need to hate.
Now all their will is worthless, none will lose
And none will suffer though their courage fail.
The tension in the brain is loosened now,
Its taut decisions slack: no more alone
– How I and each of us has been alone
Like lone trees which the lightnings all assail –
They are herded now and have no more to give.
Even fear is past. And death, so long so near,
Has suddenly receded to its station
In the misty end of life. For these will live,
They are quit of killing and sudden mutilation;
They no longer cower at the sound of a shell in the air.
They are safe. And in the glimmer at time's end
They will return – old, worn maybe, but sure –
And gather their bits of broken lives to mend.

John Jarmain

MIDWINTER

Gone are the mountains, gone Il Gran Sasso, every peak,
    every cliff and outcrop, gaunt and black, craggy hard
swallowed by the mist;
and gone the fresh little mole mounds, no sooner heaped up
    than beaded with frost, here in the prison yard
no bigger than my fist.

Gone too the country-roads like rods of ebony that cut
    these fields of snow into strict squares of black and white,
rigid rectangles;
and gone the tiny tracks of snails that looped themselves
    round a clean cobblestone shining as beautiful and bright
as jingling bangles,
spooring the gutter's edge, crisscrossing the mess-kitchen
    steps, sparkling even in this crude half light
with the sheen of spangles.
And from the eaves the long, sharp-pointed icicle – winter's
    dagger with hilt and shaft silver-chased – stabbing the
    sight
no longer dangles.

We have come to the dead end of all our days, all our nights:
    these four blank walls a drab red brown by day, pitch
    black by night. There is no turning
Backward or forward from this.
This is our life, our death-in-life: this gloom, this ghostly
    pallor above each cot at noon, the cold at day's meridian,
    as cold as ice but burning, burning
Even as war's embrace, the blazing battle's bitter kiss.

Through the chinks, the cracks in the wide wooden door,
    the shattered window, the mist seeps. Its wisps cluster,
    drift and veer,
above each wooden bed.
The floor is of cement. There is no stove or fire. In two
    long rows we lie freezing under our blankets. In this
    grey whiteness lingering around us, drooping, drear,
from which all speech, all sound has fled,
no one speaks. All the old battles, desert scraps, dogfights,
    crashes on the desert's deck, swimming around in the cold,
    dark Med. before the slow red dawn, all the heroism and
    gallantry, all the cowardice and the horror and the fear,
nothing, nothing has been left unsaid.

*   *   *

We have come to the end of all our small talk, our tether, our
    high hopes, ambitions. We have exhausted even the bicker-
    ings, the stupid quarrels, the sneer, the snarl. We have
    foregone all that we loved, cherished, held most dear
and all our books are read.

            *   *   *

This is a dead world, a lost world and these are lost men, lost each
    in his own separate limbo, banished from his own memories,
    exiled even from himself.
    Here
even dreams are dead.

Uys Krige

PRISON LIFE

The stress of prison life is strange
Each human key-board has a range
An octave high an octave low
Of which an untried man can't know
Until some new restraint imposed
Upsets the balance in repose.

Alan Campbell

*The wounded and the crippled also suffered. The Guinea Pig Club used to
sing a song after being treated for burns by the great surgeon Archibald
McIndoe at Queen Victoria Hospital, East Grinstead.*

THE GUINEA PIGS' SONG

We are McIndoe's Army,
We are his Guinea Pigs,
With dermatomes and pedicles,
Glass eyes, false teeth and wigs.
But when we get our discharge
We'll shout with all our might –

'Per Ardua ad Astra,
We'd rather drink than fight.'

John Hunter runs the gas works,
Ross Tilley wields the knife,
And if you are not careful
He'll have your ruddy life.
So Guinea Pigs stand ready,
The surgeons call, 'tis said,
And if their hands aren't steady
They'll decapitate your head.

MY RIGHT LEG WAS GERMANY

Each morning at ten the little caravan rolled through the ward. First the Captain, then the nurse, and last the ward boy pushing the surgical wagon. The surgical wagon is shaped like a tea-caddy. It's double-tiered; on the top shelf stands a jar of instruments, bottles of alcohol and bi-chloride. On the lower shelf is a pile of old 'Stars and Stripes.' When a dressing is changed a newspaper is spread over the sheet to catch the fluid and dirty lint.

This is the day for Carruthers' dressing. We all know it. And as the caravan moves over the glazed linoleum down the aisle of beds, the tension mounts like shuffling footsteps on a thick rug, building up a static charge. I see Emmet hitch himself out of bed and hump toward the latrine. He always manages to get out of the ward when Carruthers' dressing is to be changed. It is very difficult for him to walk. Other times he calls for a duck or bed-pan, but every fourth day at ten he hobbles to the latrine. Emmet has seen and heard too much. His face is continually wincing.

Carruthers' foot is exposed now. The heel and part of the sole are very clean and waxy. The rest of it is a bloody gruel. The Captain is bending over it, prodding the gruel, picking out threads of lint with a pair of tweezers. Carruthers' sobs have a rockabye beat. Don't, Doc. Don't do it, Doc. Don't, Doc. Don't do it, Doc. The ward boy is wrestling with his other leg. I have heard many men scream and sob but in the heat of movement and in the egoism of peril. It's worse lying in bed. The Captain is a small man. He has plump swift hands. The boys like him.

In the long twilight the girls come from town. Cora has smuggled three bottles of stout to me. She pulls them from her handbag and I put them under my pillow. Stout is a heavy dark ale. The girls wear

275

old sweaters and awkward skirts. The skin of their hands is ingrained with dirt around the knuckles and at the base of their fingernails. I give Cora a couple of bars of soap, and she kisses me on the mouth. The boys yell and whoop with joy. I take a lot of kidding about Cora because I have a back injury and she is a big passionate-looking girl. They say she'll finish the job the Germans began.

Remember Daisy in the beautiful book whose voice was full of money? Darien's voice is full of death – the rattling whisper of it, the meemie song of it. Overtones. He speaks and you hear the words but back of the words his voice is saying good-bye, good-bye.

The Lieutenant who led his platoon, Darien said, had a habit of jumping into a jeep and 'checking with the old man' when the going got tough. The men formed an opinion of him. Finally he noticed the change and spoke to the platoon sergeant.

'What's the matter with the men?' he asked. 'Why are they acting like this?'

'Well,' the sergeant said, 'they think you're yellow.'

'Why?'

'When it gets hot, you're not here. You're in your jeep.'

'Do you think I'm yellow?'

'I don't know.'

So the Lieutenant stayed with his men. Two days later he and the platoon sergeant and Darien were in advance estimating the flow of a river which had to be bridged. A shell hit and killed the Lieutenant and the platoon sergeant, and tore Darien's arm open.

'So we never did find out if he was yellow,' Darien said.

My greatest fear is of groaning. I groaned loudly one night and woke Pop – broken pelvis, shattered knee-cap – and he didn't get back to sleep that night. Now when I wake I stuff the sheet in my mouth and bite down. To groan fills me with loathing shame. I lie awake trying to figure out a plan to steal the sleeping pills which are locked in a metal cabinet. I know I can't get them, but I have to think of something with enough ramifications to keep me completely awake. For it is in the regions bordering sleep that my danger lives. I used to keep myself awake by straightening my legs. But in a while pain itself became personified and took a role in the crazed scenarios. That night my right leg was Germany and my left leg was a green land of refuge. Pain was King and sat on a throne of spooled bone. He was heedless. The thick worm of his neck nodded like a stalk of grass. King Pain on his vertebrated throne. My hands were brothers and a windy voice blew calling me Mr. Francis.

Circumlocutions – identifications. I am a bald red-cheeked bad-smelling Scotch lawyer spinning arguments of intricate dusty law.

Fencing of sheep ranges, dark mansions float like cold globes. Bubbles full of wreathing smoke perch upon my long barrister nose. Clownish and without laughter. I feel their obscene feathery touch like the filthy feet of a fly. A devil dance involving my face and cold globes of Scottish law. Everything is beautifully, cruelly, sharply detailed. A meticulous grotesque of my deepest concepts. These images which dog me in the jungle-land of half-sleep obey a most precise logic. But the premises are diseased. They well tidally from deepest places and bear with them memory's rubbish shards and stinking jetsam of foundered dreams. Sometimes I think these waking nightmares are the most personal belongings I have. And as night comes on my terror grows. I've been a fool. Why didn't I think of it before . . . This afternoon I told Cora to get me sleeping pills in town. She said she would. She said she would go to the chemist's. Now I will sleep. When she brings the pills I will double or triple the amount prescribed and will surely sleep.

Darien speaks to me in a low voice so the others won't hear. He has asked the Captain to rescind the order sending him back to the States. He wants to rejoin his outfit. The boys are riding him. He tries to defend himself by outdoing their desire to get back home. He tells them the only reason he wants to rejoin his outfit is because they will return to the States and then become training cadre. And he will be home, he says, when they are in the Pacific. He tells them that and laughs falsely and nobody believes him. He considers me his friend. He sits on my bed and says: 'I want to go back to my outfit. Maybe we'll go back to the States before we go to the Pacific. Okay. Fine. I have a girl. I'm not married. I don't know. Maybe we'll go straight to the Pacific. Okay. Anyway, I'll be with them. I've been with those guys through Africa and Sicily and in France and Germany. Of course there's only a few of the original guys left but – You don't think I'm foolish, do you? Do you think I'm foolish? . . . I don't know.'

That voice of his winds on and tells me about a man named Sewell. He was in Darien's squad. One day they were out mine-detecting and Sewell felt himself step on a shoe-mine. This is a tiny ingenious German mine which blasts off your leg to the top of your shoe. It is also an anti-personnel mine, throwing shrapnel for a ten- or fifteen-yards' radius. The squad was badly bunched when Sewell stepped on his mine. The shoe mine does not detonate until pressure is released. The other tiny German mine – the castrator – is calculated to catch a man in the scissors of his stride and detonate on contact, but does not break into shrapnel. So when Sewell felt his foot on the mine and it did not blow he knew that he was on a shoe-mine and that his squad was bunched too close to him. He kept his foot planted and said: 'Move out.'

His squad gaped at him. They didn't know why he stood so awkwardly, his lips trembling and leg rigid.

'Move out,' he said again. 'I'm on a mine. Goddam it, move out.'

They moved out of range and he stepped off.

Darien's voice winds on. It is complaining now. 'I'm not married or nothing. Why shouldn't I want to go back to my outfit? It'd be different if I was married.' But I know and he knows that he is married. Death has grown amorous and in his voice, behind his words, you can hear the wedding music play.

Emmet's face wincing in the raw sunlight during a fabulous afternoon of no-rain. I think they are going to put him in the psychopathic ward. He's not crazy. Over-sensitised. Nerves scraped of all protective gristle. He has seen and heard too much.

The amputees – the bright boys. The incredible laughing tough-talking amputees. As if their arms and legs and hands and feet had weighed grossly upon them and they were lighter now. Who has the answer? Who can translate those shining eyes? Here they come. Here comes Finkle – walking wide, japing, never forgetting for a minute that he's a funny man. He's singing in his borsht-circuit master-of-ceremonies voice. One meatball. One meatball. Can't get no bread with one meatball. That's my theme song, boys – he shouts. And the beds shout laughter back. That's my theme song. I gotta get a discharge now. I just can't spare the other one. It would never do. Clown. Catskill funny man, walking wide, talking big. He comes in every morning and makes everyone laugh.

In back of him is Joey. Joey is nineteen years old. He has lost his right leg and left arm. He trails Finkle every morning in their tour of the wards. They call themselves the Ambassadors from the Butchers Shop. Finkle's title. Joey isn't very articulate, but he imitates Finkle and thinks he is a side-splitting comedian. They have a community of laughter. Joey claims he is lucky because it was his right leg and left arm.

'If they'd of been on the same side,' he says, 'I couldn't handle my crutch like I do.'

Bernard Evslin

As Henry Treece pointed out, waiting for Victory in Europe was interminable.

from THE END OF THE WAR IN EUROPE

It's no fun, waiting for the war to end. A year ago, these days would have seemed like the anteroom to Paradise! Now, each day brings more confusions, more anxieties – and no relief. It's pretty bad on a Bomber Station here at home; on the Western Front, or in Italy, or the Far East, it must be almost unbearable.

As the front line creeps farther and farther into Germany, each day approaching the Russian line, we in Bomber Command are losing more and more of our targets. There is less and less necessity, or opportunity, to bomb the enemy.

We wait, day after day, for a signal to tell us that an operation is laid on for us – but Continent-based aircraft are coping with the enemies' supply lines, the Army doesn't need our co-operation any longer – and we smashed the Huns' last synthetic-oil target a week ago!

We are like craftsmen who are out of a job! After the night by night picnics, and the early morning flaps, of the D-day and oil-target periods, this enforced idleness is exasperating. We have keyed ourselves up, and it takes some time to relax.

We are all asking: what is the future of Bomber Command? And the answer is an empty laugh! For most of us, it seems that the Far East is the only solution.

To come to the end of a European war, and *then* to be sent abroad to start all over again, would knock me right off my perch – temporarily. I'd feel as I imagine a spider must feel when, after he has climbed half out of the bath, a swirl of water whisks him in again.

We have had a pretty good time in this R.A.F. Command, comparatively speaking. We've worked day and night, worked till we were ready to drop; we've had our losses, and sometimes very heavy ones; the enemy has from time to time brought the war right on to our doorsteps, and has bombed and machine-gunned us as we went about our work. But always we have been *at home*, on our own soil, listening to other English voices, drinking English beer, reading English newspapers, getting our mail quickly and regularly, going off fairly regularly for a 36-hour pass to an English town and perhaps even seeing our wives and friends once a fortnight. We have almost been civilian soldiers; and that has often made us feel, perhaps, a cut above other types of soldiers. We have been allowed, more than most, to be individuals . . .

And now our trade has gone from our hands – and we're wondering just where we'll turn our next penny.

It's pretty grim!

When V-E Day came, Keith Vaughan was in a camp in the countryside.

from V-E DAY

On the dung-crusted door of a stable a V had been made with red, white and blue ribbon, and inside the V, hurriedly chalked as an afterthought, a red E. In the little window of the grocer's was a newspaper cutting of the Prime Minister. It was stuck on the window with four large pieces of brown tape like a police notice. In the window that has bird seed and bottles of sauce was a gold frame with a reproduced oil-painting of two exceedingly mild and dignified lions, and in the bottom left-hand corner the word 'PEARS'. In front there was a photograph of the Royal Family in sepia, with the word 'CORONATION' underneath and a round circle of rust from a drawing-pin. All the familiar and reliable things had suddenly disclosed a secret and unsuspected threat, though it would be impossible to say exactly what it was they threatened. But when the last house was passed and there were only fields and hedges and ditches frothing with tall white cow-parsley, there was a feeling of relief and reassurance . . .

This, then, I thought, was the beginning of it all. This was perhaps the oldest thing on earth. Before cities and civilisations men had sat and watched sheep graze. In Canaan and Galilee and Salonica and Thrace, on the mountain slopes of Olympus and the Caucasus, on the plains of Hungary and the shores of the Black Sea, in Lombardy, Burgundy, Saxony, along all the routes where men had fought and followed searching for a home and a pasture sheep had grazed and men had watched them. Daphnis, Hyacinthus, Thyrsis, Corydon and the famous and anonymous sherpherds of Galilee. And I tried to remember all that had gone on as an accompaniment to that watching, the immense architecture of hope that had been built up round sheep. The burnt offerings and symbols of love and innocence; the preyed-upon, the lost and the helplessly young. Sacrificed, worshipped, or just eaten, through mankind's long adolescence sheep went on being sheep, somewhere in the background of every picture, greedy and silly and perpetually anxious. And each year the same disappointing story of promise and unfulfilment. The tiny wet thing with enormous legs first learning to kneel in the winter grass, as awkward and dangerous-looking as a child with a deck-chair. The insolent butting at the udders. The entirely beautiful and unnecessary prancing of lambs, movement purely for the sake of movement, only to be forgotten in a few months in a complacent and woolly middle age.

Out of the north a flock of Fortresses came flying high. It was time for them to come and they crossed every night. The slowly-mounting noise focused the uneasiness in the air. Then I realised that tonight they would not be carrying bombs; the meaning of all the little flags suddenly became real. It was as if one had dreamt the noise: the approaching impersonal menace, the indiscriminate individual death and obliteration of cities, then at the climax of terror, waking, recognised the cause of the dream – after all, only aeroplanes flying. A sense of absolute security closed over everything.

The sun had gone and over the horizon was left a stain of dried blood. The air was the colour of watery ink. At the camp the German bugler was blowing lights out. The sheep had finished eating and sat with folded feet, looking without concern on the first night of peace.

Victory over Japan and the final coming of the peace led to great celebrations.

V. J. DAY

My No. 19, wedged in at the Circus,
Halted beside the Eros pedestal
Still boarded over. Dusty sunlight flickered.
A flutter of torn paper drifted from
The windows of some fourth-floor offices.
The armistice, I guessed; we'd had the bomb;
War's over, so must be celebrated.
En route to somewhere far down Fulham Road
I got off before the World's End, time in hand,
So turned into the nearest.

Old crazies singing Knees up Mother Brown,
A world that even then I knew had ended.
Knees up, arms linked, the floor of the bar parlour
Bounding! Ports and lemon, bombazine!
And all you ladies dead now!

David Wright

VJ DAY

Hurray! Hurray!
this is the day
when the whole nation
joins in the celebration
of everlasting peace;
so let me hit this policeman
as hard as I can.
    Whoopee
for liberty!
    Destruction is absolutely at an end,
so I will see if I can bend
this park chair.
    There!
    Now for goodness sake let's try and make it burn.
I yearn
I aspire
to have the world's most beautiful fire,
and it would really please
me if we could have it right under the trees,
so that at any rate, God willing,
I shall have done just a little bit of killing.
    Law and order is established throughout the world.
Look! I have hurled
the No Entry sign
into the Serpentine.
    Swept from the earth are the vandals.
I have broken off the door handles
of this car,
Ah! Ah! Ah!
over she goes, give her another shove;
peace, prosperity, and brotherly love.
    This is the day for which we fought and prayed.
Call out the Fire Brigade.

Virginia Graham

The fact that world peace had been achieved only by the dropping of atom bombs on Hiroshima and Nagasaki led to anguish.

ATOMIC MAN

an anguish breeds within the bone
so dry the blood, so pale the hand,
as though the marrow fights alone
something it cannot understand

wax face with wrinkles wilting down
to frame the question on the lips,
the worried eyebrows of a clown
and nervous tapping fingertips.

the day it fell he shook and swayed
and leaned upon the reeling wall
and seemed to see all England fade
into a night beyond recall,

and still the shadow of the guilt
leans on a wall within the mind
cursing the summer day he felt
he was the last man of his kind.

Francis Scarfe

from THE HUMAN PROVINCE

August 1945

Matter is smashed, the dream of immortality is shattered, we were on the verge of making it come true. The stars, so close, are now lost. The closest and furthest things have become one, under what lightning! Stillness alone, and slowness, are still worth living. They have little time left. The fun of flying was brief. If souls existed, this new catastrophe would have struck them. So one does not wish that something exists, for what is unattainable? Destruction, certain of its divine origin, reaches into the very marrow of things, and the Creator smashes both the clay and his own shaping hand. Survival! Survival! Ignoble word! Trees were the wisest form of life, and they fall with us atom-robbers.

If we survive, a lot more will be at stake. But the thought that we may not survive is unbearable. All certitude came from eternity. Without it, without this wonderful feeling of some permanence, albeit not one's own, everything is insipid and futile.

All time was not white-hot for us with possibilities we never suspected – what a blessing! Paradise *was* at the beginning, and now it's come to an end. The thing that pains me most is the fate of other creatures. We are so guilty, that we almost don't matter anymore. One can only sleep now so as not to think of it. The waking mind feels guilty, and it *is* guilty.

The *succession* of discoveries in our history is really a tragedy. A few slight changes, and everything would have come out differently. A few decades for this or that, and it wouldn't have overtaken us. Of course, like everything, this misfortune too has its laws. But who is interested in the laws of a world that will certainly not survive.

It is not that we do not see anything ahead of us. But the future has split; it will be thus or thus; on this side, all fear; on the other, all hope. One no longer has the weight to decide, not even in oneself. Double-tongued future, Pythia restored to honour.

The sun dethroned, the last valid myth destroyed. The earth has come of age; on its own now, what will it do with itself? Until now, it was the unchallenged child of the sun, totally dependent on it, unable to live without it, lost without it. But light is dethroned, the atomic bomb has become the measure of all things.

The tiniest thing has won: a paradox of power.

Elias Canetti

DIRGE FOR THE NEW SUNRISE

(Fifteen minutes past eight o'clock, on the morning of Monday the 6th of August, 1945)

Bound to my heart as Ixion to the wheel,
Nailed to my heart as the Thief upon the Cross
I hang between our Christ and the gap where the world was lost

And watch the phantom Sun in Famine Street
– The ghost of the heart of Man . . . red Cain,
And the more murderous brain
Of Man, still redder Nero that conceived the death
Of his mother Earth, and tore
Her womb, to know the place where he was conceived.

But no eyes grieved –
For none were left for tears:
They were blinded as the years

284

Since Christ was born. Mother or Murderer, you have given
    or taken life –
Now all is one!

There was a morning when the holy Light
Was young . . . The beautiful First Creature came
To our water-springs, and thought us without blame.

Our hearts seemed safe in our breasts and sang to the Light–
The marrow in the bone
We dreamed was safe . . . the blood in the veins, the sap in the
    tree
Were springs of the Deity.

But I saw the little Ant-men as they ran
Carrying the world's weight of the world's filth
And the filth in the heart of Man –
Compressed till those lusts and greeds had a greater heat than
    that of the Sun.

And the ray from that heat came soundless, shook the sky
As if in search for food, and squeezed the stems
Of all that grows on the earth till they were dry.
The eyes that saw, the lips that kissed, are gone
– Or black as thunder lie and grin at the murdered Sun.

The living blind and seeing dead together lie
As if in love . . . There was no more hating then –
And no more love: Gone is the heart of Man.

Edith Sitwell

PEACE IN OUR TIME

Honour is saved by the national will,
The burgher throws up his cap.
Gone is the soldier, over the hill,
And the rat has defended his trap.

Howard Nemerov

9
After the War
Was Over

Osbert Lancaster, *Daily Express*, 24.6.47

"Don't be so stuffy, Henry! I'm sure that if you asked him nicely the young man would be only too pleased to give you the name of a really GOOD tailor who doesn't worry about coupons!"

The Forties, for most of us, had a precise and marked shape whose graph, in its outline at any rate, is clearly discernible.

It began with a political hang-over. We awoke one day to realise that we were prolonging a week-end that was already over. Monday morning had arrived and here we were, still in bed. Somebody had waved a piece of paper and guiltily, but secretly relieved, we had huddled back under the bed-clothes. The holiday had been extended. There was perhaps time for one more trip abroad, for one more hurried but exquisite meal in surroundings we knew we would never recognise in quite the same way again. We made a lingering exploration of Europe, touching its most nostalgic points like the body of a beloved; still beautiful but riddled with the disease of its own beauty. Already the betraying symptoms were visible.

We welcomed the war as a release from slow death. The surgeon's knife had been put into our own hands; we had to operate on our own body if we wanted to live.

The war's most obvious phenomena we accepted as inevitable stages in our recovery; the phoney war, Dunkirk, the Battle of Britain; evacuation and shelter-life and fire-wardens. Summer burned like a brittle pyre in whose flames the words of a great orator were cremated for ever in history. Then the long black-out; a time of protracted sea-battles, of security slogans and desert warfare. We learned new catch-phrases, a new jargon – 'war of attrition', 'we can take it', 'we've had it', 'wizard prangs'; dated, debased expressions like the slang in school-boy thrillers of an earlier epoch.

Gradually the tables turned. We were going to win in a definable period. That we should ultimately win we had never, at any time, doubted, but now for the first time the war acquired limits. The Americans came. There were agitations for and then an actual Second Front. The muddled, unreal celebrations of VE day arrived – a world dancing in its own ruins, looser, more happy and uninhibited than it would be again.

The General Election marked the beginning of a new emotional cycle – endurance on a peace-time level. We began to live by a blue-print framed for the age. But we had high hopes of democracy in a world loaded against it. We watched anxiously while a Government tried to survive its own bad public relations. Policies were worked out for a working man's society. Conditions and world opinion were unfavourable, but somehow a compromise evolved that committed itself on the scale of the time, and having committed itself, looked as if it might work. What failures there were came not from planning, but from the human element. And it would be the same, unpredictable human element in the end that would decide the success or failure of the whole experiment.

That at least was the outward shape of the Forties – the fortuitous, fervent, frozen and frustrated Forties. They contained a war and a social revolution; they were a period of struggle, of high promise and gradual decline. We saw public ambition, public education and public taste rise. We saw private incentive, the high water-marks of individual taste and standards of living drop. It was all, no doubt, quite proper.

Abroad, we had seen one fear, one enemy give way to another within the space of a single decade. We had seen Europe rid of one set of barriers, one kind of persecution, only to find in their place, more silently, more clumsily, a fresh range of frontiers, a new kind of intolerance. Between Iron Curtains and Dollar Imperialism we had watched the littoral of our own dreams shrink.

Alan Ross

Areas which had been closed for defence were opened.

BANNED AREA

SOUTH COAST, 1945

How like coarse angular flowers
Uncurling into shape,
Easing and sorting out
Their trampled rows, are these
Pink lodging-houses, free
To expand and straighten, now
The ban is lifted.

War
Had long been busy with
The town's economy. First
Small omen was *Belle Vue*
Become a Battery
Headquarters. Then a tea-shop,
For months about to close,
Changed overnight into
A Forces Rest-room, strewn
With Allied propaganda
And comic strips. At last,

Barely a year ago,
– The khaki deluge. Swarms
Jumping from backs of lorries
Fill all the rooms like birds
With lazy whistling: then
What fumes of animal dreams
From lumps asleep on floors
Till daybreak smears a light
On dented fenders, finds
Nothing to warm but war's
Soft altars (blankets heaped
In regulation slabs)
Hung round with votive gifts
– Mugs, webbing, towels, and each
Man's little sacrifice
Of freedom! I can hear
Rubbed on the window's drum
The shuffle of their drill.

Reliable hotels
(Their railings, porch to porch,
Holding towards the sea's
Flat unconcern, the same
Reduplicated stiff
Gesture of floral iron)
Where once Retirement dozed
While servants noiselessly
Elbowed their trays round doors,
Wince under boots; hot bodies,
Tuned-up and tingling, take
Short ease before the assault.
The Present rages in
Their blood. The Past for them
Is dumb. They cannot feel
The insipid lure of these
Brass-potted ferns, haunting
Drab landings with a hint
Of prim repose. No, here
Was sterner business hatched:
For suddenly – though months
Of kit-inspections, pubs,
Fag-ends, fatigues, had gone
And still seemed queueing up

To maunder by – in a flash
(Some message had come through)
There was a stir by night.
The usual boring day
Broke like a yawn, explored
Crescents of empty rooms.
– And now the ban is lifted.

Shyly, knowing it snaps
An iron spell, the first
Foot, buoyed on pebbles, tries
The prohibited beach, or feels
Its way with instruments
That listen to the sand.
Somebody shifts the coiled
Red skeletons that hoop
The foam with prickles; some
Get ready to restore
The pier's lost link; others
Oil the neglected grooves
Of slot-machines; while deep
In cellars under shops
Women unstrap the lids
Of trunks to hunt up postcards.

This is the danger hour,
When ghosts of a defunct
Lamented Yesterday
Return. The Past struggles
To be reborn, as though
Winter, with Spring at hand,
Were forced to reinstate
Her scattered leaves, reverse
The wind, and even on
Her budded branches, piece
Together last July.
Paused on this unmown lawn,
The soldiers gone, I hear
The first invading leaves
Drift back and eddy: jokes
Blown from their context, wraiths
Of litter, ice-cream bells,

Tears for a wooden spade
Washed out to sea, a kiss,
A threadbare stray good-bye,
Whispers and summery frills
Of holidays that went
And came again as smooth
As Sunday sun that winds
Like brooms used to propel
Along the promenade,
Shade into shine; as now,
Impatient of the last
Departing convoy, clouds
Sweep forward, glowering
Inland to obliterate
The war's retreating wheels.

Christopher Hassall

Millions of the armed forces were slowly demobilized.

HATS, DEMOB DEPOT, YORK

Arriving at a counter heaped with hats,
'Here comes another head,' thought I. 'So shrinks
Their number as more heads approach, and we
Don our old differences, hat by hat.
A hideous journey brings us to this halt.
How many have dropt out! The rest, once more
Parading, take their choice, then finally
Diverge into the oblivion of freedom.'

But suddenly, before we went our ways,
The clear impression of another hour
Flashed on the mind. There was a thoroughfare
Of waving hands, flags, handkerchiefs, and hats,
And all the windows weeping paper tears,
Weeping waste paper for the wasted years.

Christopher Hassall

MEDICAL

MILLBANK HOSPITAL, 1946

They sounded me all over like a house,
And (though the attic they had barely glanced at
Chuckled) wrote *Stable* in the column marked
MENTALITY, the word implying that
For all these dire events the property
Was still unhaunted. So they went. Footsteps
Followed them to the door. At last a shutter
Somewhere above significantly banged.
They had known their way about me like old friends,
Searched unsuspected rooms, filled up their form
Beneath each Latin name as though to take
The census of a Roman province. Then
I fell apart, and my accustomed self,
The body's tenant which had passed them by
A dozen times unnoticed on the stairs,
Grew timidly aware of its abode.
Body and spirit looked at one another:
One with its easy secret yielded up
And summarized in Latin; one, scot-free,
Already bound on journeys far beyond
The farthest reach of Earth's migrating birds.

Christopher Hassall

DEMOBILIZATION

The entered world is like a sleep,
But men the self-same vigil keep.

The future offers dreams of pleasure,
But can we now employ our leisure,

Or have we let this fragile art
Become a spectre in the heart?

The river's limpid line surrounds
The dwindling morals and the grounds

On which we start afresh to prove
The valid images of love.

The pencilled eyebrows of the face
We gaze at conjure with the trace

Of familiar and objective fact,
As shadows merge into the act.

And we are half what luck contrives
In our one or other lives.

Alan Ross

People found it difficult to adjust to the time of peace.

THE POST-WAR NIGHT

No, nowadays at night the flush of light
Reflected anxiously by urban skies, impresses eyes
In quest of soothing space between the stars, as with a sense
Of guilt, not reassurance. This is Peace,
Our nightly black-out dream; yet back to black skies fly
Our eyes disheartened by futility, to seek
Some sterner strength in the unmoonlit midnight's zenith
Above our heads rebuking light's illusions . . . *In our time
We have had vision.* Now our seeing tries
Not to find blindness everywhere it peers,
Relinquishing belief in any sight surpassing this.
*We must see how to justify ourselves
Always.* Perhaps indeed that is for ever all
Our eyes are used to look for: We must stand
Justified: – if not before the whole world then before
Ourselves: if not before the candid inmost heart,
Blandly at least before shrewd common-sense
Sole supreme tribunal in this business-driven world,
Still so remote from all the innate sense
Of human destiny that we are born with knows
To be truly our aim on earth: one God-ruled globe,
Finally unified, at peace, free to create! *That sense
Is dull in all but few to-day* . . . They are not listened to.
They seldom speak. And how absurd they sound

295

To such as do hear them, how like a child's
Sublime simplicity and sweet ineptitude,
To talk of Brotherhood and of the beautiful
Smooth-running Great Society that might tomorrow mean
Our paradise regained! How well our guilt,
Long versed in all the necessary lies
Required to run the world in practice knows
How always to remain the same calm, sane
Comfortably compromised collusionists, still safe and sound
At least as long as this false peacetime lasts.

David Gascoyne

Some believed that post-war reconstruction would solve the problems of the 'thirties. As John Manifold wrote:

NIGHTPIECE

Three men were talking in the road
And still 'To-morrow' was the word.

The night was clear, the lights did glitter;
The first man spoke and his voice was bitter,

'To-morrow, like another day
I draw the dole and rust away.'

The second one said, scared and low,
'Tomorrow I may have to go.'

And the two spoke never another word,
But drew together and looked at the third.

And the third man said, 'If to-morrow exists
It comes with streets like rivers with fists.

It's the end of crawling the end of doles,
And men are treated as human souls.'

I stood in a doorway and heard these things
As the three came past with the step of kings.

Yet in the long years of austerity and rationing in the late 'forties, people became tired of waiting for the promised land.

WHEN DOES THE PLAY BEGIN?

(A POLITICAL POEM)

Mother when does the
show begin when does

something happen hush
dear be quiet in just a

minute now but you
said that a long time

ago I want the curtain
to go up hush dear be

quiet it's never good
manners to talk when

the music is playing
but mother I'm tired

of the music and they
keep playing the same

piece hush darling in
just a minute now here

eat a piece of candy
no I don't want any

more candy mother I
want them to begin the

play I want to see the
lights go on and have

the people walk around
and talk & laugh & sing!

J. Laughlin

THE DIVIDED LIFE RE-LIVED

Once again the light refracted through the dusty crimson air
Leaves the spaces of the evening blurred and bare.
Bats that flicker round the edges of the square Victorian lawn
Symbolise the bourgeois souls from life withdrawn.

Now the nightingale arouses us upon the withered tree
With its disappointing, moving melody,
And against the chalky purple thrown by distant main-road arcs
Flow the tired suburban leaves like mouldy sparks.

Here the mower furred with grass like filings round a magnet's
        pole,
Teacups left for ants to make our fortunes droll;
While we sit and try to think that everything is not too late—
Sparrows sitting on the sad outfield of fate.

Once and only once we were in touch with brutal, bloody life
When we got in or kept out of global strife;
And in desert or in dockyard met our coarser fellow men,
Wielding friendly gun or scrubber, not our pen.

How we innocently thought that we should be alone no more,
Linked in death or revolution as in war.
How completely we have slipped into the same old world of
        cod,
Our companions Henry James or cats or God.

Waiting for the evening as the time of passion and of verse,
Vainly hoping that at both we shan't get worse;
While outside the demon scientists and rulers of the land
Pile the bombs like busy crabs pile balls of sand.

And the best that we can wish for is that still the moon will rise
Enigmatic, cracked and yellow to men's eyes,
And illuminate the manuscripts of poems that foretold
All the ruin and survival of the old.

Roy Fuller

Some felt that the total victory of the democracies had changed nothing in the world, although they should still agitate for change.

THE AGITATOR

The yellow flowers broken by his feet
Sent up their acrid warning to his heart;
The wordless signpost like a rotting tongue
Gave him no answer, and he had no chart.

Written upon his mind, behind the eyes.
The thickets where the clear-voiced blackcap sang,
The little sedge-rimmed pools between the trees
Led him to a new country where his foes were strong.

Somewhere at the end there lay a city
Where the women would greet him in their smoky houses,
Holding the knife hidden within the girdle
Or offering the slow venom in coloured beautiful glasses.

And in that city he must reject their cunning,
Outwit the foxy men who watched his step
And carry his doctrine quietly in his heart
Until the hour when daily thought would stop.

Crowds would see visions, and his thoughts, like birds
Burdened with messages, would find their homes.
Already in mind he saw the breasts of men
Opening to free the phoenix of their dreams.

The little hills that lay along his path
Shed their long shadows as the evening fell.
Beyond their wall, west by the sinking sun,
The paper gunmen waited for their kill.

George Woodcock

THE VERDICT

It was taken a long time ago,
The first pressure on the trigger.
Why complain that the verdict is so?
It was taken a long time ago.

And our grave will have many a digger,
The Mongol, the Yank and the nigger.
It was taken a long time ago,
The first pressure on the trigger.

Norman Cameron

COLOUR BAR

(Lines for a Well-appointed Lounge)

O dead men were yellow, and dead men were Red,
Dead men were black men who couldn't find bread,
And here stand the living, well-dressed and well-fed.
The living are white men, occasionally tight men –
But always the right men to have and to hold
All the world's factories, all the world's gold.
Unblackened by labour, unreddened by blood,
Their white hands have hastened to nip every bud
That might flower into plenty for poor men, and all men,
For only the white men – and not all the white men,
But only the right men, the happy and few men,
May have and may hold. Yet what if the future,
That uncertain creature, should alter their colour,
Should grieve them, should leave them black and blue men,
Or, cashless and fleshless, to depend for their whiteness,
On the pie and the vulture, the sun and the sand?

Donald Bishop

Some wondered what would happen if the whole system were to collapse.

BEHAVIOUR OF MONEY

Money was once well known, like a townhall or the sky
or a river East and West, and you lived one side or the other;
Love and Death dealt shocks,
but for all the money that passed, the wise man knew his brother.

But money changed. Money came jerking roughly alive;
went battering round the town with a boozy, zigzag tread.
A clear case for arrest;

and the crowds milled and killed for the pound notes that he shed.
And the town changed, and the mean and the little lovers of gain
inflated like a dropsy, and gone were the courtesies
that eased the market day;
saying, 'buyer' and 'seller' was saying, 'enemies.'

The poor were shunted nearer to beasts. The cops recruited.
The rich became a foreign community. Up there leaped
quiet folk gone nasty,
quite strangely distorted, like a photograph that has slipped.

Hearing the drunken roars of Money from down the street,
'What's to become of us?' the people in bed would cry:
'And oh, the thought strikes chill;
what's to become of the world if Money should suddenly die?

Should suddenly take a toss and go down crack on his head?
If the dance suddenly finished, if they stopped the runaway bus,
if the trees stopped racing away?
If our hopes come true and he dies, what's to become of us?

Shall we recognise each other, crowding around the body?
And as we go stealing off in search of the town we have known
– what a job for the Sanitary Officials;
the sprawled body of Money, dead, stinking, alone!'

Will X contrive to lose the weasel look in his eyes?
Will the metal go out of the voice of Y? Shall we all turn back
to men, like Circe's beasts?
Or die? Or dance in the street the day that the world goes crack?

Bernard Spencer

Although he stayed at home, V. S. Pritchett did not feel that the war had changed him much as a writer.

from *MIDNIGHT OIL*

There is not much more to say about the war. In one of Elizabeth Bowen's stories a character is made to say of the Blitz – and by extension of the war itself: 'It will have no literature.' In that sense it was like a car smash or pile-up. English writing did not vanish, but for years the experience exhausted us mentally and physically. And then, there is nothing as dead as a dead war and, as the pace quickens, the latest war kills the one before it quickly. One is ridiculous to be still alive and the best thing is to keep one's mouth shut. Looking at the war egotistically from a writer's point of view, it was a feverish dispersal and waste of one's life. It is often said that this was a good time when all private defences gave way, especially the defence of class differences, and that we all came together for once; and one hears regrets that after the war this revolution spent itself and that we went back to our traditional privacy. We did; though not to the old kind. I am not sure that to be so drowned in the mass was good for the act of writing, for the kind of humanity required of artists is not the same thing as the united public humanness we felt as citizens. A writer soon finds himself wondering how large a helping of human beings his talent can manage, without being swamped by the huge amount of social reality that is forced upon him. The unconscious benefits may be deep; the anarchy of war is a release for a time: the ultimate effects are indirect.

Without the pressure of war, the British people reverted to their natural ways.

THE BRITISH

We are a people living in shells and moving
Crablike; reticent, awkward, deeply suspicious;
Watching the world from a corner of half-closed eyelids,
Afraid lest someone show that he hates or loves us,
Afraid lest someone weep in the railway train.

We are coiled and clenched like a foetus clad in armour.
We hold our hearts for fear they fly like eagles.
We grasp our tongues for fear they cry like trumpets.
We listen to our own footsteps. We look both ways
Betore we cross the silent empty road.

We are a people easily made uneasy,
Especially wary of praise, of passion, of scarlet
Cloaks, of gesturing hands, of the smiling stranger
In the alien hat who talks to all or the other
In the unfamiliar coat who talks to none.

We are afraid of too-cold thought or too-hot
Blood, of the opening of long-shut shafts or cupboards,
Of light in caves, of X-rays, probes, unclothing
Of emotion, intolerable revelation
Of lust in the light, of love in the palm of the hand.

We are afraid of, one day on a sunny morning,
Meeting ourselves or another without the usual
Outer sheath, the comfortable conversation,
And saying all, all, all we did not mean to,
All, all, all we did not know we meant.

A. S. J. Tessimond

In the shoddy cities, a new breed of criminal and profiteer arose, providing scarce goods and services.

A THOUGHT FOR DENMAN STREET

Young man in a purple suit,
balanced on pointed ginger feet
at the corner of Denman Street,
selling illicit silk stockings
with fancy clockings
in the furtive half-light
of a dirty drunken Piccadilly night;
young man in a purple suit
doing a little business on the side,
it was not for you my son died.
    He died (not that you care)
because once, long ago, you were
kind to your mother,
and because at one time or another
you have spoken the truth.
    For Truth and Love he seemed, in his youth
to die,

but by and by
you will find, when you come to count the cost,
it is you we mourn, you who are lost,
young man in a purple suit.

Virginia Graham

SMART-BOY

I am the Lad: the wide-awake, the smart-boy,
The one who knows the ropes and where he's going,
The easy smiler with the easy money.

I was the kid who got no praise or prizes
Who's now the man to get the peachbloom lovelies:
Black Market Boy with my good mixer manner.

I'm your tall talker in the fug of bar-rooms,
Quick at a deal, an old hand on the dog tracks,
Knowing in clubs, stander at Soho corners.

Go-between guy, I'm wiser than to work for
What the world hands me on a shiny salver,
Me the can't-catch-me-dozing razor-sharp-boy

Ready to set my toe to Order's backside:
Big-shot-to-be, big-city up-and-comer:
Quickstepper, racer, ace among you sleepers.

A. S. J. Tessimond

There were still twenty thousand deserters from the armed services after demobilization was ended.

THE DESERTER

Born with all arms he sought a separate peace.
Responsibilities loomed up like tanks,
And since his manhood marked him of our ranks
He threw it off and scrambled for release.

His power of choice he thrust on the police
As if it burnt his hands; he gave the banks
His power to work; then he bestowed with thanks
His power to think on Viscount Candlegrease.

Claiming the privileges of the dead
Before his time – the heart no blood runs through,
The undelighted hands, the rotting head –

Strong in his impotence he can safely view
The battlefield of men, and shake his head
And say, 'I know. But then what can I do?'

John Manifold

It was hard to settle down. The trains still brought together and divided those who loved.

DEPARTURE PLATFORM

Always to look like this
At the unmeeting place:
Scrambling of crowds and air
When the gilt clock-hands move
Across the wet moon-face
(Seen, cheek touching lip,
Through your distracting hair)
To enter time again
Where disappointments live
In shabby comradeship.

All this is nothing new

Still on the stroke of four
A wilderness of rail
Into which we have come
Feeling like all the lost
Ten tribes of Israel,
Maybe to see and hear
The hobbled tree of steam
Lofting between the wheels
Its paradisal hiss

305

Under a dripping roof;

The rain still falling now

To share a jealous dream
Of pert and slithering heels
In the rain's puddled glass,
Who have the time I leave,
And all the afternoon
A bitter nail, a clove,
A high, blind window pane
When the black pistons drive
Where but away from love.

Now there is nothing new

Kenneth Allott

Many could not give up the memories of war.

MEMORY

War's image crosses constantly my mind
and leaps a flame to flicker in my heart
and guns continue restless, as the wind
subtle and swift as leopard carries hurt

deep to the dark recess of memory
where the last images incredulous move
of cities breathing out their agony
of grief and patience in a flame of love.

Who would not clasp the hand of his redeemer
or listen to the laughing voice upraised
in song and silver story to refute

the lies with which we celebrated summer
the rivulets of dread with which we praised
the simple dogmas issuing from his throat.

Alan Rook

THE REUNION

After so many years
To come together again
Meeting as once they met
With wonder and glad tears,
After such bitter pain
Seeking what they forget:

Here in the self-same room
They talk the difference out
As silent the sun goes down
And dies in the wintry gloom.
Only the lamp of doubt
Shines on, its flame unblown.

Changed is the furniture,
Familiar things they knew,
The wise books on the shelves,
Table and bed and chair –
All changed. The only clue
To themselves lies in themselves.

And they must again explore
That labyrinth and tread
Those half-forgotten ways
They went in once before,
Knowing, though lost, the thread
Still lies within the maze.

Could they but find that prize
They'd follow where it runs
Back through the wasted hours,
Back, back . . . until their eyes
Start with the sudden sun
And the gay-blowing flowers.

J. C. Hall

1944 AND AFTER

Pinned down in the little valley – in its way
A trap, or would be if they had the strength.
Not very dangerous, with a little care.
Still, a long day
Pressed into hollows in the rocky, bare
Untrenchable soil, without food or drink
Or anything much to think
About, damp, coldish, shiny air . . .
Until, near dusk, at length
A few guns, manhandled across the bridgeless
Black ravine, suppress
The enemy strong-points, in a thundering glare.

Later, lost love pinned him down for years
But the relief came up at last – again
Covered the breakthrough to the warm, wide plain.

Life itself, some say, is just such waiting
Hemmed in a closed cirque of one's own creating
As cramped decade after decade runs
Towards the dusk. – But where are the guns?

Robert Conquest

*Ambiguities ruled. There seemed to be no truths or distinctions or categories
any more. As Louis MacNeice wrote in his preface to:*

HOLES IN THE SKY, 1947

What is truth? says Pilate,
Waits for no answer;
Double your stakes, says the clock
To the ageing dancer;
Double the guard, says Authority,
Treble the bars;
Holes in the sky, says the child
Scanning the stars.

HIATUS

The years that did not count – Civilians in the towns
Remained at the same age as in Nineteen-Thirty-Nine,
Saying last year, meaning the last of peace;
Yet eyes began to pucker, mouth to crease,
The hiatus was too packed with fears and frowns,
The would-be absent heart came forth a magnetic mine.

As if the weekly food queue were to stretch,
Absorb all future Europe. Or as if
The sleepers in the Tube had come from Goya's Spain
Or Thucydides' Corcyra – a long way to fetch
People to prove that civilization is vain,
Wrapped in old quilts; no wonder they wake stiff.

Yes, we wake stiff and older; especially when
The schoolboys of the Thirties reappear,
Fledged in the void, indubitably men,
Having kept vigil on the Unholy Mount
And found some dark and tentative things made clear,
Some clear made dark, in the years that did not count.

Louis MacNeice

THE 'BLACK' COUNTRY

'But it is not Black,' they will tell you, 'any longer, not really
    Black.'
And of course they have the right ideas, and are right.
Progress is always changing colour: blushes more deeply, or now
    scowls darkly, or turns pale.
True, how can it be called Black? – with its shining cubes of
    metallic branch-groceries,
And the tin gleam of the fish saloon, tiled like a public lavatory,
Where the fried fish floats, in Sargasso seas of chips.

It is not Black, in the sense that the desert is Red
With a history of running sores, or that the grass was Green.
Not Black as Babylon was Scarlet, or the Blood,
As violets are Violet, as Pythagoras' thigh was Golden, or corn
    is –
Not Black as the satin back of this black horse is Black.

So we shall call it the Grey Country, out of deference.
But Grey is slyer than Black: 'Why, I am practically White.'

D. J. Enright

The corruption and ambiguity of the post-war world was brilliantly portrayed in The Third Man, *which Graham Greene wrote for Carol Reed to film in Vienna, then divided between the four Great Powers. Harry Lime (played by Orson Welles) took Holly Martins (played by Joseph Cotten) to the top of the Big Wheel in the fairground. He was killing children by supplying them with bad drugs on the black market.*

MARTINS: You've never grown up, Harry.
HARRY: Well, we shall be old for a very long time.
MARTINS: Have you ever seen any of your victims?
  HARRY *takes a look at the toy landscape below and comes away from the door.*
HARRY: I never feel quite safe in these things. *He feels the door with his hands.* Victims? Don't be melodramatic. Look down there.
  He points through the window at the people moving like black flies at the base of the Wheel.
HARRY: Would you really feel any pity if one of those dots stopped moving for ever? If I said you can have twenty thousand pounds for every dot that stops, would you really, old man, tell me to keep my money – or would you calculate how many dots you could afford to spare? Free of income tax, old man. Free of income tax. *He gives his boyish, conspiratorial smile.* It's the only way to save nowadays.
MARTINS: You're finished now. The police know everything.
HARRY: But they can't catch me, Rollo. They can't come in the Russian Zone.
MARTINS *looking out of the window*: I should be pretty easy to get rid of.
HARRY: Pretty easy.
MARTINS: Don't be too sure.
HARRY: I carry a gun. You don't think they'd look for a bullet wound after you hit *that* ground.
MARTINS: They dug up your coffin.
HARRY: Found Harbin? Pity.
  Again the car begins to move, sailing slowly down, until the flies are midgets, are recognisable human beings.
HARRY: What fools we are, Rollo, talking like this, as if I'd do that to you – or you to me. *Deliberately he turns his back and leans his face*

against the glass. In these days, old man, nobody thinks in terms of human beings. Governments don't, so why should we? They talk of the people and the proletariat, and I talk of the mugs. It's the same thing. They have their five year plans and so have I.

MARTINS: You used to believe in a God.

That shade of melancholy crosses HARRY'S *face.*

HARRY: Oh, I still *believe*, old man. In God and Mercy and all that. The dead are happier dead. They don't miss much here, poor devils.

London was also a divided city.

LONDON

I am the city of two divided cities
Where the eyes of rich and poor collide and wonder;
Where the beggar's voice is low and unexpectant,
And in clubs the feet of the servants are soft on the carpet
And the world's wind scarcely stirs the leaves of *The Times* . . .

I am the reticent, the private city,
The city of lovers hiding wrapped in shadows,
The city of people sitting and talking quietly
Beyond shut doors and walls as thick as a century,
People who laugh too little and too loudly,
Whose tears fall inward, flowing back to the heart.

I am the city whose fog will fall like a finger gently
Erasing the anger of angles, the strident indecorous gesture,
Whose dusk will come like tact, like a change in the conversation,
Violet and indigo, with strings of lemon streetlamps
Casting their pools into the pools of rain
As the notes of the piano are cast from the top-floor window
Into the square that is always Sunday afternoon.

A. S. J. Tessimond

ON THE WAY HOME

Like questing hounds
The lechers run through London
From all the alley-ways
Into all the thoroughfares

Until, shoulder to shoulder, they vanish
Into the main line stations
Or the Underground traps them.

A moment of promiscuity at nightfall
Their feet go homewards but their attentions
Are on the nape of a neck or the cut of a thigh
Almost any woman

As Schopenhauer noted
Being more interesting to them than those
Who made their beds that morning.

C. H. Sisson

*The poets and the artists were leaving the London bars, dispersing. There
was nothing to be found in there in the end.*

THE PEARL

In my 'forties days, of Soho and Fitzrovia,
The Bricklayers' Arms, affectionately known
To all its regulars as the Burglars' Rest,
Could serve a decent plate of fishcakes, or of shellfish.
I found a pearl in a mussel once
And showed it to the barman. He dropped it on the floor,
And being no bigger than a small pin's head
It was quite irrecoverable. This kind of thing
Tends to occur with all the pearls I get.

John Heath-Stubbs

SONG IN A SALOON BAR

We are here for fear we think of
    Things that we would rather not;
We are here lest we remember –
    But we have forgotten what;

Here we need not judge, decipher,
    Justify or understand,
And we fathom nothing deeper
    Than the half-pint in our hand;

Here we turn from ghosts and, turning,
    Turn the amber, honey-bright,
Frosted-gold or copper-tawny
    Glassful in the smoky light;

Somewhere yesterday-tomorrow's
    Closing like two closing claws,
But, in here, each mild-and-bitter
    Makes the cunning clock-hands pause;

Let us cluster and stand closer
    Lest we've room to turn and run;
Time for one more round, old man, for
    Time for, time for . . . one, for one . . .

We are here for fear we think of
    Things that we would rather not;
We are here lest we remember –
    But we have forgotten what.

A. S. J. Tessimond

It was hard to keep going after the war and to hold on to a dream of the new age of the peace.

A BALLAD FOR HARD TIMES

I may be no great shakes – but damn it all!
    Sometimes the Muse has turned her steps to me,

And I have listened to her dark footfall
   Where, quiet as a reed beneath a tree,
   I waited for her coming – sometimes she
Who is female and vagrant, in my ear
Sings what the public will not pay to hear.

Sometimes I think I ought to end it all,
   Because I cannot live by poetry,
Also because I know that people fall
   Like sacks of bricks for bards, when dead – and we,
   Esteemed, if unpaid, by society,
Are sure of not intoning from a bier
Words that the public does not like to hear.

Why don't I get a job that's cultural?
   The British Council, or the B.B.C.?
Or lecture blockheads in a county hall?
   Or write reviews or novels? T.S.E.
   Worked in a bank or something, didn't he?
I'll get a job, and find the time to spare
For words the public does not want to hear.

Sir, after office-hours I, like the clerk
   Who builds a fretwork model railway-station
Out of bus-tickets and old bits of cork,
   Hope to create a first-class piece of work,
And give it buckshee to the bloody nation.

David Wright

1948

Reading among the crumbs of leaves upon
The lawn, beneath the thin October sun,
I hear behind the words
And noise of birds
The drumming aircraft; and am blind till they have gone.

The feeling that they give is now no more
That of the time when we had not reached war:
It is as though the lease

Of crumbling peace
Had run already and that life was as before.

For this is not the cancer or the scream,
A grotesque interlude, but what will seem
On waking to us all
Most natural –
The gnawed incredible existence of a dream.

Roy Fuller

NEW AGE

To-night the wind comes screaming up the road
Like a train in the tube. Over my cringing head
Gas-lamps are ghosts of the still-marching dead
Whose butchered eyes, blown open,
Pity our cold condition.
Here, in this rotting air,
The traffic lights ripen
From green to yellow, from yellow to red;
And I, with a cobweb of rain in my hair,
Trudge between tram-lines, seeking a world's salvation.

Only the lost are with me, only the late
And the last, lonely stragglers in the street:
A drunkard in the lamplight, on whose coat
Something still glistens;
The frosted whore who marks
My footfall on the stone,
Sniffs in the wind and listens
Under the red lamp of the traffic light;
And a flash boy, adrift in the pin-stripe rain,
Edging towards the privacy of parks.

These, my cold company; whose nailed feet
Scrape on the pavements of eternal night;
The down-at-heel, who drift in the wet light,
Seeking a wind to blow
The spent leaf from its stalk;
Who long for death,
As the leaf longs for snow.

These only are unafraid, who throng to meet
The wind that bears a world's end in its breath.
O Christ, have pity on them, where they walk.

Raise Your nailed hand! Unwedge the window-frame
Of the sleek man in bed. Shiver the dream
That muffles his drugged ear to the crack of doom
And let him hear the shriek
Of the relentless wind
And the loose casement, rattling.
Listen. The clocks strike,
Heard by the lost; unheard in the locked room
Under the sheet where the sly hands go shuttling
This night and evermore, world without end.

Paul Dehn

10

The End of the War Decade

At the end of the decade, London was still a city of ruins.

'THE FLOWERING WEN' - JULY, 1950

Five years since the last rocket fell. And from a facade left standing, an elevation cleared of its ornament, comes the unanswerable assertion that often the bomb was a better designer than the builder. Yes, the war in London did a number of things besides killing people, imposing a curfew and encouraging the study of good books. It took the lid off poverty, the edge off reserve. It broke down the serried ugliness of the view. As Hopkins remarked of flower forms that nature left to itself makes miraculous patterns, so here destroying chance had introduced beauty. Some of these ruins, that still give a weary tug to the heart of the Londoner, are inspired Follies.

Nature gave us also the accidental rock garden. Catastrophe, we found, could sprout flowers. At first, the discovery shocked. Kilt, willow herb – what the devil were *they* doing there? One had a vision of all the seeds borne along streets in earlier Augusts, of worms perhaps waiting to push up through cracks in the pavement.

With the years, the weeds have grown thicker and taller; and not only weeds, but grasses, saplings, wheat and barley from horses' nosebags, tomato plants from the discarded sandwich crust. The number of these flowering plants and ferns on ruined sites rose after a few seasons to 126: among them – pleasant to name, if hard to distinguish – Bulbous Buttercup, Codlins-and-Cream, Musk Mimulus, Swine's Cress, Gallant Soldiers, White Goosefoot or Fat Hen, York-shire Fog, Fool's Parsley, Evening Primrose, Timothygrass, Meadow Fescue, Bittersweet. And Rosebay Willow-herb, the commonest of all in Central London today, has brought with it the elephant hawk-moth whose grubs feed on its leaves.

Nature left to itself works miraculous patterns. But next time, we are told – ah, next time! – we may not be so lucky. Atom bombs will level and the radio-active particle will pursue: ruin absolute, death without flower or worm!

G. W. Stonier

John Betjeman wrote in praise of the general shabbiness.

'IN PRAISE OF DIRT'

Once I used to wallow in a hot bath every day. I admit that I didn't do much washing in it. I used it for thinking and for shaving when the

319

weather was too cold to be standing up in naked air. Those sybaritic times are over. I am posted to a cold climate where there is a fuel shortage, and I am lucky to get one bath a month: and then the water comes out tepid. My skin has developed a protective coating after the manner of the Tibetans who, I understand, never wash at all, so that they do not have to wear vests. The result is that, instead of catching a cold once a fortnight from October to May, as I used to do in the old days, I only catch one once a month, after bath night. This is the only hygienic argument in favour of dirt: all my other reasons for liking it are aesthetic.

But before I come to them, it is fair to outline some of the horrors of cleanliness:

The house where they put down newspaper over the carpet in the hall and in the parlour, so that you shall not bring mud in;

The room where you are offered a cigarette but where there are no ash-trays – only paper flowers in the grate and everything so much in order that there is no obscure corner where you can drop ash and a cigarette end without being noticed;

Taking books out of cases, rubbing the backs off with a duster, and replacing them upside down;

The habit of 'turning out' a room which is in an order you understand, though it may look like disorder to the spring cleaner;

Cleaning and polishing linoleum so that you fall down on it;

Cleaning 18th century monuments in a church with a scrubbing brush so that all the fixture of the marble and the colour from the lettering is scrubbed away;

Cleaning ornaments which look better when obscured by dirt.

Not that I have any objection to people removing yesterday's cabbage from the interstices of a fork, or cleaning a visitor's lipstick off the rim of a teacup. My arguments against cleanliness are purely practical.

And when it comes to dirt, there is so much to say in favour of it, that it is hard to know where to begin.

How often have I seen a pretty face ruined by too much washing! Out of a factory or a farmyard there comes a girl in her working clothes, freckled face, tip-tilted nose, and a smudge on her cheek. She is full of character. An hour later she appears dressed up for the evening out. She has rubbed her cheeks in linseed oil, hidden her freckles under powder, removed the smudge and painted her lips, and she looks just like every other girl on an evening out. She has no character left at all: she looks no more than a sepia photograph in the fashion pages of a woman's magazine or, worse still, one of the colour plates.

The same argument applies to toys. My little son has a Teddy bear. When it was given to him two years ago it had no character at all: glass eyes and an expression like an inexorable Civil Servant. Two years of affection have worn away some of its fur and flattened out the rest, the glass eyes have been replaced by woollen ones, a grey film has appeared on its forehead and nose so that the dear old thing is now full of character and looks like a benevolent Beefeater.

I am told that in the wine trade, when there was wine to be sold, unscrupulous merchants would spray rubber solution on bottles which looked too new, so as to give them the vintage appearance of being hung with cobwebs. To this day the same principle applies (in terms of genuine dust instead of fake cobwebs) to the antique and second-hand book trades. I, for one, would never buy old books or furniture if they were all smartened up and clean. I would think that I was going to be charged too much for them and that I would be paying a tax to the interfering brute who had bothered about them enough to want to remove the dirt. The shrewd dealer reckons on dirt to make people think he doesn't know the value of what he is selling.

Many places depend on the dirt in them to make them hospitable. What is more naked and ashamed than the public house when it has just opened its doors? There are the shining floor, the ash-trays empty, the windows steamless, the bar glistening and deserted, the palms quivering from their wash, and the whole place reeking of disinfectant. He is a confirmed dipso who can give the first order in such an atmosphere, a nicotine-fiend who can light the first cigarette. But in two hours' time cigarettes have been trodden into the sawdust, beer lies in rings on bar and tables, crowds thicken, voices rise, the piano begins.

Yet of all the beauties of dirt, the most beautiful is dirt on buildings. 'Dear, old, dirty Dublin,' 'Dear, old, dirty London,' 'Dear, old, smoky Manchester.' You will notice how 'dear' goes with 'dirt' and 'smoky.' You couldn't say 'Dear, old, dirty Welwyn Garden City' or 'Dear, old, dirty Bournville,' because they aren't dirty and they are not 'dear.' I notice when I return to London that it has not been painted for some time. Stucco has even more grace as it peels from late Georgian terraces; neo-Georgian banks and post offices are mellowed down by smoke from staring red to smoky golden-brown: even those ghastly cliffs of commercial-Renaissance in New Regent Street look a little less pretentious and a little less forbidding without their annual wash.

They can never take on the exquisite texture of black and silver-white which smoke of centuries has given to Wren's Portland stone churches and Cathedral, but they look much better than they will when their owners wash them after the war.

I do not know what particular kind of dirt has given the Georgian squares and terraces of Dublin the Guinness-washed reds and browns of an old aquatint. But dirt has transformed those miles of brick into miles of elegance.

The fog descends on Manchester. It blackens the old Cathedral, it blackens many a Victorian church and Venetian-Gothic warehouse until they, too, begin to look as venerable as the Cathedral itself. It will, please God, blacken the new Library.

The mists from the Mersey wrap round Liverpool, the new estates begin to look less hygienic and more habitable, St. George's Hall is blacker and grander than ever, the Royal Liver building greyer and more extraordinary.

Time's dirty fingers touch the towns with texture. And they do not forget the country. At Bourton-on-the-Hill, no one has been along with a long-handled broom and brushed the flaking stone from wet Cotswold roofs. Moss has grown in the dirt and brought more dirt and grown more moss. Uneven stone roofs are gold and black and green.

I am coarse of mind, coarse of texture, a prey to most of the vices to which man is subject; but the one kind of dirt I do not enjoy is the dirt of the dirty story. It breaks up consecutive thought, it muddles conversation, it is generally apropos of nothing. A braver man than I am says to people who try to make themselves pleasant with this form of dirt: 'Do you know me very well?' 'No.' 'Then what right have you to tell me that story?'

And now I hear the water running for my monthly bath.

The Festival of Britain in 1951 promised a brighter future.

from MAGOG

One hundred years it had been since the Crystal Palace, iron and glass rising in cupolas over the trees, the sparrows shitting down on England's industrial might and Queen Victoria and the grand old Duke of Wellington, who sent up hawks after the damned defilers above, he knew how to clear a rabble out of trees or Waterloo woods. One hundred years since the Great Exhibition, when the godly prophets of disaster had warned of turning Bayswater into a giant Sodom, of pox and plague being spread by visiting Papist hordes, of fire and brimstone smashing the domes down onto the idolators beneath, only to see the revelation of the age of pride and assurance, *imperium in imperio*, steam engines and crinolines, crankshafts and fossils, spindles

and doilies, power looms and high hats, a full third of the people of
England walking through the halls of glass and wonder, their vision
stretching beyond the curved and skiey space that murmured with the
power to girdle the globe with machines and good manners. One
hundred years ago, and now the Festival of Britain.

It rained for two days out of three that January and February and
March, and the site on the South Bank turned into a morass, and the
new pleasure gardens in Battersea which were meant to rival the
Georgian elegance of Vauxhall and Ranelagh looked like the shell-
holes of Passchendaele where the Tommies had drowned in the mud.
And Magog and Radzen cursed like all sensible people at the waste of
public money and of scarce building materials for a mediocre memorial
to muddle and muck. But May proved that once again the British
could survive their own forebodings. At the first preview, visitors
advanced into the Festival grounds as the workers retreated before
them across the river, hammering a last few nails and details into their
right place. The Skylon glowed in the spring light, airily astonished at
being able to stand at all, a landmark as exclamation mark for the
whole exhibition. Beyond, the Dome of Discovery, concrete scallop of
grandeur, enclosing radar screens and cricket-bat makers and the cogs
and the sinews of British industry and invention. Dominant, the
Festival Hall for the lady harpists and the tuba players beloved of
postcard jokes. Not to forget the Lion and Unicorn Pavilion, where
whimsy reigned in the clutter of regality and spoofery that told of the
country of Shakespeare and Edward Lear, greatness knowing its own
absurdity even in its decline.

Andrew Sinclair

*The future society of England seemed to lie more in the suburbs and the
bungalows than in the great cities.*

THE BUNGALOWS

In lofty light the towers dissolve
Of yellow elms this tranquil day,
Crumble in leisurely showers of gold
All Turneresque in bright decay.

The elms disperse their leaves upon
A nineteen-thirty builder's row

Of speculative dwellings, each
An unassuming bungalow.

Like concave shells, or shades, or shields
That guard some life or light aloof,
Like hands that cup a flame, or keep
Some frail and captured thing, each roof.

If high-pitched hopes have gone to roost
Where low-pitched roofs so smoothly slope
Perhaps these autumn rays diffuse
A deeper anodyne than hope.

Between the vast insanities
That men so cleverly invent
It may be here, it may be here,
A simulacrum of content.

Though separate only from the road
By five-foot hedge and ten-foot lawn
Each semi-isolationist
Seems almost from the world withdrawn,

Except that from a roof or two
Those thin and wand-like aerials rise
That suck like opium from the air
Bemusement for the ears and eyes.

The denizens of each hermitage,
Of 'Nellibert' and 'Mirzapore',
Bird-watchers all, in love with dogs,
Are primed with useful garden-lore:

Cabbage the emblem of their life –
Yet mauve the michaelmas-daisy glows
And under reddening apples gleams
A pearly, pure, belated rose.

Begrudging vulgar fantasy
To cheap and ordinary homes,
Discrimination might deplore
That concrete frog, those whimsy gnomes,

Nor see them as blind tribute to
The rule of dreams, or as a last
Concession to the irrational,
The old, wild, superstitious past.

The commonplace needs no defence,
Dullness is in the critic's eyes,
Without a licence life evolves
From some dim phase its own surprise:

Under these yellow-twinkling elms,
Behind these hedges trimly shorn,
As in a stable once, so here
It may be born, it may be born.

William Plomer

The poets wrote their own mocking obituaries and laid the past to rest.

OBITUARY OF R. FULLER

We note the death, with small regret,
Of one who'd scarcely lived, as yet.
Born just before the First World War,
Died when there'd only been one more:
Between, his life had all been spent
In the small-bourgeois element,
Sheltered from poverty and hurt,
From passion, tragedy and dirt.
His infant traumas somewhat worse,
He would have written better verse,
His youth by prudence not so guided
His politics been more decided.
In the event his life was split
And half was lost bewailing it:
Part managerial, part poetic –
Hard to decide the more pathetic.
Avoiding China, Spain and Greece,
He passed his adult years of peace
In safe unease, with thoughts of doom
(As birth is feared inside the womb) –
Doom of his talent and his place,

325

Doom, total, of the human race.
This strange concern for fellow creatures
Had certainly some pathic features.
He could not understand that death
Must be the lot of all with breath,
And crudely linked felicity
With dying from senile decay,
Finding no spiritual worth
In guided missiles, torture, dearth.
Quite often he was heard to babble
'Poets should be intelligible'
Or 'What determines human fate
Is the class structure of the state'
Or 'Freud and Marx and Dickens found
And so do I – souls not profound'.
These views were logically a feature
Of his rude, egotistic nature –
So unemotional and shy
Such friends as he retained would cry
With baffled boredom, thankful they
Were not part of his family.

If any bit of him survives
It will be that verse which contrives
To speak in private symbols for
The peaceful caught in public war.
For there his wavering faith in man
Wavers around some sort of plan,
And though foreseeing years of trouble,
Denies a universal rubble,
Discovering in wog and sailor
The presages of bourgeois failure.
Whether at this we weep or laugh
It makes a generous epitaph.

Roy Fuller

LAMENT

When I was a windy boy and a bit
And the black spit of the chapel fold,
(Sighed the old ram rod, dying of women),
I tiptoed shy in the gooseberry wood,
The rude owl cried like a telltale tit,
I skipped in a blush as the big girls rolled
Ninepin down on the donkeys' common,
And on seesaw sunday nights I wooed
Whoever I would with my wicked eyes,
The whole of the moon I could love and leave
All the green leaved little weddings' wives
In the coal black bush and let them grieve.

When I was a gusty man and a half
And the black beast of the beetles' pews,
(Sighed the old ram rod, dying of bitches),
Not a boy and a bit in the wick-
Dipping moon and drunk as a new dropped calf,
I whistled all night in the twisted flues,
Midwives grew in the midnight ditches,
And the sizzling beds of the town cried, Quick! –
Whenever I dove in a breast high shoal,
Wherever I ramped in the clover quilts,
Whatsoever I did in the coal-
Black night, I left my quivering prints.

When I was a man you could call a man
And the black cross of the holy house,
(Sighed the old ram rod, dying of welcome),
Brandy and ripe in my bright, bass prime,
No springtailed tom in the red hot town
With every simmering woman his mouse
But a hillocky bull in the swelter
Of summer come in his great good time
To the sultry, biding herds, I said,
Oh, time enough when the blood creeps cold,
And I lie down but to sleep in bed,
For my sulking, skulking, coal black soul!

When I was a half of the man I was
And serve me right as the preachers warn,

327

(Sighed the old ram rod, dying of downfall),
No flailing calf or cat in a flame
Or hickory bull in milky grass
But a black sheep with a crumpled horn,
At last the soul from its foul mousehole
Slunk pouting out when the limp time came;
And I gave my soul a blind, slashed eye,
Gristle and rind, and a roarers' life,
And I shoved it into the coal black sky
To find a woman's soul for a wife.

Now I am a man no more no more
And a black reward for a roaring life,
(Sighed the old ram rod, dying of strangers),
Tidy and cursed in my dove cooed room
I lie down thin and hear the good bells jaw –
For, oh, my soul found a sunday wife
In the coal black sky and she bore angels!
Harpies around me out of her womb!
Chastity prays for me, piety sings,
Innocence sweetens my last black breath,
Modesty hides my thighs in her wings,
And all the deadly virtues plague my death!

Dylan Thomas

*The deaths of the leading Soho publisher and Scots artist of the war
decade were commemorated by poets who remembered them in their time.*

FUNERAL MUSIC FOR CHARLES WREY GARDINER

A cold, dull day in a tardy spring:
As the coffin enters the chapel, a black crow,
Like a corny image from a neo-romantic
Nineteen-forties poem, flies over and croaks,
'Dear God,' I think, 'this is going to be depressing,
More than the general run of funerals.'
There is no music here – only an apparently
Automatic and electronic organ
With tremolo permanently on, as if it was shivering
Somewhere in outer darkness.

Now I remember him,
Myopic and spry as an old grey rat,
Penning his memoirs in a crumbling house
Eaten piecemeal by women and by drink.
'The answer to life is no,' he said, and sometimes
He really seemed to mean it. God help us all
If so indeed he did – that gate leads
Only into the 'nothing, nothing, nothing, nothing,'
Which he averred the sum of things.

Burying him, we bury part of ourselves
And the poetic forties, – we, the mourners,
Ageing survivors of an abused
Unfashionable decade. Bohemians, drunks,
Undisciplined and self-indulgent – so, perhaps, we were.
And yet I think we still believed in poetry,
More than some who now possess the scene:
Dot-and-carry Long John Silvers with small dried-up
Professors perched upon their shoulders.
At least our parrots had real and gaudy feathers.

Out in the air, the sun
Is not yet attempting to shine. Among the bushes
That straddle over the gravestones – another trite symbol:
Redbreasts are singing. Those charitable birds,
The tale tells, strewed with dead dry leaves
The sleeping siblings, poor babes in the wood.
What, in this last resort, are any of us but
Sad lost children under the dark thorn?

John Heath-Stubbs

A STROLL IN SOHO

I. M. Robert Colquhoun – 1914–62

Mooney's – a gentlemen's outfitter. The Old Queen's Head
An employment agency. Sic transit, you might say.
Expense-account restaurants have taken over
The meeting-places of the unstable and unsober.

And these evening passers-by, uniform, amenable –
There is not one whose government insurance is not paid,
Who will not be receiving a pension at sixty-five.
Where are those whose lives were disorderly but had meaning?

I see no evidence that the human animal is not dead
But deduce, citizen, from your inhalation
And exhalation of the unrationable atmosphere
That you are organically alive and inhabit those garments.

Soho – wraiths bristle as I turn the square.
Colquhoun's gone into his last coma,
His ghost joins the throng on the pavements.
Citizen, step aside, it is more alive than you are.

David Wright

A new breed of poet showed a different sensibility in dealing with the events
of the war decade.

REJOINDER TO A CRITIC

You may be right: 'How can I dare to feel?'
May be the only question I can pose,
'And haply by abstruse research to steal
From my own nature all the natural man'
My sole resource. And I do not suppose
That others may not have a better plan.

And yet I'll quote again, and gloss it too
(You know by now my liking for *collage*):
Donne could be daring, but he never knew,
When he inquired, 'Who's injured by my love?'
Love's radio-active fall-out on a large
Expanse around the point it bursts above.

'Alas, alas, who's injured by my love?'
And recent history answers: Half Japan!
Not love, but hate? Well, both are versions of
The 'feeling' that you dare me to. Be dumb!
Appear concerned only to make it scan!
How dare we now be anything but numb?

Donald Davie

330

Index of Contributors